Intercultural Language Activities

Cambridge Handbooks for Language Teachers

This series, now with over 40 titles, offers practical ideas, techniques and activities for the teaching of English and other languages providing inspiration for both teachers and trainers.

Recent titles in this series:

Intercultural Language Activities

John Corbett

Consultant and editor: Scott Thornbury

CAMBRIDGE
UNIVERSITY PRESS

CAMBRIDGE UNIVERSITY PRESS
Cambridge, New York, Melbourne, Madrid, Cape Town,
Singapore, São Paulo, Delhi, Mexico City

Cambridge University Press
The Edinburgh Building, Cambridge CB2 8RU, UK

www.cambridge.org
Information on this title:
www.cambridge.org/9780521741880

First published 2010
Reprinted 2013

Printed and bound in the United Kingdom by the MPG Books Group

A catalogue record for this publication is available from the British Library

Library of Congress Cataloging-in-Publication data
Corbett, John, 1959–
    Intercultural language activities / John Corbett.
        p. cm. – (Cambridge handbooks for language teachers)
    ISBN 978-0-521-74188-0
    1. English language—Study and teaching—Foreign speakers—Aids and
devices.   2. Intercultural communication.   3. Multicultural education.
4. Language and culture.   I. Title.   II. Series.

    PE1128.A2C69335 2009
    370.117—dc22

2009035018

ISBN 978-0-521-74188-0 paperback and CD-ROM

Contents

Thanks and acknowledgements

I would like to thank the many colleagues, friends and students who, wittingly and unwittingly through the years, have contributed ideas to this book; in particular, Joina M. Almeida, Mariza Riva de Almeida, Wendy Anderson, Vanessa Andreotti, Dave Beavan, Mike Byram, Susan Holden, Clarissa Jordão, Christian Kay, Gabriele Linke, Peih-ying 'Peggy' Lu, Andrea Matos, Ron Martinez, Martin Montgomery, Robert O'Dowd, Alison Phipps, Alan Pulverness, Andrea Assenti del Rio, Jack Scholes, Cicero Menezes de Sousa, and all the students and teachers who have participated in the 'Intercultural Connections' project organised by Glasgow University's Department of English Language. No doubt you will recognise your own fingerprints on the following pages. Sincere thanks also go to Scott Thornbury, Tracy Jakes and Barbara Thomas for their unflagging enthusiasm and advice during the writing and editing process, and to the team at Cambridge University Press for its support. Teresinha Rodrigues Alves graciously afforded me her hospitality and allowed me to commandeer her computer for a happy summer spent drafting much of this volume. Augusta Rodrigues Alves supported, cajoled, read a full draft thoroughly, and made innumerable constructive suggestions with sensitivity and insight. The book is better for their creativity, energy and wisdom.

The authors and publishers acknowledge the following sources of copyright material and are grateful for the permissions granted. While every effort has been made, it has not always been possible to identify the sources of all the material used, or to trace all copyright holders. If any omissions are brought to our notice, we will be happy to include the appropriate acknowledgements on reprinting.

Text

For the text on p. 1: © *Council of Europe*; For the screenshot on p.13: reprinted with kind permission of www.epals.com; For the screenshots on pp. 110 and 209: Data cited herein have been extracted from the British National Corpus Online service, managed by Oxford University Computing Services on behalf of the BNC Consortium. All rights in the texts cited are reserved.; For the screenshot on p. 111: Davies, Mark. (2008–) The Corpus of Contemporary American English (COCA): 400+ million words, 1990–present. Available online at http://www.americancorpus.org; For the poem titled 'A Martian sends a postcard home' on pp. 124–125 by Craig Raine, copyright © Craig Raine, 1979; For the text in 7.3a on p. 135: Reproduced with permission of Marc Fennell; For the text in 7.3b on p.135: Reproduced with permission of Dustin Putman; For the screenshots on pp. 140 and 143: Davies, Mark. (2007–) TIME Magazine Corpus (100 million words, 1920s–2000s). Available online at http://corpus.byu.edu/time; Text on p. 148: © Yiannis Tziortzis; Text on p. 150: © Copyright of Vietnam Investment Review; For the poem on pp. 157–158: 'Kidspoem / Bairnsang' taken from *The Colour of Black and White* by Liz Lochhead is reproduced by permission of Polygon, an imprint of Birlinn Ltd (www.birlinn.co.uk); Text on pp. 207 and 214: © Jeremy MacClancy.

Photos

For the photo on p. 25: © Corbis/ Claro Cortes IV/ Reuters; John Corbett for supplying the photos on p. 71; © Alamy/ David Robertson for p. 83 (left); © Alamy/ Arch White for p.83 (right); For the photo on p. 114: © Alamy/ Jon Arnold Images Ltd; © Scran for p. 115 (top); © Corbis/ Bernard Bisson/ Sygma for p. 115 (bottom); © Alamy/ Blend Images for p. 127 (top); © Alamy/ Blickwinkel for p. 127 (bottom); © Alamy/ Chad Ehlers for p. 152 (top); © Alamy/ Andrew Rodriguez for p. 152 (middle); © Alamy/ Phovoir/ FCM Graphic for p.152 (bottom); © Getty Images/ Hulton Archive for p. 168 (top left and top right); © Alamy/ RIA Novosti for p. 168 (bottom left); © Getty Images/ AFP for p. 168 (bottom right) and p. 178 (bottom); For the photo on p. 175: © Alamy/ Jordi Salas; © Alamy/ John MacTavish for the photo on p. 178 (top); © Getty Images for p. 187 (left); © Alamy/ H Mark Weidman for p.187 (right); For the photo on p. 202: © Getty Images/ Peter Poulides.

Introduction

Intercultural learning and teaching

This book is a starting place for the observation, description and evaluation of different cultures, the learners' own, and those of speakers of other languages. The concept of *inter*cultural activities may possibly still require some explanation, although the development of intercultural language learning and teaching has now been ongoing for over two decades. The principles of intercultural language education are firmly embedded, for example, in the *Common European Framework of Reference for Languages: Learning, Teaching, Assessment* (Council of Europe, 2001). There, its aims are summarised as follows (p.1):

> *In an intercultural approach, it is a central objective of language learning to promote the favourable development of the learner's whole personality and sense of identity in response to the enriching experience of otherness in language and culture.*

Intercultural learning and teaching raise some fundamental challenges to previous models of language education. First of all, they challenge the conventional goal of language education as 'native-like proficiency'. For many learners, this is a distant, even unattainable goal. It is also, many teachers now argue, an unnecessary one. In a world where English is increasingly used as a *lingua franca*, it seems sensible to accept that it is more important for a language learner to communicate effectively in a range of more or less familiar contexts, than to be able to mimic the linguistic conventions found in, say, the USA, Australia or Great Britain.

Even so, the displacement of 'native-like proficiency' as the main goal of a language curriculum is not a trivial matter. Something of substance must occupy the vacuum. Intercultural language learning substitutes for 'native-like proficiency' the more immediately achievable goals of 'cultural exploration and mediation'. Intercultural learners *use* language to explore different cultures, and to mediate in those situations where cultural misconceptions occur. They do this with increasing sophistication, drawing on their accumulating cultural knowledge and developing skill in using the resources of the target language. They are also encouraged to employ personal qualities such as empathy, open-mindedness and respect for others.

Crucially, intercultural exploration involves discovering one's own culture as well as the cultures of others. Many of the activities in this book focus first on the *home* culture; an extensive resource that has hitherto been largely neglected in the second language classroom. Through the activities, learners look anew at their own community's behaviour, practices and values and prepare to explain them to people whose behaviour, practices and values differ. In order to accomplish this, learners need to develop skills in cultural observation, description, explanation and evaluation. Furthermore, learners require a forum in which to share and discuss their findings with people from other cultures. In some teaching situations the class will itself be multicultural, and therefore it will naturally provide an arena for intercultural exchange and discussion. In many situations, however, learners may share their linguistic and cultural insights with others via electronic media such as web-based discussion forums or virtual learning environments. This book gives advice on how to set up online intercultural communities, and how to promote online discussions.

Intercultural communicative competence

An intercultural language curriculum, then, has language goals complementing the competences and skills required for cultural exploration and mediation. The detailed specification of intercultural communicative competence is still a developing project, although much work has been accomplished in this area by Michael Byram and his colleagues. In documents such as the *Common European Framework,* intercultural communicative competence is conceived of as a set of knowledge, skills and attitudes. With reference to Byram's work, we can summarise these as follows: (a) knowing the self and the other; (b) knowing how to relate and interpret meaning; (c) developing critical awareness; (d) knowing how to discover cultural information; and (e) knowing how to relativise oneself and value the attitudes and beliefs of others. Let us consider how this book addresses these five aspects of intercultural communicative competence.

Knowing the self and the other

Intercultural language learners need to acquire an understanding of how interaction works, and how individuals relate more generally to those around them and to society at large. People often find a way of relating to others by joining certain clubs or leisure groups or taking up particular hobbies. In these settings, they often bond with others by gossiping, and telling stories or anecdotes about their lives and experiences, thus offering the opportunity to dramatise and negotiate their personal and group values. Intercultural language learners can be encouraged to explore, describe and compare social groups and see how they use patterns of communicative interaction to sustain a sense of identity.

The impulse to explore and categorise requires a counterbalancing caution. Individual learners are, as every teacher knows, real people who rightly resist stereotyping as a 'typical' member of this or that group. 'Knowing the self and the other' therefore depends on understanding the complex interactions between individuals and groups, and how individuals actively negotiate their multiple identities in the context of different communities. The language activities suggested in this book encourage learners to enhance their knowledge of the dynamic relations between individuals and groups by examining, for example, how people dramatise their values through the stories they tell, and how people interact through their silences and gestures as much as their words.

Knowing how to relate and interpret meaning

The exploration of language and culture is, at heart, a search for meaning. Meaning can obviously be communicated via spoken or written language, in a variety of genres – a lecture, a conversation, a shouted warning, a newspaper report, a scholarly article, an email, a posting in an internet chat room, a blog, or even an old-fashioned letter. Learners need to be exposed gradually to an ever-increasing range of such genres, each of which serves a particular purpose for the community of speakers and writers that uses it. Many genres are governed by a relatively stable set of linguistic conventions which are appropriate to their cultural purpose. The style of a blog, for example, will not be the style of a scholarly article, just as the style of an informal conversation will not be the style of a lecture. As learners become familiar and confident with the conventions governing different genres, their communicative repertoire expands.

Meaning is also communicated non-verbally, through facial expressions, gestures, and even more general forms of behaviour. A beckoning finger or a nod of the head might have a particular meaning in a given culture. Of

3

course, interaction works differently in different communities – periods of silence between conversational utterances, for example, have different lengths and a different significance for different speakers. Interruptions can also have different implications, even within a single community, depending, say, on whether the person who is interrupting is male or female. It has been suggested by some scholars that men tend to interrupt in order to take control of conversational topics, while women's interruptions are generally more cooperative, and are designed to support the speaker. Personal preferences such as the wearing of black eye-shadow or covering one's head also have a variable set of meanings, depending on who and where you are. Preferring one type of car to another, following a particular rock band or classical composer, manicuring one's nails or adopting a vegetarian lifestyle – all these types of behaviour can also send out a message about the kind of person you are and the values you hold. The very instability of meaning makes non-verbal behaviour a perennially fascinating resource for cultural exploration.

Culture is the expression of the values and beliefs of a community – and the community, in turn, may be defined in terms of age, gender, profession, ethnicity, social class, nationality, or even affiliation to some social activity such as sport, theatre-going, consumption of literature, and so on. A dance class that is held in a particular city will have its own 'culture', its unwritten rules of acceptable behaviour, and its participants might even share a special language, of, say, reels, jigs and strathspeys. But there are also trans-national cultures of professionals such as business people or scientists, football fans, music fans and film fans, and adherents to political or social causes. Migration and the mass media have accelerated and intensified the transcultural flow of ideas, practices and behaviours that are global in extent but local in inflection. Chinese restaurants, for example, can be found in many countries around the world – but the menus found in San Francisco or Dublin will be different from those found in Beijing. Reggae music has expanded from its Jamaican roots, but its manifestations in other countries express their own regional identity. Ultimately, all cultural phenomena generate meanings that have to be interpreted in relation to the local conventions and values of the specific community that has created or adopted and adapted them.

The intercultural activities in this book, then, focus on different kinds of community at home and in other countries. Some of the activities focus on the organisation, symbols and language used in these communities. These activities encourage learners to develop skills in interpreting these cultural symbols and language, and to relate them to the values, expectations and purposes that have generated them.

Developing critical awareness

Intercultural language education begins with the assumption that contact between cultures should be mutually enriching for the individuals and communities involved; however, it is undeniable that contact between cultures has historically taken place in conditions of invasion, colonialism, forced immigration and economic migration. In short, the conditions of contact between languages and cultures have too often been marked by differences in power, opportunity, and access to intellectual and material resources. Intercultural language learners have to acknowledge these historical processes and be critically aware of their continuing impact. For example, language learners need to be critically aware and politically engaged with the negative consequences of globalisation, such as the potential erasure of local cultural traditions. However, multiculturalism has been criticised for going too far the other way by treating all cultural values as equally acceptable, and therefore, for example, for tolerating oppressive practices against women or minority groups, if those practices are sanctioned by tradition. Intercultural language education treats all cultural values as open to debate, and subject to critical examination and negotiation. That said, these debates should ideally be characterised by principles of empathy and respect for others.

Some of the chapters in this book, then, directly address topics such as politics and religion that, in the past, some language teachers have rightly treated cautiously. The intercultural classroom, at best, can become a safe space for engagement with differences in belief and ideology, not so that some false consensus can be imposed, but in order to promote genuine understanding and respect.

If its emphasis is solely on direct political engagement, however, intercultural language education can appear to be overly solemn and earnest. That is not the case with most of the activities in this book which are designed to encourage the exploration and celebration of everyday life and behaviour, from walking in the park to enjoying a performance by street artists. Even so, some of the intercultural activities are explicitly designed to engage learners with social issues, to invite learners to consider alternative ways of being and acting, and to foster respectful ways of questioning cultural practices that seem unacceptable.

Knowing how to discover cultural information

The intercultural language learner is one who develops an increasingly sophisticated means of discovering cultural information. The two pillars of this approach derive ultimately from the academic pursuits of *ethnography*; the systematic observation and description of cultural practices, and *semiotics*; the observation, description and analysis of sign systems, such as language itself, but also systems like non-verbal communication, visual symbolism, fashion and dance.

This book follows many others in arguing that ethnography begins at home. The description of the learners' home culture can be a rich and motivating stimulus to second language learning, particularly if the home culture is to be shared and discussed with people from other cultures. And so we invite learners to visit familiar places, the better to observe and describe local linguistic and cultural practices in such everyday settings as supermarkets, hairdressers and cafés before comparing and discussing their descriptions with classmates and then sharing their insights online with 'e-partners' elsewhere around the globe.

The second major strand in the book is semiotic. Many of the activities invite learners to consider how conversational conventions work in first and second languages, how non-verbal behaviour impacts on communicative acts, such as greeting and persuading, and how visual communication is used publicly in genres such as advertising, and privately in contexts such as dressing up for an evening out. As well as developing an ethnographic imagination, then, intercultural language learners should, over time, become adept at 'reading' and interpreting an ever broader range of linguistic and cultural practices.

Knowing how to relativise oneself and value the attitudes and beliefs of others

Intercultural language education should not lead to uncritical acceptance of the values and beliefs of others, and intercultural language learners should develop inquiring and open minds when faced with otherness. Many of the activities in this book address issues that the learner might at first find strange in the culture of others – for example, attitudes to food, beauty, religion and politics. One way of encouraging respect for the unfamiliar is to make the familiar strange, by 'decentring' one's perspective of one's own culture. Literary texts and other cultural forms of expression, like film and music, have long been recognised as effective means of dramatising strangeness in other cultures, as well as effective ways of defamiliarising the everyday, and they are used in this book, too, to stimulate discussion of other ways of being.

This book addresses a set of skills and competences that have come to be seen as integral to intercultural language education. It does so in a world that is rapidly changing, particularly in the opportunities afforded to learners in different countries to engage in communication directly with speakers and writers from other cultures. Whereas a mere decade or so ago many learners might complain that they would never have the opportunity to use their second language with other speakers, now the revolution in global communications has made contact between language users worldwide instant and inexpensive.

The Internet and intercultural language education

The arrival of the Internet has already reshaped intercultural language education for many learners. But the challenge to intercultural language educators is how to combine classroom teaching with the manifest opportunities offered for formal and informal learning. On the plus side, learners today have unparalleled access to channels of instant, interactive communication with English users worldwide. Never before have they enjoyed such rich opportunities for 'authentic' language use and the comparison of different cultural practices. On the negative side, unhappier experiences of online discussions can show learners easily becoming frustrated by the different expectations of their 'e-partners', in, for example, the time, enthusiasm, and seriousness that they invest in their electronic interactions. Also, in some cases, the widely different political values of partners in an online exchange undermine the building of respect and empathy necessary for an effective exchange of views.

Effective online exchanges, like other educational initiatives, need to be managed, and even then, their success is never guaranteed. Nevertheless, the rewards of building an effective online community of learners outweigh the various risks that teachers and learners face. Many of the activities in this book, then, assume that learners will have access to the Internet, whether in the classroom, the home or through an Internet café. Most of the activities can still be done without such access, but the activities will be greatly enriched if you can help learners find and participate in an online intercultural community. The initial activities in this book are directed towards supporting you and your learners in finding such communities, and in making good use of them. Technology is now outpacing educational practices in many ways – online communities are facilitated by social networking programs like Facebook, Bebo and Orkut, while a resource such as Tag Galaxy (www.taggalaxy.de) facilitates the sharing and display of photographs taken by participants from every corner of the planet. Ben Goldstein's *Working with Images* is one of a range of books that, like the present volume, seek to acknowledge and exploit many online resources now available to learners. The activities in *Intercultural Language Activities* encourage you and your learners to participate in more structured online projects than are presently offered by social networking programs, but the skills and attributes developed by the activities here can be transferable to different online environments.

Of course, the Internet is not only a forum where people from different cultures can meet; it is also an inexhaustible source of information about different cultures and societies. Some of the activities in this book invite learners to explore the wealth of information provided by the Internet. The activities encourage the use of internet resources to *discover* information by the critical reading of news websites, for example, or the use of online corpora to investigate language use. They discourage learners from simply finding a suitable website and cutting and pasting facts without processing them.

The Internet is also, like many powerful tools, open to abuse. It goes without saying that, particularly when establishing an intercultural community where children are exchanging information online, care must be taken to ensure that there is no exploitation of participants. The websites suggested in this book are of organisations that have a reputable track record of twinning educational institutions such as schools. In addition, one of the activities focuses explicitly on developing awareness of 'netiquette', the dos and don'ts of online intercultural exchange.

The organisation of this book

The book is intended to support a wide range of teachers who are involved in general English courses with teenagers and adults, working either in English-speaking communities or in non-English-speaking countries. The book can be dipped into for individual activities, or the activities can be followed in a sequence appropriate to the interests and language level of the learners.

The activities are intended to supplement the main syllabus or coursework adopted by an educational institution; the section on *Icons*, for example, would naturally extend language practice in the description of people, while the debate on blood sports or politics gives further practice in the language of argumentation. Many of the topics and activities demand a certain level of maturity and are designed for teenagers and adults, with a language level of intermediate or above. They are intended to build on a basic knowledge of the world and to excite an interest in discovering more. The activities should help learners to enjoy making links between the familiar and the strange, the easy and the less comfortable, the self and the other. You will no doubt adapt these activities for the levels, needs and interests of your own learners, some activities being more suitable for younger learners than others. I trust, however, that the activities will help you and your learners to make many unpredictable and exciting intercultural connections.

Chapter 1 *Setting up an online community* gives practical advice on setting up computer-mediated intercultural exchanges, and some suggestions on how to start and develop online discussions. As noted above, simply providing a technological platform for online discussions does not guarantee their success, and the opening chapter of this book suggests ways of supporting learners as they become used to communicating through online discussion groups. Not all such discussions, however, are smooth or unproblematical. A key component of intercultural communicative competence is the ability to mediate between people in conflict, whose misunderstanding might well arise from differences in cultural perspective. Chapter 2 *Mediations* offers a set of activities encouraging learners to deal with incidents that potentially involve misunderstanding and disagreement. Chapter 3 *Domestic life* deals with the everyday nature of culture, and invites learners to look afresh at their own home lives and see themselves as others might see them. This chapter is complemented by the next one, 4 *Public spaces,* which moves outside the domain of the home to explore the public places of leisure and commerce. Chapter 5 *Face to face* builds up learners' understanding of aspects of conversation, with an emphasis on storytelling, body language and informal expression. The theme of oral communication is extended in Chapter 6 *Interviewing* to those particular skills necessary for learners to investigate culture through interviews with people from different walks of life. From oral skills, Chapter 7 *Interpretations* turns to reading and writing, with a series of activities designed to enhance the learners' engagement with written material, whether that material is traditional 'hard copy' or online resources such as freely available, searchable corpora of digitised texts.

At this point, the book turns to a series of what might be termed 'intercultural issues'. These chapters are topic-based and involve learners in reflecting on aspects of their own cultural experience and comparing these with the experiences of others. Chapter 8 *Childhood* invites learners to recall the period of their formation as individuals, and their integration into the community through school. Chapter 9 *Icons* focuses on the roles that famous figures and celebrities play in local, national and international life, paying particular attention to the values and qualities that they embody for different communities. Chapter 10 *Sport* considers, for example, how tribal loyalties are expressed by spectators, fans and cheerleaders and looks at unusual sports. Chapter 11 *Food* encourages learners to explore the different cultural meanings expressed by food, restaurants and supermarkets in different places. Chapter 12 *Politics* and Chapter 13 *Religion* broach sensitive subjects that new teachers of language are often warned against – for good reason. Even so, learners are often highly engaged with their political and religious beliefs, and, for this reason, despite the obvious challenges, these topics merit a place in an intercultural language curriculum. These topics also offer potential for integration of language classes with other courses across the curriculum, most obviously in the areas of history and the social sciences. At first glance, the final chapter, 14 *Presenting an image*, is less controversial, with its focus on fashion and appearance, and yet it addresses the no less serious issue of the messages we send to others in the ways we mould our personal appearance.

Using the CD-ROM

There are many photocopiable extracts in this book, varying from dialogues to observation schedules. All of these are to be found on the accompanying CD-ROM as PDF files. These can be projected in the classroom, or they can be printed out and handed to your learners. There are also photos on the CD-ROM and all the material is cross-referenced in the book so you can find the materials you need quickly and easily.

Website

For further information and extra materials please visit www.cambridge.org/elt/intercultural

1 Setting up an online community

The last 30 years have seen an unprecedented revolution in communications technology. Whereas only a few decades ago, many learners of English worldwide might never actually have encountered another speaker of English outside their classroom or school, now email, internet chat rooms, discussion boards, blogs and instant messaging have made communication across languages and cultures commonplace, quick and easy. Computer-mediated communication has given a whole new impetus to the integration of culture-learning with language-learning. Many teachers have consequently taken the opportunity to set up collaborative online partnerships with other teachers and learners of English worldwide.

While most of the activities in this book can be accomplished without participating in an online intercultural exchange, many of the tasks can be brought alive by the involvement of 'e-partners' from around the globe. Learners will therefore need access to the Internet to take part in the intercultural exchange. This first chapter gives guidance to those who are thinking of establishing an online community of learners of language and culture. *Setting up an online intercultural exchange* (1.1) prepares the class and helps you to arrange an online collaboration with appropriate e-partners elsewhere. *Describing an e-partner* (1.2) helps learners build relationships with their e-partners. *Starting an online discussion* (1.3) and *Developing an online discussion* (1.4) focus on the kind of language that is required to start and develop a successful discussion thread online. Early on in an online collaboration it might be a good idea to establish ground rules, and *Netiquette: devising rules for an online community* (1.5) is designed to ensure that the expectations amongst the members about, say, the quantity and nature of the online communication are clear to all. *Exploring culture through a virtual mascot* (1.6) suggests a way for younger learners to compare cultures and *Intercultural film club* (1.7) focuses on sharing observations and opinions on films from different cultures; while the final activity, *Journal of intercultural discussions* (1.8), encourages learners to keep a reflective journal of their intercultural encounters online.

1.1 Setting up an online intercultural exchange

Outline	You set up an online exchange for your learners, to connect them to speakers and learners of other languages worldwide (e-partners). The class chooses a partner school or institution to collaborate with, and rehearses an ice-breaking activity in class.
Focus	Familiarising learners with the idea of e-partners and motivating them to begin a series of dialogues with them. Basic personal description.
Level	Lower intermediate and above
Time	15 minutes in the first lesson and 30 minutes in the second lesson
Preparation	Learners will need access to a computer with an internet connection, here and in other activities in this chapter. Learners will also need sheets of paper and copies of Box 1.1a. Alternatively, you could project it from the CD-ROM. Several institutions that support online exchanges for language learning are listed in *Further reading and resources* on p. 257. This activity should be spread over two lessons.

Procedure

1 Explain to the learners that they are going to link up with e-partners in another country to learn about different cultures. With the class choose a country that learners want to find out more about. Various websites can be used to put teachers and learners in touch with each other. For example The Global Gateway, managed for the Department of Children, Schools and Families by the British Council, is a website that puts teachers in contact with each other, and learners themselves can use the 'ePals' network (suggested websites are given on p. 257).

2 When the class has chosen a partner school, and you have contacted the partner school and established an online collaboration with another class, the learners can use email or web-based forums to begin a discussion with their e-partners. A sequence of emails and responses is usually called a 'discussion thread'. Depending on the communications technology used, the learners' familiarity with it, and their language level, you can match up individuals into partnerships, or allow the learners to find their own partners. As in most social situations, however, learners first need to get to know each other. Explain that the learners will be posting messages on an online discussion board so they can get to know their e-partners. The messages should have the following format:

   • Introduce yourself: say who you are and where you are from.
   • Give four words that you think describe you.

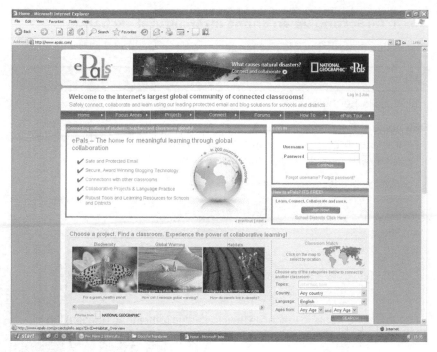

The 'ePals' website (www.epals.com)

The example in Box 1.1a shows a typical exchange between two e-partners. This example can be used with less advanced learners to show how one e-partner gives some basic information about herself, and the other e-partner responds with some friendly comments and further questions.

3   To practise, the learners take a sheet of paper, write an introduction about themselves and four words that describe them. Put learners into pairs and ask them to swap their introductions.

4   In their pairs, they respond to each other's message by writing a question. They return the sheet of paper to their partner.

5   They answer the question and swap the sheets of paper again.

6   Choose some of the exchanges to discuss in class and ask learners to suggest ways of extending or improving them.

7   Once you have set up the exchange with the partner institution, the learners go online and post their introductions, their four words, and, later, their responses to their e-partners.

Box 1.1a: Setting up an online intercultural exchange

Discussion thread: Sample exchange

From: Ciorsdan

Salut, hallo, hej, hola, oi

My name is Ciorsdan (which is Scottish Gaelic and pronounced 'Kirsten'). I'm from the north of Scotland, in between Inverness and Aberdeen - I basically live in a field near a town called Huntly.

Four words to describe me are:
sociable
smiley ☺
ambitious
open-minded

Bye for now

Ciorsdan

P.S. If anyone wants to teach me their language (other than English) I'm willing to learn!!

From: Alfredo

Hi Ciorsdan, what a beautiful name!

I've always wondered what it is like to live in a field. What's the weather like there? I'll propose something to all of you. Why don't you tell us what it is like where you live and what you like to do.

It would be fun for us to know how people from different places actually live every day and how they see their world, wouldn't it?

Eso es todo por el momento.*

Alfredo (from Argentina)
BTW if anyone needs a little help with their Spanish I'll be here and I'm sure my Argentinian friends will too.

© Cambridge University Press 2010   PHOTOCOPIABLE

* = That's all for the moment.
BTW = by the way

Note: The discussion threads contain some errors as they are written by students.

1.2 Describing an e-partner

Outline	Learners begin discussions and build relationships with their e-partners by exchanging personal descriptions of themselves.
Focus	Descriptive language.
Level	Elementary
Time	20 minutes in the first lesson and 20 minutes plus in the second lesson
Preparation	This activity will need to be spread over two lessons.

Procedure

1   Either pair learners up with an e-partner, or ask them to choose an e-partner for themselves. They are going to write a description of themselves for their e-partners. If necessary, pre-teach some descriptive language, e.g. *tall/medium-height/short, brown/dark/red/blonde/fair hair, blue/brown/green eyes*, and elicit some of the learners' likes and dislikes.

2   Learners practise writing a brief description of themselves, e.g.
   My name is . . . and I was born in . . .
   I'm tall/short with . . . hair and . . . eyes.
   I've got . . . brothers/sisters.
   I like . . . and I dislike . . .
   My favourite music / football club / film star is . . .

3   Circulate and check learners' work. Next, with the class, discuss a polite way of asking the e-partners for information about themselves, e.g. *Hi! My name's Maria. I'd like to get to know you better. I was born in . . . Tell me about yourself! I look forward to hearing from you!*

4   The learners go online and post their descriptions.

5   When replies have arrived from the e-partners, tell learners that they are going to compare their partners with themselves. To introduce the language of comparison, ask a learner to come to the front of the class. Find out something about their preferences – what does he or she like? Compare their appearance and preferences with your own, and write some model sentences on the board, e.g.
   We have both got blue eyes.
   We both like/dislike the films of . . .
   My partner has got brown hair and I have got fair hair.
   I like . . . but my partner doesn't.

6   The learners write a comparison of themselves and their e-partners. Afterwards, nominate some learners to read their descriptions aloud.

1.3 Starting an online discussion

Outline	Learners prepare for more elaborate online discussions with their e-partners.
Focus	The structuring of effective discussion 'starters'.
Level	Lower intermediate and above
Time	30 minutes plus
Preparation	You will need a computer and projector to project Boxes 1.3a and 1.3b on the board. Alternatively photocopy them for learners. Boxes 1.3c and 1.3d can be used instead with lower-level learners.

Procedure

1   Inform the learners that they are going to practise starting an online discussion on a topic of their choice. Elicit some possible topics from the class and write these on the board, e.g. food and drink, leisure activities, and so on. A popular discussion starter is to ask for a 'top 5' list, e.g. 'my favourite 5 songs/singers', or 'my favourite 5 films'. Or discussion starters could be more unusual, such as *What is the best name for a pet snake?* or *What is the best wallpaper design for a hotel bedroom / office / prison cell?* Ask the learners to write three or four sentences that they hope will prompt an interesting response from their e-partners.

2   Next, hand out copies, or project onscreen, the two examples of discussion starters in Boxes 1.3a and 1.3b. (Variations and instructions for learners with a more basic knowledge of language are suggested at the end.) Ask the learners to read each of the starters, and answer the following questions:

   • What expressions does each writer use to show any of the following:

      modesty   sincerity   politeness   interest in the answer?

   • What expressions does each writer use to share his or her own views?

   • Which of the starters do you think will be more effective? Why?

Suggested answers:

Discussion starter A has various modesty and politeness formulae, e.g. *This might seem like a bit of an odd question but. . .*; *Hehe* [i.e. laughter] *a bit of a dull subject I know, but. . .* It also indicates a sincere personal interest in the topic, e.g. *I thought it might be interesting*; *I would very much appreciate everyone's thoughts and ideas.* It offers views as well as asks for others' (*Mine would have to be...*) and is therefore the more effective starter.

Discussion starter B is polite and friendly, but the question looks as if it has really been asked by a teacher. The topic is very general and no examples are given. There is no indication that the writer has any personal interest in the question whatsoever.

Box 1.3a: Starting an online discussion

Discussion thread: Starter A

From: Laura

This might seem like a bit of an odd question but I was just wondering what everyone's favourite drink is? (Not including alcohol!!!!) Mine would have to be that old British favourite, tea, although I know many others prefer coffee . . . Hehe a bit of a dull subject I know, but I thought it might be interesting to see how much we all differ in our basic preferences. I would very much appreciate everyone's thoughts and ideas . . .

Cheers!

© Cambridge University Press 2010   PHOTOCOPIABLE

Box 1.3b: Starting an online discussion

Discussion thread: Starter B

From: Pearl

Hi, nice to meet you. May I ask you a question? What's your opinion about the transformation of women's status in your society in the past and in the present, in the west and in the east? Thank you for your help!

© Cambridge University Press 2010   PHOTOCOPIABLE

3 Ask the learners about how they would respond to the two discussion starters shown.
4 Invite the learners to review their own discussion starters and check for:
   - politeness
   - the offer of their own opinion
   - evidence of sincere interest in the topic

The learners revise their discussion starter and write it at the top of a piece of paper.
5 Put learners into groups of four. Each member of the group passes their discussion starter to the person on their right who writes a response to it. Then they pass it to their right again and continue until they receive the paper with their own starter. They read all three responses to their starter.
6 After rehearsing their starters in class, the learners go online and try their discussion starter out on their e-partners.
7 Once learners have received replies from their e-partners, get them to feed back their findings to the rest of the class. If necessary, model language for learners, such as, *X is from Japan and her favourite drink is . . .*

Variation for lower-level learners
One popular option is to ask the members of the online community to compose a list, such as their favourite game shows, sitcom stars, or a 'bucket list' of things they would like to do before they die (or, colloquially, 'kick the bucket'). For learners with a more basic language level, you might wish to substitute the following discussion starters instead of step 2:

Box 1.3c: Starting an online discussion

Discussion thread: Variation starter 1

From: Adriana

Hi!

I am really interested in the three things that people want to do before they 'kick the bucket' (die) ☹. I would like to (1) visit the Pyramids in Egypt, (2) drive a Lamborghini, and (3) do a bungee jump from the Golden Gate Bridge in San Francisco. Pretty selfish, I know! But what would you like to do?? I look forward to hearing from you! ☺

© Cambridge University Press 2010   PHOTOCOPIABLE

Box 1.3d: Starting an online discussion

Discussion thread: Variation starter 2

> From: Hui
>
> Hi!
>
> May I ask you a question? I want to know the three things you would do before you die. This is called a 'bucket list' because it lists things to do before you 'kick the bucket'. Thank you for your help.

© Cambridge University Press 2010   PHOTOCOPIABLE

1.4 Developing an online discussion

Outline	Learners rehearse the kinds of discussion to be found online using the example topic 'pets'. They are then encouraged to identify other possible topics for an online discussion. This task follows on from *Starting an online discussion* (1.3).
Focus	Developing an online discussion.
Level	Lower intermediate and above
Time	30 minutes plus
Preparation	Learners will need copies of Box 1.4a and pieces of paper. You may also like to show learners example responses in Boxes 1.4b and 1.4c.

Procedure

1 Begin by asking learners how they would start an online discussion about 'pets'. Together, the class drafts a discussion starter. This can be compared with the example in Box 1.4a, and modified or refined, if necessary.

2 On a sheet of paper, each learner writes a short response to the class discussion starter. After finishing the response, the learners pass the sheet of paper to a partner.

3 Each partner now writes another response to the first learner's response, and they pass the sheet of paper on again, to another member of the class – until the page is filled up.

4 Next, select some responses, discuss them, and get the class to think of ways to improve and elaborate on the responses and questions. For a variation for more advanced learners, see pp. 21–22.

5   Finally, the learners go online, introduce and discuss the topic of pets with their e-partners.

6   You can prompt the learners to use their textbooks and watch television programmes or films from other countries to identify possible discussion topics and bring them to the next lesson. Sometimes the most productive are about surprisingly everyday topics, for example, *what do newsagents/newsstands sell in your country?* There are many differences between countries, e.g. in some countries newsagents also sell alcohol, sandwiches, bus tickets, parking permits, ice cream, DVDs, etc. An ideal discussion is one that encourages learners to look afresh at their own community and their own behaviour, while comparing it to another community and its behaviour.

Box 1.4a: Developing an online discussion

Discussion thread: Example starter

From: Jo
Hi everyone!
Does anyone have a pet? How are animals treated in your culture? Here in Britain, we have the reputation of being crazy about our pets. My pets are treated like family members. How are pets viewed in your culture and do you guys have any or want any?
I have a dog called Buster, fish (who don't have names) and a lizard called Vegas ☺. Do you have organisations to look after sick animals? What sort of animals are kept as pets? Do you have pet shops?
I look forward to hearing from you!

© Cambridge University Press 2010   PHOTOCOPIABLE

Variation for more advanced learners

You can introduce the sample responses in Boxes 1.4b and 1.4c, and discuss some of the language features used, e.g. personal opinions:

> *I am not a great fan of (insects).*
> *I am definitely a (cat) lover!*
> *I think (feeding Poldi) is disgusting.*
> *I do like (dogs) as well.*

and comparisons:

> *There is no great difference between (Great Britain) and (Germany) in terms of (pets).*
> *(Dad) loves (Tigerle) as much as I do.*
> *(Dogs) need a lot more (looking after) than (cats).*

Box 1.4b: Developing an online discussion

Discussion thread: Sample response to Jo

From: Angie

Hi,

I have a cat called Tigerle (little tiger) and I miss him very much. At first, my dad didn't want a cat ('And who is going to look after him when we want to go on holiday?' etc.), but now he loves Tigerle as much as I do. ☺

I think there is no great difference between Great Britain and Germany in terms of pets. We have organisations to look after animals, etc. and we even have 'animal hotels' where people take care of your pet while you are on holiday. Who looks after Buster, Vegas and your fish when you are not there? Are you responsible for them or does the whole family take care of them?

An old friend of mine has a lizard, too. His name is Poldi and I had to feed him insects sometimes when she wasn't there which was quite disgusting as I am not a great fan of insects. . . What does Vegas eat?

Say hi to your pets, enjoy your day,
Angie

© Cambridge University Press 2010   PHOTOCOPIABLE

Box 1.4c: Developing an online discussion

Discussion thread: Sample response to Angie

From: Paul

I am definitely a cat lover!

My cat (Bilbo Baggins) pulls the funniest faces. His expressions are priceless. He clearly thinks that he's head of the household (he tries his best at trying to take over all the comfortable places in the house and he thinks that he has the right to all food) and is in a constant battle with my dad about it, who tries his best to enforce some discipline on him. But, really, how can you discipline a cat? They know their own minds far too well.

It's the best at meal times when, all of a sudden, this little head will pop up above the table with ears flattened and nose sniffing. He generally tends to look a bit miffed. I think it's because he doesn't get invitations to dinner. But he always manages to sneak into the kitchen some way or another.

Even though I've been rambling on about how great my cat is, I do like dogs as well. They just need a lot more looking after than cats, so I'd probably always choose cats over them. Actually, Bilbo is dog-like in that he comes on walks with me. It's true, he will always follow me when I go on walks across the fields and around the country lanes and he always makes this cute wailing noise, as if to say "Hey, where are you going?". Or, actually, he might be trying to say "Hey you. Where do you think you're going? I want feeding!!"

Paul

© Cambridge University Press 2010   PHOTOCOPIABLE

* The discussion threads contain some errors as they are written by students.

1.5 Netiquette: devising rules for an online community

Outline	Learners cooperate with their e-partners to devise a set of 'rules' governing acceptable behaviour in the online community.
Focus	Ensuring learners and their e-partners have similar expectations about how to behave online.
Level	Intermediate and above
Time	30 minutes in the first class; the list of rules can be reviewed and amended in 10–15 minutes in later classes
Preparation	You will need a board or overhead projector. This activity will need to be spread over a few lessons.

Procedure

1   This activity should be done early in the process of establishing an online intercultural exchange. Invite the learners to think about what they like and do not like when they are using email or chat rooms. For example, do they care about prompt responses, politeness, or accurate spelling and punctuation? Put learners in groups and get them to brainstorm ideas for a list of acceptable online behaviour.

2   Each group reports back and you draw up a list, on the board or overhead projector, which might cover the following:
   * The minimum number of expected mails/postings per week is . . .
   * The expected response time to a mail/posting is . . .
   * The maximum length of a mail/post should be . . .
   * The maximum size of an attached file should be . . .
   * Taboo discussion topics will include . . . (or there are no taboo topics).
   * DON'T USE CAPITAL LETTERS (it seems as if you are shouting).
   * Treat participants with respect. Do not use abusive language. Do not assume that the values and beliefs of others are the same as your own.
   * Do not write anything when you are feeling tired or emotional.
   * Humour or irony is sometimes difficult to understand across languages and cultures, and so should be explicitly signalled, e.g. by ☺.
   * Do not criticise or correct other people's spelling or grammar.
   * When quoting others, do not change the words of their postings or mails.

3   Select a learner to post the provisional list of 'rules of netiquette' online for negotiation with the group of e-partners. After an online discussion, the class and the e-partners agree a final version to act as a framework for the collaboration. Appoint another class member to edit the provisional list and then post the final version online.

1.6 Exploring culture through a virtual mascot

Outline	The class and their e-partners make and exchange paper mascots which they use to discuss aspects of culture. This activity works particularly well with younger learners.
Focus	Writing brief descriptions of everyday life in one's own culture, and reading brief descriptions of life elsewhere.
Level	Pre-intermediate
Time	40 minutes in the first class and 20–30 minutes in follow-up classes
Preparation	It is assumed that the class is involved in an online intercultural exchange with learners of the same age elsewhere. Sturdy paper and colouring pens are needed for the creation of the mascot, which needs to be posted or scanned in and sent to the class of e-partners. Learners can take photographs of the visiting mascot enjoying aspects of their culture. You will also need photos of mascots for step 1. Alternatively, use the photo on the CD-ROM in Box 1.6a. This activity may need to be spread over a few lessons.

Procedure

1   Introduce the concept of a mascot, i.e. a person, animal or mythical being used to represent a group, community or company. You could look at football mascots or search online for Olympic Games mascots, e.g. Sam the eagle, USA (1986), Hodori the tiger, Korea (1990). Alternatively, show learners the Olympic mascots in Box 1.6a ('good luck dolls' or *fuwa*, China 2008).

2   As a class, the learners brainstorm possible ideas for a mascot, e.g. will it be a person, an animal or a mythical creature? They then decide what will represent them as a class.

3   Explain to the learners that they are now going to design their mascot and send it to their e-partners. Elicit from the class some of the features of your mascot – for example, has it got pointed ears, big blue eyes, long, hairy legs? Either you or one of the learners draws the mascot on the board in response to suggestions from the class. Then guide the class in a group composition, to give the mascot a brief biography:

• What is its name?
• Where does it come from? (This should be somewhere local.)
• What does it like to eat?
• What are its hobbies?

Box 1.6a: Exploring culture through a virtual mascot

Photo: Olympic Games mascots

© Corbis/Claro Cortes IV/Reuters

From *Intercultural Language Activities*
© Cambridge University Press 2010   PHOTOCOPIABLE

---

4   The class then sends the mascot to the e-partners with its biography.
    They may do this physically, by sending the mascot through the post or,
    alternatively, they can scan or photograph their mascot and email its
    image to the e-partners. The class receives a guest mascot in return from
    their e-partners.

5   Once the guest mascot has been received, get the class to decide on
    experiences that it should have in the local community. For example, the
    class might decide to do some of the following activities:
    • take the guest mascot to a local restaurant or café
    • take the guest mascot to a school sports' event
    • take the guest mascot to a local beauty spot
    • take the guest mascot to the local shops or market

6   Next, divide the class into groups and get each group to select a different
    activity to do with the guest mascot, either together or taking turns with
    their families. When they have completed the activity, each group should
    write about it for the e-partners (e.g. *We took X to a local restaurant for
    lunch. There was a big menu, which included* ...). If possible, photographs

should be taken, to show the e-partners their mascot having these experiences.

7 The class members then post a report so that the e-partners can read about their mascot.

8 The class members also read about the experiences of their own mascot in another culture. Where appropriate, they can discuss their own mascot's experiences in class. For example, if their mascot visits a local landmark or participates in a local festival, then together, you can rehearse some follow-up questions, and send them to the partner class. This can be a good way of learning more about the partner class's environment, history and customs. If the mascot visits a local castle, ancient building, temple or gallery, the class can ask their partners about when it was built, why it was built, who owns it, who visits it now, and so on.

Variation

Instead of writing their reports of the mascot's experiences, the learners can write emails or postcards as if they are from the guest mascot (e.g. *Today I went to a local restaurant for lunch. There was a big menu, which included . . . I tried the . . . It was delicious/disgusting!*).

Note

This activity is inspired by Joina M. Almeida and a group of Brazilian teachers who participated in an exchange using the popular children's character 'Flat Stanley'. Information about the character and similar projects is available at http://www.flatstanley.com and http://www.flatstanleyproject.net/

1.7 Intercultural film club

Outline	Learners watch films from different cultures and share their observations and opinions of those films, ideally online, with people from those cultures.
Focus	Describing films and making evaluations.
Level	Intermediate and above
Time	30 minutes in the first class and 20–30 minutes in follow-up classes
Preparation	Learners will need access to DVDs or films from the countries participating in the online intercultural exchange. You should check they are in a usable format. Learners watch the films outside the class. Box 1.7a should be copied for learners. This activity should be spread over a few lessons and includes homework

Procedure

1   Ask the class whether they watch films in a language that is not their first language. If they do, make a list on the board of a few of the films suggested, and one or two opinions of them, e.g.

Film	Director	Language	Opinion
The Leopard	Luchino Visconti	Italian	'beautifully shot', 'badly dubbed', 'too painful to watch'
Infernal Affairs	Siu Fai Mak & Wai Keung Lau	Cantonese	'stylish thriller', 'a study of good and evil'
Behind the Sun	Walter Salles	Brazilian Portuguese	'bleak but beautiful', 'slow and depressing'

2   Explain that learners are going to watch films for homework which will be in English, with English subtitles, or dubbed into English. Ideally the class should use DVDs that have subtitles in English; learners can then listen to the dialogue and read it as well. In conjunction with the learners and their e-partners, devise a list of available films from their different cultures to watch for homework.

3   Introduce the class to the observation schedule in Box 1.7a, and explain they should complete it while they are watching their film.

4   Get learners to watch the films outside class. Encourage learners to look at other reviews of the film online, for example on the www.rottentomatoes. com website. Ask learners to note down useful vocabulary.

5   Afterwards, get learners to post their observations online to their e-partners. Encourage them to start a discussion about anything they found strange or puzzling about the behaviour of the characters in the film. Get them to find out how closely it reflects life in the e-partner's culture. (You should monitor the postings, but refrain from intervening. The discussion space should be for the learners alone.)

> ## Box 1.7a: Intercultural film club
>
> ### Observation schedule: Describing a film
>
> 1 Title of the film:
>
> 2 Name of the director:
>
> 3 Year it was made:
>
> 4 Original language:
>
> 5 Locations in which it is set:
>
> 6 Summary of the plot:
>
> 7 A surprising or confusing incident in the film:
>
> 8 An interesting cultural difference or similarity:
>
> 9 My overall opinion about the film:
>
> © Cambridge University Press 2010   PHOTOCOPIABLE

1.8 Journal of intercultural discussions

Outline	Learners reflect systematically on their experience of online intercultural communication. They keep a regular journal of their online intercultural 'encounters' and monitor the language they have learnt, and their cultural insights.
Focus	Personal narrative.
Level	Intermediate and above
Time	30 minutes plus
Preparation	Learners will need a notebook or computer access to keep their journal entries in, and copies of the suggested template for journal entries in Box 1.8a. You will also need a computer and projector to display the sample discussion thread (Box 1.8b) in class, or copies of the discussions for learners to read.

Procedure

1 Show the template of the journal (Box 1.8a) and discuss with the class the benefits of keeping a journal of their intercultural discussions, e.g.

- Keeping a regular journal is proof of learning, and so good for motivation.
- Reviewing a journal is good for the memory.

- Reviewing a journal helps give richer insights into language and culture.
2 Practise completing the journal with the learners by going through the sample discussion thread (Box 1.8b) with them.
3 Using the template in Box 1.8a as a prompt, the learners keep a journal based on their own interactions, on a regular basis (ideally, weekly). They may either submit their written records to you for comment, or email you their computer files on a regular basis.

Variation for lower-level learners

Learners with lower language levels could keep a journal of intercultural encounters in their mother tongue, using only some expressions in English. You can encourage them to use more and more English expressions in the journal until they have the confidence and skills to write wholly in English.

Box 1.8a: Journal of intercultural discussions

Journal: Online intercultural discussions

1 Your name:

2 Date:

3 Journal entry number:

    a) What was the topic of the online discussion?
    b) Who else was involved in the discussion?
    c) Did you learn anything new from this discussion? If so, what?
    d) How did you feel about what you learnt? For example, were you . . .

    surprised   disappointed   amused   confused   pleased   angry   saddened

    e) Put yourself in the position of the other people in the discussion. How do you think they felt about what they learnt?

    I can see that many of the people involved felt the same way about . . .
    I can see that many of the people involved felt differently about . . .

    f) Looking forward, I now want to find out more about . . .

                             PHOTOCOPIABLE

Box 1.8b: Journal of intercultural discussions

Discussion thread: A discussion starter and three responses

Topic: Sundays

From: Lydia, in Spain

I was just wondering what you think about Sundays? I was just looking outside, and all the trees are bare, the sun is not shining, it doesn't appear to be any different from other days, but still it has got a Sunday feeling to it. Do Sundays have a different feeling for you too? One of calmness?

How would you describe a perfect Sunday? I think for me it would be a long breakfast, maybe taking a walk, reading, and watching a nice movie.

From: Kinga, in Scotland

I come from Poland, but I'm studying in Glasgow now. On Sundays I usually try to read some stuff for uni, however as this is 'Sunday' it's quite hard. I had a two year gap between studies filled only with working Mon-Fri, so Sat/Sun were my days for being lazy. It's quite hard to shift and change my habits to working and studying on Sunday too.

P.S. Going for a walk is a really good idea ...

From: Verena, in Germany

Well, a perfect Sunday for me would start with a long, long sleep until nearly 11 o'clock. Then I would have a long breakfast. I would relax all day, just do nothing important. I try to do all the important things like homework or stuff like that on Saturday, so that I would have a free Sunday.

I also think that taking a nice walk would be a great idea, especially on the beach in Warnemünde on the Baltic sea, but reading and watching TV are also my favourites.

Bye and have a nice Sunday!

From: Chun-Chen, in Taiwan

Hello! I usually see a movie if I have free time on Sunday. I always have many things to do like preparing homework or practicing the guitar. And I like to go to the seaside, because my city is near the Taiwan Strait. I also like to read novels on a Sunday. I enjoy it.

PHOTOCOPIABLE

Note: The discussion threads contain some errors as they are written by students.

2 Mediations

One of the key roles played by intercultural speakers of different languages is that of mediator between people from different social and cultural backgrounds. The effective intercultural speaker is someone who can identify and explain cultural differences that might make others uncertain, or even uncomfortable. The activities in this chapter help develop learners' mediating skills. They fall generally into the categories of critical incidents and strategies for conflict resolution.

'Critical incidents' are widely used in education to encourage reflection and develop strategies for effective communication. They are examples of miscommunication or misunderstanding, usually caused by different cultural expectations held by the participants in the interaction. Learners develop a means of analysing critical incidents by:

- *describing* what has happened
- *interpreting* and *explaining* what has gone wrong with the communication
- *suggesting* alternative ways of communicating

By developing analytical skills, learners raise their awareness of the cultural factors that contribute to effective and ineffective communication. The activities encourage learners to develop skills in analysing critical incidents, before inviting them to identify, explain and discuss critical incidents of their own. Often no single solution can be found; however, the identification and analysis of critical incidents is useful in probing the cultural assumptions that underlie communication. *Levels of formality* (2.1) invites learners to observe and reflect on possible areas of difficulty arising from choosing a formal or informal means of expression in different situations. The next activity, *Job interview* (2.2), asks learners to apply their observational and explanatory skills to a particular situation, a job interview, which might mean different things to different people. *Gender and sympathy* (2.3) encourages learners to explore the expectations that males and females bring to everyday conversation. *Personal critical incidents* (2.4) acts as an introduction to critical incidents as a concept, and encourages learners to reflect on similar situations in their own experience, and to develop systematic strategies for dealing with them.

Critical incidents can result in some discomfort, embarrassment, or, at worst, conflict. One of the most demanding competences that intercultural language learners are expected to develop is mediating between different sides in conflict. This level of expertise is delicate, sophisticated and demands sensitivity and maturity. Sensitivity and maturity are not necessarily qualities that can be taught in the language classroom; however, intercultural language activities do at times require engagement with these qualities. Some of the activities in this chapter therefore focus directly on uncomfortable situations where misconceptions, disagreements or conflict might well occur, within and across cultures. There is, of course, no guaranteed 'formula' for resolving disputes and disagreements whether within or across cultures. However, teachers can expose learners to situations where disagreements are likely to arise, and, in the 'safe space' of the classroom, learners can practise recognising some of the signals of conflict, and so develop strategies for dealing with it. In this light, *Styles of conflict resolution* (2.5), considers different styles of dealing with conflict, *Conflict mediation* (2.6) gives an example of a role play involving conflict, and *Reflecting on conflict* (2.7) encourages learners to reflect on conflicts that they see on TV and in films and to explore the language and strategies used to manage them. To conclude, *Questioning and defending a belief* (2.8) helps learners to develop appropriate strategies for discussing issues that they feel strongly about.

2.1 Levels of formality

Outline	Learners identify and discuss communication problems that others are having and suggest solutions.
Focus	Introducing, requesting, inviting and complaining. This activity is a good follow-up to classes which deal with the language of formal or informal introductions.
Level	Intermediate and above
Time	40 minutes plus
Preparation	Copy the sample dialogues and situation cards for learners in Boxes 2.1a to 2.1e, or project them from the CD-ROM.

Procedure
1 Begin by explaining to the learners that they are going to look at situations in which people encounter communication difficulties.

Read out the following example:

An American and a Chinese professor of English are attending a conference. At the opening reception, the American professor notices the Chinese professor is standing alone and looks lonely. The American decides to say hello.

Next, brainstorm with the class what the American professor might say in a situation like this, and how the Chinese professor might respond. Divide the class into pairs, and get each pair to make up a short dialogue that they can act out. The learners' dialogues will probably be similar to the one shown in Box 2.1a.

2 After the class has practised their dialogues in pairs, ask them to reflect on some of the basic decisions each of the participants has made, e.g.
   - whether the speakers should address each other formally or informally
   - whether the speakers should use each other's first name or title plus surname
   - how close they should stand to each other
   - how much eye contact they should use

3 After discussing these issues, give the pairs the dialogue in Box 2.1a and ask them to read it aloud. They then discuss how to change the level of formality and they role play it. There is an example in Box 2.1b which shows both professors being less formal. The learners can then discuss how the change in formality changes the nature of the relationship between the two men.

Box 2.1a: Levels of formality

Model dialogue A: Formality level

American professor:	Good evening. May I introduce myself? I'm Professor Joe Williams from UCLA.
Chinese professor:	Good evening. My name's Xiao Zheng.
American professor:	I'm delighted to meet you, Professor Zheng. Have you travelled far to the conference?
Chinese professor:	Yes, I've travelled from Shanghai.

© Cambridge University Press 2010   PHOTOCOPIABLE

Box 2.1b: Levels of formality

Model dialogue B: Formality level

American professor: Hi there, how're you doing? I'm Joe Williams from UCLA.
Chinese professor:　Hello. My name's Xiao Zheng.
American professor: Pleased to meet you, Xiao. Where are you from? Beijing?
Chinese professor:　No, I'm from Shanghai.

© Cambridge University Press 2010　　　　　　　　　　PHOTOCOPIABLE

4　Ask the pairs to reflect on how they felt about changing the level of formality in this exchange. Did they feel more comfortable with an informal or a formal exchange?

5　Explain that different people might have different expectations of everyday encounters like this. For example, the American professor might feel more comfortable with an informal style of introduction, and consider formality a sign of unfriendliness. However, the Chinese professor might prefer a more formal style of introduction, and consider informality a sign of disrespect. To get on with each other, then, the two speakers are going to have to make some adjustments.

6　Distribute the role card for Situation one in Box 2.1c to all the learners and tell them that they should take the role of Speaker A, while you take the role of Speaker B. Give the learners some time to think about what they will say, and then nominate some learners to suggest ways of requesting permission to leave early. Elicit more and less formal ways of asking for permission, e.g.

Speaker A
(formal) *Excuse me for asking, Mr/Ms X, but is it possible for us to leave the class before it ends? It is necessary for us to pray at specific times during the day.*
(informal) *Look, [first name], there's a bit of a problem. We have to leave the class half-way through to pray, you know? That's going to be ok with you, isn't it?*
Speaker B
(formal) *I realise that this is important to you and I'm happy for you to leave the class as long as you do the work you miss afterwards.*
(informal) *Sure, not a problem. Thanks for letting me know. Check with me later to see what you've missed.*

34

With the class discuss which level of formality they are more comfortable with.

Ask the learners to think of other situations when they might need to ask permission to leave school or work early, e.g to visit a doctor, to pick up a child from school, etc. How would they ask for permission?

Note: Praying can be a sensitive topic so you may wish to adapt this activity. Alternative suggestions are learners needing to open a bank account or have time off for a special celebration, e.g. Chinese New Year.

7 Distribute the role cards for Situations two and three in Boxes 2.1d and 2.1e and ask the learners, in pairs, to think about what they would say in the situations described. They should think particularly about the formality of the language they will use and then rehearse their dialogues in pairs.

8 After the rehearsals, nominate some learners to re-enact their dialogues in front of the class. The class members should:
- listen to the exchanges
- summarise the problem
- suggest ways in which the speakers could improve their dialogues.

Box 2.1c: Levels of formality

Role card: Situation one

> Speaker A: You represent a group of Middle Eastern students who have travelled to Britain to learn English. You are meeting the teacher for the first time. Explain to the teacher that the students will have to leave class half-way through in order to pray.

> Speaker B: You teach English in a college in Britain. You are in charge of a new group of students from the Middle East. You are meeting the group representative for the first time.

Box 2.1d: Levels of formality

Role card: Situation two

Speaker A: You live in a city in Argentina. A new neighbour has moved into the area from another country, and you want to be friendly. Invite your new neighbour to a traditional South American barbecue, with lots of great local beef!

Speaker B: You have just arrived in Argentina from another country. You are settling in, but the diet is difficult. For health reasons, you do not eat meat.

© Cambridge University Press 2010   PHOTOCOPIABLE

Box 2.1e: Levels of formality

Role card: Situation three

Speaker A: You and your family live in a large block of flats. You have two children in their late teens. Last week, you and your husband/wife went away on holiday for a few days, leaving your children at home.

Speaker B: You have just moved into a large block of flats. You have a new job, and you are working hard. Unfortunately, your neighbour is having lots of parties at night. The music is so loud that you cannot sleep. Go to your neighbour and complain about the noise.

© Cambridge University Press 2010   PHOTOCOPIABLE

2.2 Job interview

Outline	Learners look at different cultural expectations within the format and function of a job interview.
Focus	Asking and answering questions; varying expectations about how to behave in a formal interview.
Level	Intermediate and above
Time	40 minutes plus
Preparation	Copy the example interviews and job advert in Boxes 2.2a and 2.2b for learners or project them from the CD-ROM.

Procedure

1 Explain to the class that people from different cultures often have different expectations of what happens in certain common situations. To illustrate this, the class is going to explore how different expectations influence a candidate's success or failure in a job interview.

2 Give the learners the example of a job advert for a van driver in Box 2.2a.

Box 2.2a: Job interview

Advert: Van driver

Speedy Couriers require Van Drivers

Must have clean UK driving licence

Basic salary: £280.00 per week

© Cambridge University Press 2010   PHOTOCOPIABLE

With the class brainstorm the kinds of questions that an employer and a candidate might ask at the job interview, and write them on the board, e.g.

Employer questions
- Have you got a clean driving licence?
- Have you got much experience of driving a van?
- Have you got any other work experience?
- What is your current job?
- Will you be able to work irregular hours/evenings and weekends?

Candidate questions
- Is there the opportunity for overtime?
- How many hours work is there per week?
- Is there the possibility of further training?
- What is the holiday entitlement?

In more advanced classes, you can elicit one or two questions, and then ask the learners in groups to come up with three or four more of their own.

3 Divide the class into groups of three, with two learners in each group taking the role of a job interviewer, and the third taking the role of a candidate for the job. Each group role plays an interview for the job. After

37

each interview, the 'candidates' from each group can circulate between 'employers'.

4 After each 'candidate' has been interviewed three or four times, you can end the role play. In a whole-class setting, if appropriate, the 'employers' and 'candidates' can discuss and rate each other's performance.

5 After the class discussion, ask the learners to imagine a situation in which two candidates had very similar work experience, but they answered the questions differently. Show the class the two exchanges in Box 2.2b and ask the learners to discuss in groups which of the two candidates they would choose to employ – and to give reasons why.

Box 2.2b: Job interview

Dialogue: Two example interviews

Candidate one

Employer: Have you got a clean driving licence?

Candidate one: I've never broken the law, no.

Employer: I see. Have you got any other work experience?

Candidate one: Yes, I've done lots of different things. I've never had any complaints.

Candidate two

Employer: Have you got a clean driving licence?

Candidate two: Yes, I've been qualified to drive vans since I was 18.

Employer: I see. Have you got any other work experience?

Candidate two: Yes – I've worked as a security guard and as a gardener. They didn't involve driving, but they did involve irregular hours and weekend work.

© Cambridge University Press 2010   PHOTOCOPIABLE

---

6 After the groups have chosen their preferred candidate and given their reasons to the rest of the class, comment on the expectations of each candidate. Candidate one treated the interview as a test, and believed that the employer's questions were intended to find out if they had a criminal record or a poor work record. Candidate two did not treat the interview as a *test*, and believed that the employer's questions were intended to give an *opportunity* to talk about their experience and how it relates to the job advertised. Candidate two is more likely to get the job.

7 Ask the class *why* the employer asks the following questions:
   • Have you got a clean driving licence?
   The employer probably wants to know something positive about the candidate's driving experience, for example, how long he or she has been qualified to drive a van.
   • Have you got much experience?
   The employer probably wants to know something positive about the candidate's relevant work experience, e.g. other driving jobs.
   • What other jobs have you had?
   The employer probably wants to know something positive about the candidate's experience of other types of job with similar conditions, e.g. involving travel, irregular hours, etc.

   After discussing what the employer *really* wants to know, ask the learners to rephrase the employer's questions so that they are more direct and explicit, e.g.
   • How long have you been qualified to drive a van?
   • Have you had other driving jobs?
   • Have you done any other jobs that required irregular hours or weekend work? Have you done any other jobs that demanded reliability and punctuality? Etc.

8 After this discussion, reorganise the learners into different groups of two employers and two candidates each, and ask them to role play the job interviews again, one candidate after the other. This time, the candidates must decide if they are going to treat the interview as a *test* or an *opportunity*. The employers must also decide if they are going to ask *explicit* or *indirect* questions.

9 Finally, the employers then decide which of the two candidates they wish to hire.

2.3 Gender and sympathy

Outline	Learners focus on the different expectations that males and females often bring to everyday conversation.
Focus	Past narratives; conversational storytelling; exploring what different genders expect from conversations.
Level	Intermediate and above
Time	40 minutes plus
Preparation	This activity might best be done after *Sharing stories in conversation* (5.1) and *Supporting talk* (5.2). Copy the reading text and situational role cards in Boxes 2.3a and 2.3b for learners.

Procedure

1 Ask learners the following questions:
   - Is it true that women are better listeners than men?
   - Is it true that men interrupt more than women?
   - Is it true that men are less sympathetic than women?

   The members of the class offer their opinions, and you then inform them that they are going to read some research on this topic. Give out the reading text in Box 2.3a. As a general pre-question, ask the learners if they agree with the description of typical male and female behaviour.

2 After they have read and discussed the points made in the reading text, read the following story to the class and ask the learners to think about how a male and a female might respond to it:

   I've had a terrible day. I was going to work this morning, wearing a new pair of high-heeled shoes, and one of the heels broke. Fortunately, I didn't hurt myself, but the shoes are ruined. I had to break the other heel myself, so that I could walk properly! I was going to go to the shoe store to complain, but I've lost the receipt, and I know that they won't exchange the shoes without proof that I bought them there. I just feel awful!

   Ask learners for typical male and female responses according to the reading text. The class might suggest that a woman would make lots of sympathetic noises and tell a similar story about ruining shoes or clothing, or losing a receipt. A man, however, might simply nod and then suggest that the woman keeps her receipts in a safe place in future.

3 Next, nominate particular learners to demonstrate 'typical' male and female responses, while you retell the story of the shoes.

Box 2.3a: Gender and sympathy

Reading text: Gender and differences in sympathy

Women often complain that men are not good listeners – but does this complaint have any basis in fact? Linguists think it does. Some language specialists have studied the conversations of men and women, and they have concluded that males and females do behave differently when they are talking.

Typically, when a woman is complaining about something to another woman, she gets sympathy from her listener. A sympathetic female listener will listen, say she understands, and talk about similar situations that she, too, has experienced.

But when a woman is complaining about something to a man, the story is very different. Males do not understand that the woman is simply seeking sympathy; a man believes that a woman is bringing a problem to him so that he can solve it. So, instead of talking about similar situations that he has experienced, the average man tells the woman what she should do in future. This is not what the average woman wants, and so she feels hurt and misunderstood. She also feels that the man is hard and unfeeling. The poor man, on his part, cannot understand why the woman is so upset. He's solved her problems, hasn't he?

© Cambridge University Press 2010   PHOTOCOPIABLE

---

4   After this, invite the learners, in pairs, to share and respond to the situations in the role cards in Box 2.3b. Distribute the cards randomly and get each learner to take it in turns to describe the situation. The listeners in each pair can choose either to share a similar experience, or provide a solution to the situation described.

5   Finally, lead a class discussion in which the learners reflect upon their performance. Issues that might arise include the following: the role cards are designed so that the stories can be told by a female or a male – but are some stories (like the hairstyle anecdote) more likely to be told by females? Do the males in the class feel comfortable telling this kind of story? Is it actually true that women sympathise and men problem-solve or are these typical responses stereotypes? If men sympathise and women problem-solve, are they breaking the expectations of their respective genders?

Box 2.3b: Gender and sympathy

Role cards: Three different situations

Situation one: You were driving to work and your car broke down. You are a member of an automobile rescue service, but when you looked in your purse/wallet, you didn't have the card with the telephone number. You must have left it at home.

Situation two: You spent a fortune on a new hairstyle at the weekend. When you were leaving the hairdresser's, the rain started. It was a real downpour, so you decided to phone a taxi. You took out your mobile phone but the battery was flat. You got soaked waiting for a bus, and your hair was a total mess.

Situation three: You have a pet cat who is always getting into trouble. Last week, your neighbours went on holiday, and when they were taking their cases to their car, your cat went into their apartment. They didn't notice and locked your cat inside. You heard your cat crying inside the apartment, and you have been dropping food through your neighbour's letterbox for five days now. The carpet must be a mess!

© Cambridge University Press 2010   PHOTOCOPIABLE

2.4 Personal critical incidents

Outline	Learners apply the skills they are developing, in the analysis of critical incidents, to their own lives.
Focus	A written explanation of a critical incident and proposed mediation, i.e. suggestions about how to resolve the problems that arose as a result of them.
Level	Intermediate and above
Time	20 minutes in the first lesson and 30–40 minutes in the second lesson
Preparation	Learners need copies of the reading text in Box 2.4a. This activity will need to be spread over two lessons and includes homework.

Procedure

1   Explain to the class what is meant by a 'critical incident', i.e. an example of misunderstanding caused by people having different cultural assumptions, values or expectations. Here you can give an illustration from your own experience, or give learners the reading text in Box 2.4a. If you use this reading text, the learners can be asked how they would explain the problem to the British couple and their Brazilian hostess.

Box 2.4a: Personal critical incidents

Reading text: An example of a 'critical incident'

A British couple were invited to stay with a Brazilian family. The Brazilian hostess prepared large meals for the British couple, because it is considered a sign of good hospitality to offer more food than her guests can eat.

However, the British couple felt terrible. Where they came from, it was considered polite to finish eating all the food that was offered to guests. Therefore they forced themselves to eat everything that was given to them.

The Brazilian hostess was surprised at her guests' appetites, and provided more and more food for each meal. The British couple ate it all up, and gained more and more weight. At the end of their stay, they were grateful to leave – and the hostess was very happy to see them go!

© Cambridge University Press 2010   PHOTOCOPIABLE

---

2   Ask the class, over a few days if necessary, to think of an example of a critical incident in their own lives. If necessary, you can further prompt the learners by suggesting situations such as misunderstandings about punctuality, exchanging gifts, dress code for a party, etc.

Each learner should describe the critical incident in writing before they come to class, and they could consider the following questions:
- Who was involved?
- Where did the incident take place?
- When did it take place?
- What happened?
- How did the participants in the incident react?

- How would you classify the critical incident? For example, is it to do with gender expectations / age differences / professional differences / religious differences / ethnic differences / social class differences / nationality?

3 During the next lesson, put learners into groups. They share their stories, and attempt to provide explanations for the incident. They can also suggest some strategies for improving the communication between the participants.

4 Each class member then revises the written description of their critical incident and adds:
   - a possible explanation of why it occurred
   - possible ways of avoiding the miscommunication, or improving understanding

5 Collect in and assess the descriptions, analyses and strategies.

Follow-up

After you have assessed the learners' work you can select a few of the learners' critical incidents and invite them to make a presentation about the incident to the full class, for discussion and debate.

2.5 Styles of conflict resolution

Outline	Learners reflect on different approaches to conflicts within and across cultures.
Focus	Language of conflict; conditionals.
Level	Upper–intermediate and above
Time	40 minutes plus
Preparation	Copy the questionnaires, table and worksheet for learners in Boxes 2.5a to 2.5d. The sample questionnaire in Box 2.5a needs to be adapted to the situation of the learners.

Procedure

1 Tell the learners that they are going to explore the language and behaviour that occurs when people are in disagreement. Explain that individuals from different cultures tend to have different ways of coping with disagreements and conflict. Begin by eliciting learners' own experiences of disagreements, by circulating a questionnaire such as the one in Box 2.5a.

2   Next, group the learners in pairs, and get them to ask each other the questions on the questionnaire. After they have finished, ask the learners to raise their hands if they have ever been in a disagreement with others.

Box 2.5a: Styles of conflict resolution

Questionnaire: Conflict

Have you ever been in a disagreement . . .

with your parents/children about staying out late at night?	YES	NO
with your teachers about a homework deadline?	YES	NO
with friends about their political opinion?	YES	NO
with colleagues about the quality of their work?	YES	NO
with your employer about your pay and conditions?	YES	NO
with neighbours about their responsibilities?	YES	NO
about something else? (Say what it is. . .)	YES	NO

© Cambridge University Press 2010   PHOTOCOPIABLE

---

3   Tell the learners that there are various ways of dealing with disagreements and conflicts. Hand out copies of the questionnaire in Box 2.5b and ask learners to tick the boxes depending on whether the statement is true or false for them. Encourage learners to be as honest as possible. When they have finished, ask them to compare their responses with their classmates.

Box 2.5b: Styles of conflict resolution

Questionnaire: Ways of dealing with conflicts

Ways of dealing with conflicts	True	False
I don't mind conflicts because I have a strong personality and I find that I usually get my own way.		
When there is a conflict, I prefer to work with others to find a new, imaginative solution that suits both parties.		
When I am involved in a conflict I usually just give in to the other parties' demands.		
I avoid conflicts whenever I possibly can.		

© Cambridge University Press 2010   PHOTOCOPIABLE

---

4   Next, explain that the four options in the questionnaire represent four possible strategies for dealing with disagreement, namely:

- Confrontational
- Collaborative
- Accommodating
- Avoiding

With the class brainstorm the kind of language and behaviour appropriate to each of the four strategies, building up a table based on the one in Box 2.5c.

Box 2.5c: Styles of conflict resolution

Table: Strategies for dealing with conflict – appropriate language

Ways of dealing with conflicts	Suggested language
Confrontational: I don't mind conflicts because I have a strong personality and I find that I usually get my own way.	*I'm afraid you/we must . . .* *You/we have to . . .*
Collaborative: When there is a conflict, I prefer to work with others to find a new, imaginative solution that suits both parties.	*Let's look at this from a fresh angle.* *Why don't we . . .?* *We could . . .*
Accommodating: When I am involved in a conflict I usually just give in to the other parties' demands.	*Ok, I'll let you . . .*
Avoiding: I avoid conflicts whenever I possibly can.	*I don't wish to discuss it.*

© Cambridge University Press 2010   PHOTOCOPIABLE

5   After the class has suggested some language for each of the four strategies for coping with disagreement, ask the class to choose one of the situations from the questionnaire in Box 2.5a. Together, you and the class brainstorm a dialogue that illustrates the disagreement and possible strategies for coping with it. The class can then discuss which strategies are likely to be most successful. A possible dialogue is given in Box 2.5d.

Box 2.5d: Styles of conflict resolution

Model dialogue: Parent-child conversation

Parent: You were out far too late last night. I'm afraid you're going to have to be home by nine o'clock from now on. *[confrontational]*

EITHER

Child: OK. *[accommodating]*

OR

Child: Sorry, but look . . . you gave me this great new mobile phone for my birthday. I could phone you every half hour after nine o'clock to let you know where I am. *[collaborative]*

OR

Child: I'm not going to argue about this again. I'm going to my room! *[avoiding]*

© Cambridge University Press 2010   PHOTOCOPIABLE

2.6 Conflict mediation

Outline	Learners explore and reflect upon the demands made on mediators dealing with a conflict that involves different styles of communicating.
Focus	Listening to complaints; understanding and resolving differences; making suggestions and seeking consensus.
Level	Intermediate and above
Time	40 minutes plus
Preparation	Copy the role cards in Box 2.6a.

Procedure

1   Explain to learners that they are going to explore an imaginary conflict situation and that they will have to resolve the conflict which is between two people from different cultural backgrounds. The people involved have different values and goals, and also different ways of communicating.

2   As a warm-up, ask the class how they understand the following two general styles of communication. You could select two pairs of learners to mime the communication styles silently, before the rest of the class.

Intimate
Someone stands very close to you and looks at you straight in the eye when they are talking to you. He or she touches your arm briefly while talking.

Distant
Someone stands at a distance from you and looks down when they are talking to you. He or she avoids touching you.

3 After the class has discussed the two communication styles, explain that they may well be interpreted differently by different people. For example, the first speaker's behaviour might be interpreted as friendly, engaging or, alternatively, as forward, impolite or even aggressive. The second person's behaviour might be interpreted as respectful and polite or, alternatively, as cold, unfriendly or even suspicious. Add that misunderstandings between people with different values or opinions can be intensified if they have different styles of communication.

4 Put learners into groups of three and tell them that they are going to role play a situation in which two people with different communication styles are in conflict. A third person is charged with the task of listening to each participant and suggesting a way forward that will be acceptable to the two people in conflict.

5 Explain the following situation to the class:
The two people in conflict are learners of English from different countries, both attending a residential summer school in the United Kingdom. Speaker A is part of a group of people who spend much of their evenings and nights noisily partying and chatting in the halls of residence. Speaker B is part of a group of people who are trying to study and sleep when the others are partying. Speaker B has complained to Speaker C, a school counsellor, about the behaviour of Speaker A and his/her friends. Speaker C has brought the two together to discuss the situation and to try to find a solution.
Once the learners have understood the situation, point out that they can choose a communication style for the role play. Are they going to be intimate or distant?

6 Learners are assigned one role card each from Box 2.6a in their groups of three. They then rehearse the role play.

7 After the groups have finished their rehearsal, invite one group to perform the role play in front of the class. Encourage learners to reflect

on the way Speaker C has handled the complaint. What options were open to him or her? What kind of language could he or she use to make the situation better (or worse)? Was the solution achieved realistic? How did the communication styles chosen affect the outcome? How do A and B feel about the resolution suggested? How will the learners behave in such situations in the future?

8 Finally, invite the class to reflect on the qualities needed to be a good counsellor. For example, which of the following qualities are most important for a counsellor to have?

- empathy (the ability to understand the feelings and values of different people)
- authority (the ability to make a decision and communicate it clearly)
- vision (the ability to think of a new solution to a problem and to gather enthusiasm to achieve that solution)

Box 2.6a: Conflict mediation

Role cards: Resolving a conflict

Speaker A: You are attending a residential language course in the UK. You are one of a group of people who spend much of your evenings and nights noisily partying and chatting in the halls of residence. A counsellor has called you for a discussion. (Remember to choose a communication style: *intimate* or *distant*.)

✂ ---

Speaker B: You are attending a residential language course in the UK. You are part of a group of people who are trying to study and sleep when others are partying noisily. You have complained to a school counsellor who has called you for a discussion. (Remember to choose a communication style: *intimate* or *distant*.)

✂ ---

Speaker C: You are employed as a counsellor at a residential language school in the UK. Some of the students are unhappy and you have decided to bring them together to discuss the problem and to try to find a solution. Perhaps the best way to begin the discussion is to thank the two learners for coming to see you and then say something like: *Now, I understand there has been a bit of a problem. . .Can you explain to me. . .?* (Remember to choose a communication style: *intimate* or *distant*.)

© Cambridge University Press 2010   PHOTOCOPIABLE

2.7 Reflecting on conflict

Outline	Learners reflect on conflicts and on the language and strategies used to manage them.
Focus	The language of conflict and mediation.
Level	Upper-intermediate and above
Time	15–20 minutes in the first lesson and 30 minutes plus in the second lesson
Preparation	Learners find their own incident from a story, film or TV programme that illustrates a situation of conflict, or select a dramatic scene for them. Possible examples are the attempted suicide near the beginning of *Dirty Harry*, or the attempted robbery of the café at the end of *Pulp Fiction*. This activity should be spread over two lessons and includes homework.

Procedure

1 Explain that this activity invites learners to reflect on situations involving conflict or argument and how these situations might be managed.

2 For homework, learners find, think about and describe an incident from a film or TV programme in which a conflict was dramatised, e.g.
   - an argument between family members or friends
   - a hostage incident or robbery
   - a disagreement between a senior and junior employee, or between an employer and an employee

   They should consider the following questions:
   - Where did the incident happen?
   - Who was involved?
   - What exactly happened?
   - What did the characters say to each other?
   - How did the incident end – well or badly?
   - Was a different ending possible? If so, what?

3 In the next lesson, divide the class into groups of three or four and ask them to report back on their findings. The groups choose one incident to dramatise, and rehearse it. Tell learners they can change the ending to make it better or worse. Circulate, giving advice on language where necessary.

4 Select some of the groups to perform their dramatisation in front of the whole class. Encourage learners to comment on how well or badly the conflict was handled. Elicit whether the participants could resolve their conflict more effectively.

2.8 Questioning and defending a belief

Outline	Learners engage directly with the issue of questioning and defending beliefs – and develop appropriate strategies for doing so. Note that any activity that deals with beliefs can elicit strong emotions, including defensiveness or hostility. Be prepared to deal sensitively with such emotions if they arise.
Focus	Asking questions, stating opinions, defending positions – politely and impolitely. Intonation and the use of 'hedging' phrases to soften the force of statements.
Level	Upper-intermediate and above
Time	40 minutes plus
Preparation	None.

Procedure

1   Explain that this activity will assist learners in questioning and defending beliefs and that they are going to focus on the language of argument. Tell the learners that some of them are going to role play discussions between people who hold different beliefs. The discussions might result in a constructive exchange of views, or they might become hostile arguments.

2   As a warm-up to the discussions, write a bald statement and a hostile question on the board or screen, e.g.

Controversial statement   Strong challenge
The earth is flat.   *Are you serious?*

With the class, brainstorm ways to make the statement and question 'softer' by using hedges or 'harder' by using intensifiers to defend a belief. The use of a sympathetic or hostile tone of voice is also important.

Hedges
From my point of view, the earth seems flat.
The earth looks flat to me.
I'm not sure that I understand what you're saying.
If I understand you correctly, you're suggesting that the earth is flat?

Intensifiers
The earth is obviously flat!
There's no doubt at all that the earth is flat!
Are you really suggesting that the earth is flat?
Are you seriously saying that the earth is flat?
You cannot, surely, be saying that the earth is flat!

3   Next, explain that some people hold beliefs that many others think are
    strange. For example, the Flat Earth Society was formed in the 1950s and
    there are many websites devoted to 'flat earth' theories, which generally
    state that the earth is shaped like a dinner plate, with ice at the edges
    keeping the water in. Invite the learners to suggest some of the questions
    and comments that they might put to a group of 'Flat Earthers' in a
    discussion of their theory, e.g.

Have you got any evidence to support your ideas?
Are you saying that science is completely wrong?
Don't you worry that people think you are crazy?
That's ridiculous!
How do you explain . . . ?

4   Tell the learners that another belief that Flat Earthers (and others) uphold
    is that the Apollo moon landings in the 1960s and 1970s were a hoax,
    organised by the US government. List these beliefs on the board or screen,
    and, with the class, add other 'controversial beliefs' to the list, e.g.
    • The earth is flat.
    • The Apollo moon landings were faked.
    • Aliens from other planets have visited earth.
    • The Loch Ness Monster / Yeti / Bigfoot exists.
    • Elvis is alive.
5   Invite the class to choose one of these beliefs to debate and then divide
    them into two groups; one group arguing for the belief, and the other
    against it. If necessary, they should research their arguments.
6   Pair up members of opposing groups, and get them to debate their
    beliefs. Circulate and give advice where necessary and then nominate
    two or three pairs to re-enact their discussion in front of the whole class.
    Alternatively, learners can have a class debate. Ask one learner from each
    group to sit in the centre of the classroom, and start debating the issue.
    Encourage other learners to then come in and take over from them, until
    everyone has had a turn.
7   As they debate, the class rates each learner's attitude according to the
    following scale:

1 Hostile   2 Quite hostile   3 Neutral   4 Quite friendly   5 Friendly

8   Finally, discuss which approach worked best. Did learners feel a hostile
    or friendly approach was more successful?

3 Domestic life

It is often said that 'culture is ordinary', that it is concerned with the attitudes, beliefs and values that are expressed in everyday behaviour. In other words, different people in different places do ordinary things in different ways because, at a deeper level, they hold different attitudes, values and beliefs. This chapter and Chapter 4 explore this assumption by inviting learners to reflect on aspects of their own everyday life. Learners are invited to consider a number of very ordinary activities that concern home life, or the private sphere of family and personal identity. As with any set of activities that address the values and beliefs underlying everyday behaviour, some sensitivity is required: while many learners will enthusiastically embrace the opportunity to reflect on their everyday practices, other learners, or their relatives, might be less comfortable with their home lives being used as the basis for classroom language practice. If the learners resist the invitation to share information about their habits and the habits of their families, their privacy should naturally be respected. However, if the learners accept the invitation, then the classroom should be presented as a safe site for a rich set of supportive and reflective experiences.

Our house, my territory (3.1) asks learners to consider the organisation of the home, and is followed by *Sofa studies* (3.2), which focuses on the changing function of a common piece of furniture, the sofa, and compares how it is presented in advertisements with how it is actually used at home. Attention then shifts to activities that take place in the home: *Television viewing habits* (3.3) gets learners to observe their family's viewing habits, while the distribution of domestic duties amongst the family is investigated in *Domestic duties* (3.4). *Which song reminds you of...?* (3.5) explores the personal associations that learners have established between songs and key topics of their life, such as home, love and childhood. Finally, *A day in the life* (3.6) connects the learners' own everyday life to events in the community, the country and the world.

3.1 Our house, my territory

Outline	Learners investigate the layout of living accommodation in different cultures, and reflect on the ways in which the different functions of different spaces are communicated. In particular, learners consider how they identify their space within the home. This activity is aimed particularly at young adults.
Focus	Language of physical description.
Level	Intermediate and above
Time	40 minutes plus
Preparation	Copy the questions in Box 3.1a for all learners and copy Box 3.1b for less advanced learners.

Procedure

1   With the class, brainstorm a list of different kinds of living accommodation. Write the list on the board, e.g.
   • apartment in a block of flats
   • semi-detached house
   • detached house

2   Check with the learners how many have their own room and how many share a room. Ask about different ways in which learners personalise their room, e.g.
   • a sign on the door (saying what?)
   • posters (of whom or what?) or other decorations on the wall?
   • arrangement of furniture (desk, bed, chairs?)
   • lighting arrangements (wall lights, bedside light?)
   • a display of sports trophies, or other collections?

3   With the learners, brainstorm the different possible spaces that might exist within or adjacent to an apartment or house. Write a list on the board. Spaces might include: entrance hallway or porch (to separate public from domestic space), living room/area, kitchen, dining room/ area, 'den' or TV room, bedroom(s), bathrooms / shower rooms / toilets / en-suite, study, balcony or veranda, garden, garage.

4   Invite the learners to think about how their home as a whole organises three types of activity, using Box 3.1a which focuses on interaction and communication between people, e.g. family and friends; the seeking of personal privacy, or greater intimacy with a family member; the expression of the inhabitants' personality.

Distribute the questions in Box 3.1a below and ask learners to consider their answers individually. Then they discuss them in groups. They can either look at all sections of the worksheet, or each group can look at one section of questions only. Each group then reports back to the class.

Box 3.1a: Our house, my territory

Questions: How accommodation is organised

Family

a) Where in the accommodation does the family meet as a whole?

b) What activities does the family do together?

c) Does the organisation of the accommodation help these activities or make them more difficult?

Friends

a) Where do friends meet in the accommodation?

b) What activities do family members do with friends?

c) Does the organisation of the accommodation help these activities or make them more difficult?

Layout

a) Which rooms are closest/furthest away from the front door or main entrance? (These are usually the most private.)

b) In accommodation of more than one storey or level, which rooms are upstairs and which are downstairs?

c) Which rooms are used for work or study? Who uses them?

Ambience

a) In the accommodation, are the doors to different rooms kept open or shut? Which doors?

b) In different rooms, what lighting (e.g. spotlights, lamps) is there?

c) How is sound (e.g. from an audio system) used in different rooms?

d) How many computers are in the accommodation? Where are they?

e) What pictures and ornaments are used in different rooms? What do they say about the people that live there?

© Cambridge University Press 2010   PHOTOCOPIABLE

5   Next, the learners work in pairs (A and B). In each pair, the learners take turns to describe their homes while their partner draws a floor plan of their description, paying attention to issues such as number of inhabitants, layout, organisation of furniture, etc. After the plan has been finished, the learners ask their partners questions about how the layout of the accommodation helps interaction, individual privacy, and expresses the personalities of the inhabitants. Ask some pairs to report back what they found out about their partner's home.

6   If the learners have e-partners, they can write a description of their own living accommodation and post their descriptions for comparison and discussion online.

Variation for lower-level learners
Use Box 3.1b instead of steps 4, 5 and 6. Get learners to ask a partner the questions. They then draw a plan of their partner's home.

Box 3.1b: Our house, my territory

Questions: Description of someone's home

a) What kind of accommodation do you live in, e.g. house, apartment?

b) How many levels or storeys do you have?

c) How many people live with you?

d) How many rooms do you have?

e) Where is each room?

f) Tell me about the furniture in each room.

g) Where does the family usually meet together?

h) Where do family members meet their friends?

i) Describe your own room to me in detail.

j) Do you think your room reflects your personality? If so, how?

k) Do you think your home reflects the personality of the different members of your family? If so, how?

© Cambridge University Press 2010   PHOTOCOPIABLE

Variation for elementary learners
1 Draw a diagram of an apartment on the board, or project one onscreen, e.g.

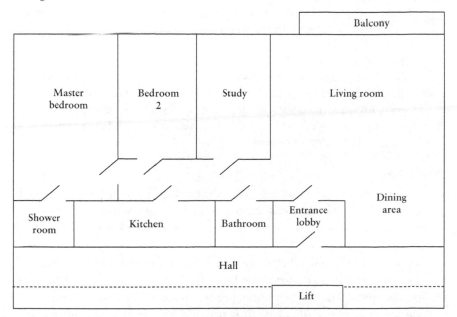

2 Ask learners where to put particular items of furniture and household goods, e.g.

Where does the washing machine/TV, etc. go?

You can then ask more general questions about the apartment, e.g.
- How many people live here?
- Which rooms have carpets / wooden floors / tiled floors?
- Is anything missing in this apartment? (e.g. maid's room, cupboards, nursery)

There are likely to be differences in the answers to the above questions. For some learners, it will be natural to have the washing machine in the kitchen; for others not. Some learners will not expect to have carpets in the shower room or bathroom.

3 After discussing the apartment on the board, learners draw and label their own house. They can then compare and discuss their homes with a partner.

3.2 Sofa studies

Outline	Learners reflect upon one of the most important and expensive items of furniture – the sofa.
Focus	Language of physical description and everyday domestic activities. Comparing and contrasting (everyday uses versus images in advertising).
Level	Intermediate and above
Time	30 minutes in the first lesson and 30 minutes plus in the second lesson
Preparation	Photocopy Box 3.2a. You might also like to collect some advertisements for sofas from glossy magazines, furniture catalogues, etc. This activity will need to be spread over two lessons and includes homework.

Procedure

1 Explain that the class is going to do some research on the design, use and meanings of one of the most important and expensive items of furniture. Ask learners if they can guess what it is (the *sofa*, also known as the *couch* or *settee*).

2 If you have collected advertisements for different kinds of sofa, these will come in useful here. If they are in English, they provide useful vocabulary for describing sofas, or you could pre-teach some, e.g. *classic, stylish, comfortable, with cotton/linen/silk mix/leather upholstery, armrests, feather-filled cushions, and solid oak/beech/metal legs and feet, chintz, plain/patterned. Available in brown/charcoal/green/grey/red/purple/ white*, etc.

Find out from the learners how many live in a house with a sofa, and ask them some questions about this item of furniture:

- Name all the ways people sit on sofas, *e.g. they sit upright, slouch on it, lie along it*, etc.
- Name some things people do on sofas, *e.g. watch TV together, read, drink and/or chat*, etc.
- Where do people buy sofas? *e.g. at furniture showrooms on the edge of town, on the Internet*, etc.
- Ask learners what their sofa looks like. Does it have armrests, a low or high back, is it straight or L-shaped?
- How many does it seat? Two, three, four . . .?
- Is it an individual piece of furniture or part of a three-piece suite?
- Is it plain or patterned? What colour is it? Is it chintz (a highly patterned cotton print)?

- What fabric covers it? PVC, leather, cotton?
- Where is it positioned? Before a fireplace, in front of the TV, or opposite another sofa?

3 Ask the learners to consider how advertisements link certain *meanings* with different styles of sofa. **Answer:** they do this by showing sofas being used in different kinds of setting, and by different kinds of people.

- How are *leather* sofas represented in advertisements? *Often they are shown in settings that are associated with wealth and good taste, and used by rich, 'stylish' owners.*
- How are *chintz* sofas represented? *In the UK they are often associated with traditional values, and advertisements might show them with older users, in rather more old-fashioned homes.*

Note: Cultural associations change from place to place and over time – do your learners associate leather sofas with good taste and chintz ones with old-fashioned values? Do advertisements still reinforce these stereotypes?

4 Ask the class if they know what 'couch potato' means (someone who spends much of their life on the sofa, watching television and does not have an active lifestyle). Tell the class that for homework they are going to do some practical research about sofas and their uses. The research will be in two parts. In the first part learners will describe their own sofa, and the everyday activities that the sofa facilitates. The second part will investigate the sofa in contemporary television and magazine advertising. Tell learners that they will need to collect sofa advertisements for this.

5 Introduce the worksheet in Box 3.2a and make sure the learners know what is expected of them.

6 In the next lesson, allow learners to spend some time comparing their sofa with the sofas they found in advertisements. The learners then compare their results in groups. Select members of each group to report back to the whole class. Or if learners have e-partners, get them to describe their findings to them in an online intercultural exchange.

Box 3.2a: Sofa studies

Worksheet: Your sofa and sofas in advertisements

Part one

a) Describe your sofa in a couple of paragraphs. (If you do not have a sofa, describe the main piece of furniture in your living area.)

b) Choose an evening and keep a record of the main activities that people do on the sofa. (For example, do people watch television, read, eat, drink, chat?)

c) How do people sit on the sofa? (Do they sit upright, slouch, lie flat, sit with their legs tucked under them?)

d) What does your sofa say about you and your family?

Part two

a) Collect three or four advertisements for sofas from magazines or look at sofa websites. Describe the sofas in the advertisements.

b) In the advertisements, what activities are people doing on the sofas?

c) In the advertisements, how do people sit on the sofa?

© Cambridge University Press 2010   PHOTOCOPIABLE

Variation
This activity can be extended to other consumer items that make a statement about the status and personality of the owner, such as dining room tables, mobile phones, personal audio equipment, laptops, or cars.

3.3 Television viewing habits

Outline	Learners do some simple research-based tasks, using the family as a source of data.
Focus	Present simple for habitual actions. Expression of preferences.
Level	Lower intermediate and above
Time	15–20 minutes in the first lesson and 30 minutes plus in the second lesson
Preparation	Copy the observation schedule in Box 3.3a for learners. For less advanced learners, you can copy the observation schedule in Box 3.3b. This activity will need to be spread over two lessons and includes homework.

Procedure

1 Explain to the learners they are going to do some research into TV viewing habits. Hand out copies of the observation schedule in Box 3.3a and go through it with the class, ensuring they understand the questions.
2 Instruct the class to gather data from their own, or a friend's, family before the next lesson.
3 During the next lesson get the learners to share their findings in groups of four.
4 Each learner then writes a few paragraphs to report his or her findings. Learners check and correct for accuracy the English of each other's paragraphs.
5 If the class is participating in an online intercultural exchange, the learners share their revised paragraphs with their e-partners.
6 Finally, ask the learners to create an ideal TV schedule for one evening's viewing (with a minimum of five programmes). The schedule should have the starting time, title, and a brief description of each programme in two or three sentences. After they have created the schedule, the learners can compare their choices. Which kind of programme is most popular? Which are the strangest choices?

Box 3.3a: Television viewing habits

Observation schedule: My family

Number of televisions in the home:

Location of television(s):

For each family member, identify THREE favourite television programmes.

Favourite TV programmes	Family members				
1					
2					
3					

For each family member:
Identify ONE programme that is 'unmissable' and describe it briefly:

Identify the LAST programme they recorded or downloaded:

For each family member, rate the following types of television programme from 5 = excellent to 0 = terrible.

a) news
b) sports
c) documentary
d) arts
e) comedy
f) soaps

g) reality shows
h) game shows
i) cartoons
j) drama
k) music
l) talk/chat shows
m) other _____

If the family watches television together, who has the remote control?

Observe your family watching television and answer the following questions:
Does anyone do any other activity while watching (e.g. knitting, ironing, playing, reading a newspaper)?

Do members of your family react verbally to what is on the TV? If so, what do they say and when?

PHOTOCOPIABLE

Variation for less advanced learners

An easier observation schedule can be completed, based on the viewing habits of one family member, e.g. *My mother likes . . .* With the class, devise an observation schedule or use the one in Box 3.3b.

Box 3.3b: Television viewing habits

Observation schedule: My mother

My mother usually watches TV from . . .   until . . .

My mother's three favourite TV programmes are:

1

2

3

My mother's favourite person on TV is . . .

While my mother is watching TV, she also . . .

© Cambridge University Press 2010   PHOTOCOPIABLE

3.4 Domestic duties

Outline	Learners use a questionnaire to investigate who in the family is responsible for different everyday domestic duties.
Focus	Questions about daily routines; organising information for class presentations.
Level	Beginner and above
Time	30–40 minutes in the first lesson and 30 minutes plus in the second lesson
Preparation	You might like to make copies of the model questionnaire in Box 3.4a. This activity should be spread over two lessons and includes homework.

Procedure

1   Tell the class that they are going to investigate who in a family is mainly responsible for everyday domestic duties, such as cooking meals, washing up, ironing, polishing shoes, etc.

2 With the class, produce a list of about ten domestic duties that might be performed by the father, mother, grandparents, children or someone outside the family (e.g. a maid, or a technician). Depending on circumstances, possible duties might include: cooking meals, washing up dishes, washing clothes, ironing clothes, polishing shoes, cleaning the house, putting younger children to bed, taking children to school, shopping for food, setting the DVD/recorder, fixing electrical equipment or plumbing, watering indoor plants, watering outdoor plants, mowing the lawn, serving visitors food or drink, putting the rubbish out, walking the dog.

3 Look at the questionnaire in Box 3.4a which identifies who lives in a house and lists possible domestic duties. With the class, discuss any changes they might want to make before interviewing their own and then another family, e.g. the family members in the column headings and the duties. Explain to learners that in and across cultures, people live in different kinds of family. Some people live in *nuclear* families (i.e. father, mother and children) while others live in *extended* families (i.e. with grandparents, aunts and uncles, cousins, etc.). In many countries, servants, such as a maid, live with the family, or visit the family on a daily or weekly basis. Sensitivity may be required in the construction of the questionnaire, since it is very possible that some learners will live in households whose members face difficulties such as divorce or bereavement.

4 Explain to learners some of the questions may be sensitive and personal, and ensure when they are interviewing another family that they are aware of the potentially intrusive nature of such questioning. Tell learners they can use polite and sensitive language to ask for information, such as:
   I wonder if you could help me with some research?
   Do you mind if I ask you a few questions about your family?
   Is it okay to ask you a few personal questions?
   If you would prefer not to say, that's ok.

5 Ask a learner to interview you in front of the class, to model the interview.

6 In the next lesson, when the interviews are completed, the learners form groups of four or five and look for patterns in their data, e.g. is the washing or ironing done by males or females? The groups then present and discuss their findings with the class.

Box 3.4a: Domestic duties

Model questionnaire: Household structure and duties

Who is mainly responsible for . . .	You	Partner/wife/ husband	Mother	Father	Male child	Female child	Grandmother	Someone outside the family	Not done
cooking meals?									
washing clothes?									
ironing clothes?									
polishing shoes?									
cleaning the house?									
setting the DVD/ recorder?									
serving food and drink to visitors?									
watering indoor plants?									
watering outdoor plants?									
mowing the lawn?									
. . .									
. . .									

3.5 Which song reminds you of . . .?

Outline	Learners recall a song with which they have strong personal associations.
Focus	Describing song lyrics and feelings, explaining associations using past tense narratives.
Level	Lower intermediate and above
Time	30 minutes plus
Preparation	You may like to make copies of the model description in Box 3.5a.

Procedure

1 Learners close their eyes and think about a song in any language that has a strong personal meaning for them. It might be a song that they would sing to represent their country at a mixed-nationality event. Or it might remind them of home, love, childhood or summertime.

2 Ask the learners to name their songs, and list them on the board or screen, along with the learners' associations with the songs.

3 With the class, review some of the language that can be used to describe their favourite songs, e.g.

> *it takes me back to . . .*   *a feel-good song . . .*
> *cheesy but fun*   *a personal favourite*
> *it always cheers me up*   *one for a true romantic*
> *a classic song*   *smooth and gentle*
> *full of energy*   *relaxing*
> *it makes me feel . . .*   *I remember . . .*
> *. . . reminds me of . . .*

4 Learners write about their three favourite songs for an online forum. The example in Box 3.5a can be used as a model.

Box 3.5a: Which song reminds you of . . .?

Model description: Favourite songs

Songs move me in different ways. My favourite song is *Sozinho* as sung by the Brazilian singer/songwriter, Caetano Veloso. It's a beautiful ballad, with really sad lyrics. It makes me cry every time I hear it. I also love *Here, There and Everywhere* as sung by Emmylou Harris. Emmylou has such a gentle, soothing voice. And, for fun, I also love *Birdhouse in Your Soul* by those funny guys, They Might Be Giants.

© Cambridge University Press 2010   PHOTOCOPIABLE

---

5   If the class is taking part in an online intercultural exchange, the learners
    can share their song associations, and find out about what songs different
    people from different backgrounds and cultures associate with their
    country, their home, love, childhood and summer.

3.6 A day in the life

Outline	Learners develop a 'portrait of a day' that combines personal and local events, national and international events.
Focus	Past tense narrative; reading and writing.
Level	Pre-intermediate and above
Time	20–30 minutes in the first lesson and 40 minutes plus in the second lesson
Preparation	Learners need A3 paper for creating a poster in step 5 if they are not involved in an online intercultural exchange. This activity will need to be spread over two lessons and includes homework. For the homework, learners will need access to the Internet, and/or a range of national and local newspapers (which can be in the learners' first language).

Procedure

1   Ask the class to think of events that took place on the previous day, and
    (if known) the time they occurred. The learners should think of:
    • an international event (e.g. political or sports event)
    • a national event (e.g. political, sports or celebrity event)
    • a local event (e.g. political, sports, community or school event, etc.)
    • a personal event (e.g. an encounter, accident, conversation, surprise,
      etc.)

2   List some of these events on the board, as far as possible in
    chronological order. For example, a list might look something like the
    following:

    18 April
    08.00   In Belo Horizonte, Brazil, Suzana had papaya, bread rolls,
            cheese and coffee for breakfast. She sent a text message to her
            boyfriend and arranged to meet for lunch.
    13.00   The French Minister of Industry announced in Paris that
            unemployment had dropped to a new low.
    15.20   Pedro was going from class to meet a friend at a café and got
            caught in a downpour. He was soaked.

16.30   MSN news reported that, in Hollywood, a Mexican actress in a popular television drama announced that her engagement to an American pop singer was over.

19.00   Sandra sat down with her family to watch an episode of their favourite soap opera on television. Her father, mother and grandmother watched the episode with her. Her younger brother stayed in his room, playing computer games.

21.14   Arsenal scored the only goal of the game against Chelsea, to move to the top of the English Premier League.

3   Explain that the list is a brief 'portrait of a day', and tell the class that they are going to make a more detailed portrait of one day in their lives. They will keep a journal, noting personal, local, national and international events that they notice. The events can be important or unimportant. But together, they will give a portrait of a unique day in their lives. Tell learners that they need to include the following:

• FOUR everyday things that happened to them, or that they did
• THREE events that happened in the local community
• TWO national events
• ONE international event

For each of these events, learners should briefly answer these questions:

• Who was involved?
• When did it happen (as precisely as possible)?
• Why did they notice it?

4   The class then discusses the date they will choose and possible sources of information about international, national and local events, e.g. websites, newspapers, advertising posters, leaflets in libraries, etc.

5   In a following lesson, the learners get into groups of four to six and choose some of the events to develop into a combined group poster of their day to display in class, or write a posting for their e-partners in an online intercultural exchange. Get the groups to compare their 'portraits of the day' and then compare them with their e-partners.

4 Public spaces

This chapter continues to encourage learners to think 'ethnographically'. The activities leave the private, domestic sphere and begin to explore public spaces, particularly places of commerce and leisure.

As in the previous chapter, the emphasis initially is on exploring the learners' own culture and their own behaviour. That being said, most of the activities can also be adapted for use on language courses in English-speaking environments. Wherever they are, the learners are sent into the cafés, shops and leisure spaces of their own everyday existence, and invited to develop their skills of systematic observation and description. They continue to observe, describe and reflect on their own rituals of daily existence – as if they were visitors from another culture. They look critically at the role of English in public spaces in their home culture in *An A–Z of signs in English* (4.1), and reflect on an important area in their village, town, or city in *Comparing places* (4.2). Learners consider the behaviour and views of people in different settings, in *Café society* (4.3), and in *At the hairdresser's* (4.4). They examine the behaviour of people in public in *Behaviour on public transport* (4.5) and in *Exploring an art gallery or museum* (4.6) while they investigate the phenomenon of street performers in *Street performers* (4.7). Learners also reflect on their own leisure pursuits: when they go out for an evening's entertainment in *Going out for the evening* (4.8) and when they go elsewhere on holiday in *Holiday photographs* (4.9). Overall, the activities offer examples of different kinds of 'field research'.

All of the activities can be done as self-contained projects, with discussion in class. However, the activities are further enriched if the class is participating in an online intercultural exchange (see Chapter 1). As well as reflection, the activities can then stimulate comparison between the learners' own experiences and those of their e-partners.

4.1 An A–Z of signs in English

Outline	Learners look systematically at the use of English in public spaces in their own community.
Focus	Learners collect and discuss examples of English used in advertising in their own community.
Level	Elementary and above
Time	15–20 minutes in the first lesson and 30 minutes plus in the second lesson
Preparation	Ideally, learners should have access to a camera to photograph signs. Alternatively, they need paper so they can copy by hand the signs they see. You will need a computer and projector to display the photographs in Box 4.1a and pieces of A3 paper for step 3. This activity will need to be spread over two lessons and involves learners looking for English signs in the community in their own time.

Procedure

1   Divide the class into groups and tell each group that its members are required to go into their community, after school, and collect examples of signs in English (and/or other languages used in the area). They can copy down the examples on a piece of paper, or, if they have digital cameras or camera phones, they could take pictures of them.

2   Explain that each group should collect signs that represent as much of the alphabet, A–Z, as possible. This will obviously depend on how much signage in English there is in the community. Show learners the photographs in Box 4.1a as examples. They can be flexible about which word in the sign represents a letter in the alphabet; for example, the sign *Just Love You* can be used to represent *J, L* or *Y*. The learners simply need to specify that 'L is for Love in *Just Love You.*'

3   In a following lesson, the learners share their signs and see how many letters of the alphabet they have covered. Then they re-classify them according to their content, e.g. advertisements for food, drink, clothes, information notices, etc. They should then produce a poster arranging the signs on it according to their content, which they can share with the other groups and discuss their findings, e.g. were most of the signs in English for food?

4   More advanced learners can then discuss some of the following questions:
   • What kinds of products are advertised in English?
   • Do any signs use a mixture of languages?
   • What reasons can you think of for using English on signs in a non-

English speaking country? Is this use of English changing the English language as a whole?

- Is the English language displacing other languages in your community?
- Is the use of English on signs something you should be angry about, or afraid of – or is it a development that you welcome?

5   If learners are participating in an online intercultural exchange, they can go online and share their experience of signs in English with their e-partners. Are similar things advertised in English in different places?

Variation for learners in an English-speaking environment

This activity can be adapted for other languages – for example, is there evidence of signs in Arabic, Chinese, French, German, Spanish, Polish or Punjabi in public spaces in Australia, the UK or USA? Particularly fruitful areas for exploration are restaurants and employment agencies.

Box 4.1a: An A–Z of signs in English

Photos: Signs

A restaurant in Taiwan

Belly dancing classes in Brazil

Poster for a café franchise in Brazil

A tattoo parlour in Singapore

© Cambridge University Press 2010   PHOTOCOPIABLE

4.2 Comparing places

Outline	Learners reflect on and describe an important area in their village, town or city.
Focus	The language of location and physical description.
Level	Elementary and above
Time	30 minutes plus
Preparation	Choose a possible local area to describe, e.g. the village, town or city centre, or the centre of the local community and find a map of it if possible. Learners will need pieces of paper in step 2.

Procedure

1 Draw a map of the local area or project it, if you have a photo, onto the board and name it, e.g. *this is the High Street, etc.*

2 Ask the learners, in pairs, to make a rough copy of the map from the board or screen, and then add four or five well-known buildings, shops or other landmarks onto their own copy.

3 Ask some of the pairs, in turn, to name one of the buildings, shops or landmarks they have chosen. When each pair names something, add it to the map on the board and introduce some language to describe its location, e.g.

   The shopping mall is at the end of the High Street.
   The town hall is opposite/beside the cathedral.
   A river runs through the park.
   The post office is inside / beside / next to / on the left of the shopping mall.

   Write out some of these sentences on the board.

4 The pairs then write a brief description of the locations of the other buildings, shops and landmarks they have named on their own map.

5 Nominate some of the pairs to read out their descriptions.

6 To practise the language of location further, ask questions such as:

   Where's the cathedral / park / shopping mall / community centre?
   It's on / beside / next to / in the middle of / behind / on the right of . . .

7 If learners are participating in an online intercultural exchange, they can post their description of their chosen locality to their e-partners, and compare responses. With the class, rehearse a discussion opener, e.g.

   Hi! I'm curious about where you live. In the centre of my city you can find . . . When you walk down the street, the X is on the left and Y is . . . I'm really interested to know more about your town/city/village!

4.3 Café society

Outline	Learners consider local and global manifestations of 'café culture' in both local, independent cafés and in international café franchises.
Focus	Observing and describing two types of café in the community as an example of ethnographic 'field research'.
Level	Intermediate and above
Time	30–40 minutes in the first lesson and 40 minutes plus in the second lesson
Preparation	To help rehearse the language involved, it would help if you could take some photographs of a local café before class, and have photos to show of the decor, the menu, the staff dress code, etc. Learners also need copies of the observation schedule in Box 4.3a. The activity needs to be spread over two lessons and involves learners visiting cafés in their own time.

Procedure

1 Introduce the topic of cafés and raise the following issues and questions:
   - Identify and classify types of café in the community, that is, independent cafés, and franchise operations, e.g. Starbucks®, Costa, etc.
   - Which (if any) do the learners prefer and why?
   - What is the process of ordering a coffee or other drink in different cafés – is there table service, do you order at a bar, is there a special language involved (e.g. *regular cappuccino to go*)?

2 Divide the class into groups and give each group the task of visiting and observing the behaviour of people in either an independent café or a franchise operation. Together work out a schedule to make their observation more systematic, or use the observation schedule in Box 4.3a.

3 Once the observation schedule has been designed, show the class photographs of a local café, and get them to answer as many questions on the schedule as possible, using the photos as input. Check the answers and help with necessary language (e.g. to describe the staff uniforms). After the lesson, learners visit a local café, and complete their schedules.

4 In a following lesson, when the groups have carried out their research, get them to prepare their presentations and then report their findings back to the class. If the class is participating in an online intercultural exchange, they can share their findings with their e-partners.

Box 4.3a: Café society

Observation schedule: Visiting a café

Name of café:

Franchise or independent?

Time of visit:

Time spent there:

What kind of drinks are available (e.g. speciality coffees, tea, alcohol, other)?

What kind of food is available?

In which language(s) is the menu?

Are the drink and food associated with particular national cultures (e.g. Italian, American, British)?

Is the decor (pictures, style of furniture, etc.) associated with a particular place (e.g. a country or a city)?

How do you order and obtain drink and food?

Are there particular expressions used to order the drinks (e.g. *grande mocha, skinny latte, cappuccino to go*)?

Are the staff in uniform? If so, describe it.

Describe the staff (age, gender, ethnicity). *Note: You may have to guess some of these.*

Describe the customers (age, gender, ethnicity, profession; single, couples or family). *Note: You may have to guess some of these.*

How do the males greet each other?

How do the females greet each other?

Are other facilities available (e.g. newspapers, magazines, wireless internet access)?

PHOTOCOPIABLE

4.4 At the hairdresser's

Outline	Learners reflect upon and observe behaviour at a local hairdresser's salon or barber's shop.
Focus	The focus is on description of different types of activity and interaction at the hairdresser's.
Level	Intermediate and above
Time	30–40 minutes in the first lesson and 40 minutes plus in the second lesson
Preparation	Permission needs to be sought from hairdressers or barbers willing to be observed for a class project; alternatively, learners might accompany a member of class who is having his or her hair cut. You could also bring to class some health and beauty magazines in English that contain advice on hairstyles, if these are locally available. Learners may need copies of the template observation schedule in Box 4.4a. This activity should be spread over two lessons and involves learners visiting a hairdressing salon or barber shop in their own time.

Procedure

1   Ask the class to brainstorm different kinds of hairdressing salons or barber shops available in the local community, and the kinds of activity and interaction that take place there. Alternatively, elicit answers to the following questions:

- Do males and females use the same or different hairdressing salons/ barbers?
- Exactly what kind of routines do males and females expect to encounter in the establishment (e.g. washing hair before and/or after it is cut, cutting and styling hair, shaving, trimming beard, massaging head and shoulders, removing hair from ears, manicuring nails)?
- How many people are involved in the activities (hairdresser and one or more assistants; someone to sweep up hair, etc.)?
- What language do customers use to describe the hairstyle they want? What kind of 'small talk' is expected? Can you list four or five expressions in your mother tongue that you would expect to use in a hairdresser's salon or a barber's shop?

2   The learners, using a dictionary, or asking e-partners who have experience of an English-speaking culture, find out the English equivalents for the vocabulary of hairdressing and the kind of small talk used while hair is being cut and styled.

3 Distribute some health and beauty magazines for men and women (if available) and ask the learners to skim and scan for expressions that describe different hairstyles. If magazines are available in English, learners can find the expressions in English. If not, they should find them in their own language and then check the English translation in a dictionary or online.

4 One consideration at the hairdressers' is the language appropriate to men and women. Introduce the expressions below and discuss with the class whether they are more likely to be used by males or females or whether they are likely to be used by both sexes:

I'd just like a tidy up, please.
I've been thinking about a perm.
Just a trim, please.
I'd like it short at the back.
I've been thinking about highlights.
I like to comb it to the side.
I'd like a manicure, please.
Could I have a wash and a cut?
I'd like a facial.
I'd like my eyebrows done.

5 Tell the learners that, in groups, they are going to observe and report back on activity in a hairdresser's salon or barber's shop. Together, they draw up an observation schedule of things to look out for. The schedule may include:

- gender of customer
- prices for males and females
- the process of 'having your hair cut' and the expressions used
- the number of people involved in the activity
- the things they talk about
- the different types of service offered (e.g. manicure, massage, etc.)

Alternatively, they can use the observation schedule in Box 4.4a opposite.

6 The groups prepare a report that they present to the class, and, if they are participating in an online intercultural exchange, share it with their e-partners.

7 Finally, get the groups to role play the parts of customer and hairdresser/ barber, using the English they have learned to associate with the activity of having your hair cut. In some instances, the customer might ask for a service (e.g. a manicure or massage) that the establishment does not offer.

Box 4.4a: At the hairdresser's

Observation schedule: Visiting the hairdresser's/barber's

Name of establishment:

Location:

Time of observation:

Number of customers: Males: Females:
                        Children (under 12):

Number of staff: Males: Females:
Staff, e.g.:   Stylist(s)
                        Assistant(s)
                        Receptionist(s)
                        Manicurist(s)/Pedicurist(s)
                        Other (give details)

Styles offered and prices:

Other services offered: Shave
                          Massage
                          Manicure/pedicure
                          Other (give details)

Typical topics of conversation:

Useful expressions (state the language, if not English, and give a rough translation):

4.5 Behaviour on public transport

Outline	Learners look closely at non-verbal behaviour on public transport.
Focus	Present simple for habitual actions.
Level	Lower intermediate and above
Time	30–40 minutes in the first lesson and 40 minutes plus in the second lesson
Preparation	Copy the observation schedule in Box 4.5a for learners. This activity should be spread over two lessons and involves learners observing behaviour on public transport in their own time.

Procedure

1 Invite the class to brainstorm different types of public transport with which they are familiar, e.g. buses, trains, trams, metro systems.

2 Ask the learners what kind of behaviour they would expect in different forms of public transport, e.g. do people stand, sit or both?
How close can people be before one person feels uncomfortable? Or elicit answers to the following questions:

   • Imagine you are sitting in a half-empty metro carriage. At the next stop, someone comes into your carriage and walks towards you. How do you react? Do you look at them and smile? Look down or away? Shift your place (very slightly)? Pretend not to notice their presence?

   • Imagine that you are sitting on a crowded bus. All the seats are taken and many people are standing. Who, if anyone, would you give your seat to? A young woman/man, an older woman/man, a child, a pregnant woman, a woman with a baby?

   • What kind of behaviour do you find unacceptable on public transport? (Are there notices forbidding this kind of behaviour?) For example, smoking, spitting, using mobile phones, talking loudly, swearing, drunken behaviour, talking and laughing with the driver, resting your feet on another seat, carrying pets such as a dog or cat? Do you say anything to people who display this kind of behaviour? If so, what?

3 Learners go out, after class, and observe people's behaviour on public transport. They should complete the observation schedule in Box 4.5a. As a rehearsal, get some learners to come to the front of the class and role play acceptable and unacceptable behaviour on a bus or train, while the rest of the class completes a schedule. Learners then compare

their completed schedules, and report back. Before doing the role plays, brainstorm together the kind of language used in likely scenarios, e.g.

Polite offers/requests and acceptances/refusals

Would you like a seat?	*Oh, yes thanks!* or *No, thanks, I'm getting off at the next stop.*
I'm afraid smoking is not allowed.	*Oh, sorry, I didn't know* or *So? What are you going to do about it?*
Do you mind not spitting? It's very unpleasant!	*Oh, I do apologise, I'm not very well* or *Do I look like I care?*

4   In the next class, put the learners into groups and ask them to report on their observations.
5   Each group then composes a set of 'Rules for Behaviour on Public Transport'. As a class, look at each group's rules. Are there any similarities or differences? If the class is participating in an online intercultural exchange, they can exchange their rules with their e-partners.

Box 4.5a: Behaviour on public transport

Observation schedule: Public transport

Type of transport taken:
Day, date and time of trip:
Duration of time spent travelling:
Were you standing or sitting?
Were there any rules and regulations visible? If so, what were they?
How many passengers were there?
Describe them, e.g. older/younger/children; male/female, etc.
Did the passengers talk to each other?
Did the passengers listen to music, or talk on mobile phones?
Did the passengers make eye contact or behave in a particular way?
Would you describe any of the passengers' behaviour as polite or unacceptable?
If it was unacceptable, how did the other passengers react?

© Cambridge University Press 2010   PHOTOCOPIABLE

4.6 Exploring an art gallery or museum

Outline	Learners observe and describe a public art gallery or museum, focusing on the contents and the behaviour of the visitors. This might be in their own country, or in the country which they are visiting.
Focus	Describing a cultural institution; ethnographic analysis; raising awareness of cultural objects and their local significance.
Level	Intermediate and above
Time	20–30 minutes in the first lesson and 40 minutes plus in the second lesson
Preparation	Learners need copies of the observation schedule in Box 4.6a. This activity should be spread over two lessons and involves learners visiting a gallery or museum in their own time.

Procedure

1 Introduce the topic of art galleries by asking questions such as:
   - Who has visited an art gallery? Which one?
   - What did you see there?
   - Did you see anything by a famous artist?
   - What did you like most?
   - What did you like least?
   - How can you describe the paintings you liked?
        I loved the . . .
        It's gorgeous.
        It's so lovely.
        The colours are so vivid.
        It's powerful.
   - How can you describe the paintings you didn't like?
        I wasn't keen on the . . .
        It was pretty unimpressive.
        I think it's over-rated.
        It didn't do much for me.
        It's not my kind of thing.

2 Divide the class into groups and direct each group to visit an art gallery or museum outside class time. The learners should spend time there and take notes in English on topics such as those suggested in the observation schedule in Box 4.6a.

3 After the visit, each group organises its observations into an oral report, and reports back to the whole class.

4   If the class is multicultural, class members can discuss the similarities
    and differences between public art galleries and museums in their home
    countries. If the class is not multicultural, the group can exchange
    a written report on the museum/art gallery they visited with their
    e-partners and then discuss similarities and differences online.

Box 4.6a: Exploring an art gallery or museum

Observation schedule: Art gallery or museum

Name of the gallery/museum:

Location:

What are the opening times?

Is there an entrance fee, or is entrance free?

Day/time of visit?

Duration of visit?

Describe the layout, content, special exhibitions, etc.

Who was exhibiting, e.g. local and/or international artists? What periods in history
were represented?

What kind of people visited the gallery/museum? (Were they individuals, couples,
family groups? What was their age, gender, ethnicity, social class, etc.?)
Note: You will have to guess some of these details.

How did the visitors behave in response to the exhibits (was there any visible
reaction of interest, pleasure, boredom, confusion)? What did they say?

Choose one exhibit and observe it for 15 minutes to see how many people look
at it and make a note of the average time spent looking at it. What were the
maximum and minimum times?

Which exhibits were the most/least popular?

Was there a gallery/museum shop? If so, what kinds of things were on sale? What
kinds of things were people buying?

4.7 Street performers

Outline	Learners observe and interview street performers in their city or town, and compare their findings with their e-partners.
Focus	Describing different types of performance (busking, juggling, human statues, etc.).
Level	Intermediate and above
Time	30–40 minutes in the first lesson and 40 minutes plus in the second lesson
Preparation	This activity should be spread over two lessons and involves learners talking to street performers in their own time. You will need a computer and projector to display the photos in Box 4.7a. Learners may need a copy of the questionnaire in Box 4.7b.

Procedure

1 Show learners the photos on the CD-ROM in Box 4.7a. Ask learners what these people are doing (they are street performers; one person is a human statue, the other person is juggling). Ask the class what kinds of street performance they have come across in their home town or city. Examples might include busking (singing and/or playing music), dancing, juggling, drawing portraits, sculpting balloons, miming or being 'human statues'. Elicit common locations for such activity (e.g. main shopping streets and parks).

2 Tell the class that, in groups, they are going to interview some of the local street performers. Together, discuss the kinds of questions that the learners might ask, and write them on the board, e.g.
   • How old are you? under 20/20–29/30–39/40–49/50–59/over 60
   • Where are you from?
   • When did you leave school?
   • Are you married or single?
   • Do you enjoy performing?
   • Is this your only job? If not, what else do you do?
   • How did you learn to do what you do?

3 In class, two learners role play the parts of interviewer and street performer (give them a role of one of the people in the photos if you wish). The other learners make a note of the answers to the questions on the board. At this stage, you can bring up some practical issues that should help the interview take place more smoothly, e.g.
   • When should the performer be approached? (Probably when s/he is resting.)

Box 4.7a: Street performers

Photos: Street performers

© Alamy/David Robertson   © Alamy/Arch White

From *Intercultural Language Activities*
© Cambridge University Press 2010   PHOTOCOPIABLE

- How might learners ask permission to interview the performer? (*'Excuse me, do you mind if we ask you a few questions? We're doing a project for our school.'*)
- Should the learners give a donation after the interview? (It would probably be appreciated!)

4 Learners are then sent out in groups to interview street performers in the town or city where they are currently living. This can be in the learners' first language or in English if they are in an English-speaking environment. A possible template for a questionnaire is given in Box 4.7b.

5 After the learners have finished their interviews, they prepare a report and present it to the class. Then they can share and compare their reports with their e-partners online.

Box 4.7b: Street performers

Sample questionnaire: Interviewing street performers

Place and date of performance:
Type of performer: *e.g. mime artist, musician, juggler, acrobat*

Introduce yourself politely, and ask if you can interview the performer for a class project.

1   What is your name – or what do you call yourself professionally?

2   How do you describe what you do?

3   Where were you born?

4   How old are you? (under 20 / 20–29 / 30–39 / 40–49 / 50–59 / over 60)

5   Are you married or single?

6   Is this your only job? Yes/No
    If not, what else do you do?

7 What is your highest educational qualification?
            None
            School certificate
            College diploma or university degree

8   Do you enjoy your work? What do you like most?
                            What do you like least?

Thank you very much for your time and help!

© Cambridge University Press 2010   PHOTOCOPIABLE

Variation for lower-level learners
Learners at less advanced levels can attempt this activity if you present more of the necessary language in advance, and spend more time rehearsing the interviews and presentations. Typical language for the presentation will be generalisations in the present simple, beginning with phrases such as:

> *All/Some/Several/One of the performers . . .*
> *According to . . .*
> *X said that he/she . . .*

4.8 Going out for the evening

Outline	Learners consider how different groups within and across cultures organise an evening out. They then attend and observe an evening out.
Focus	Describing dress, time, and leisure activities such as eating, drinking, dancing, etc.
Level	Lower intermediate and above
Time	20–30 minutes in the first lesson and 40 minutes plus in the second lesson
Preparation	Learners need digital cameras to take photos of their evenings out and a copy of Box 4.8a. This activity should be spread over two lessons and involves learners observing a night out.

Procedure

1 Ask the learners how they spend an evening out. Use the questions below as a guide:
   - Which evenings are preferred (weekdays or weekends)?
   - How many are involved (couples, groups)?
   - Who is involved (friends, family)?
   - Where do you go (cinema, clubs, bars, restaurants, the house of a friend or family member)?
   - What do you and others wear (males and females)?
   - What time does the activity usually begin and end?
   - How is the activity decided upon (by invitation, by discussion and consent, by one person taking the lead; beforehand, at the last minute)?

2 Instruct the learners, in groups if possible, to observe an evening out and report back in a future lesson. The groups should prepare a class report that covers the questions above. If possible, they should provide pictures such as digital photographs.

3 If the class is participating in an online intercultural exchange, they can share their reports with their e-partners. An example of an online posting on this topic is given in Box 4.8a.

Box 4.8a: Going out for the evening

Discussion thread: Night out

Topic: Going out
From: Andrea

Our class has decided to prepare a presentation for all of you, showing how people dress up to go to different kinds of party. In Rio de Janeiro the 'cariocas', as the local people are called, have a particular way of dressing up to go out. It depends on the kind of parties they're going to. For example, people wear specific kinds of clothes for dancing 'samba', 'forró', 'axé', 'carioca funk' or for going to a rave party. Rio is a city where the beach style is always present in the way the cariocas look. It can be seen in the pictures, taken last Saturday at a rave party.

Girls usually wear tiny shorts or mini skirts and tops. The majority wear pale colours or white to enhance their tanned skin. The same for the boys: they wear shorts and t-shirts. The majority of boys dance without t-shirts and it's not only because it is very warm but it's to show their tanned and fit bodies. So we'd like to know what the people in your city wear when they go to a party.

© Cambridge University Press 2010   PHOTOCOPIABLE

4.9 Holiday photographs

Outline	Learners reflect on what it means to be a tourist, by focusing on photographs taken on holiday.
Focus	Describing and evaluating; exploring what it means to 'go on holiday' for different groups in different cultures.
Level	Intermediate and above
Time	40 minutes plus
Preparation	Ask learners to bring in some holiday photographs. (Note that in some cultures the sharing of personal photographs is considered inappropriate, so check first.) You could bring in some of your own. Learners will need copies of the questions in Box 4.9a.

Procedure

1   Learners bring to class four or five holiday photographs.
2   Put learners into groups of three or four. Ask them to discuss their
    photographs and, in turns, answer the questions in Box 4.9a about them.

Box 4.9a: Holiday photographs

Questions: My holiday

- Where was the destination? In your home country, or abroad?
- Was a different language spoken there?
- Why was the holiday destination chosen?
- How long was the holiday? Was it long enough, too short or too long?
- How many people were in the group? Were they family, friends or strangers?
- What kind of activities did you participate in?
- What kind of things did you photograph? Why?
- What kind of things struck you as familiar in the holiday destination?
- What kind of things struck you as different?
- What was your most enjoyable experience?
- What was your greatest disappointment?

© Cambridge University Press 2010   PHOTOCOPIABLE

---

3   In their groups, learners choose one of the destinations and write a
    guide for visitors, highlighting the positive and negative aspects of
    the destination, what to do and not to do, the *must-sees* and the *don't
    bothers*.
4   Learners report back on the information in the guides to the rest of the
    class. If the learners have e-partners, they can share, compare and discuss
    their holiday experiences together.

5   Face to face

This chapter considers some of the characteristics of face-to-face communication that are important for establishing a sense of personal identity and rapport with others. These characteristics may vary from culture to culture; even if they do not vary, they still make considerable demands on second language learners. The first two activities focus on aspects of conversation that are particularly challenging for lower-level learners. *Sharing stories in conversation* (5.1) focuses on telling conversational stories and anecdotes. This is a key area in the presentation of the self in conversation: the stories we tell dramatise our values, attitudes and beliefs, and they function to show the people we are talking to how we feel about the world. *Supporting talk* (5.2) looks at 'back-channelling'. This activity is designed to raise awareness of the impression that the learners are giving to other speakers through their management of supportive talk. Being supportive is challenging to learners for two reasons. First, under the stress of communicating face to face in another language, they may concentrate so much on listening and comprehending that they neglect to give conversational support to the person who is speaking. Secondly, the appropriate amount of supportive talk, as well as its form and timing, may vary from culture to culture.

Of course, face-to-face communication is not only about the words we use. Body language, or non-verbal communication, also plays a major part in how we present ourselves to others. *Exploring non-verbal communication* (5.3) is designed to raise awareness of non-verbal communication in general, while the following activities invite learners to explore specific aspects of it. *The eyes have it* (5.4) turns our attention to the gaze; *Empathy and body language* (5.5) involves a role play which encourages learners to consider how our body language is related to the empathy we display in face-to-face communication; and *Gestures* (5.6) focuses on gestures that are used to communicate particular meanings. *In the office* (5.7) considers how body language sends messages about status and power in a workplace setting. The final activity, *Exploring informal language* (5.8), returns to conversational expression, and encourages learners to explore and record those informal, colloquial words and phrases that characterise much spoken interaction.

5.1 Sharing stories in conversation

Outline	Learners focus on how people from a range of cultures share stories.
Focus	Past tense narratives and evaluations.
Level	Intermediate and above
Time	20 minutes plus
Preparation	You need a board and an overhead projector.

Procedure

1   Introduce the idea that most, if not all, cultures tell stories and anecdotes
    to share experiences, and that stories within conversations can express
    feelings, attitudes and values. Write the following list on the board, and
    invite the learners to think about a story they would tell about one of
    them:

    something that made me excited   *something that bored me*
    something that made me happy   *something that made me sad*
    something that made me feel good   *something that embarrassed me*
    something that restored my   *something that frustrated me*
    * belief in people*
    something that made me feel brave   *something that frightened me*

2   Elicit from learners the kind of evaluative expressions that they might use
    in their stories, e.g.
    *It was so/really cool/boring/great/awful/satisfying/embarrassing/
    heartwarming/frustrating/terrifying etc.*
    *I was so/really impressed/bored/pleased/horrified/satisfied/
    embarrassed/frustrated/terrified etc.*

3   Explain that when people are talking, they often tell personal stories
    about a similar topic. So, for example, three people in a group might
    all tell personal stories about something that made them feel brave or
    frightened. An important point is that each successive story must sound
    more dramatic or intense than the one before. An increase in drama
    or intensity can be achieved by exaggerating the content, or by using
    dramatic intonation and gestures, or by emphasising the effect that the
    story had on the speaker.

4   Give an example of a story about something that was frightening, or
    use the following example, '*I can't stand spiders. They're horrible. This
    morning, when I got up and went to the bathroom, there was this huge
    spider in the bath. I was terrified! But I forced myself to turn on the tap
    and flush it down the plughole. It was awful – I felt physically sick!*' Next,

89

ask the class to suggest similar stories of their own, involving frightening insects, like spiders, or something more terrifying. Tell learners that they need to make their stories as dramatic or intense as possible.

5 Divide the class into groups of three. Each group chooses one of the topics from the list on the board, e.g. something that made me happy. Each member of the group is given two minutes to think of a personal story that illustrates the topic chosen by the group. More advanced learners could use the variation below.

6 The first speaker in each group tells a personal story based on the chosen topic. Then the second speaker tells a second story on the same topic – but tries to make it sound more dramatic or intense than the first story. Finally, the third speaker tells his or her story on the same topic – and this speaker should try to make the final story sound even more dramatic or intense than the first two.

7 After the stories have been told, the class can reflect as a whole on the way the conversations developed from the opening topic. Did the speakers stay on topic or did they shift topics? Did the members of the class tell the same kind of story? Some research suggests that males tend to tell 'problem-solving' stories in which they feature as the heroes; females, on the other hand, more often tell stories that invite sympathy and laughter. Was this true of the groups in your class? After rehearsing their stories in class, learners who are taking part in an online intercultural exchange can go online and share their stories with their e-partners.

Variation for more advanced learners

For learners in their later teens, a possible source of relevant topics and language for storytelling can be found in teenage magazines such as *Teen* and *Seventeen*, particularly in the advice and letters pages. Magazines for female teenagers often feature 'cringe stories' of embarrassing incidents. Experience suggests that male teenagers buy magazines on particular topics such as sport, music, film, motor vehicles, and so on. Ask learners to collect examples of teen magazines for both males and females (in print or online), in their first language or in their second language, and consider the kinds of personal stories that each contains. What kinds of stories are more likely to be told by females or males? They can then write their own examples of such stories in English as a rehearsal for conversations about them in class as in step 6.

5.2 Supporting talk

Outline	This activity extends the topic of conversational storytelling in *Sharing stories in conversation* (5.1). Learners raise their awareness of the impression they are making on the people with whom they are conversing.
Focus	Conversational storytelling, back-channelling and supporting talk.
Level	Lower intermediate and above
Time	30 minutes plus
Preparation	Find some video clips, for example on www.youtube.com of people talking. The clips should illustrate how learners support speakers. Advanced learners might be able to take advantage of the free materials on empathic listening, available online from the University of California at http://www.cnr.berkeley.edu/ucce50/ag-labor/7article/article40.htm Learners need copies of the supporting talk table in Box 5.2a and the scale of interest table in Box 5.2b. You will also need a piece of paper for step 4.

Procedure

1 Introduce the class to the concept of responsive and supportive listening when in conversation. Explain that speakers from some cultures offer little vocal response when someone is talking, instead keeping a respectful silence. Speakers from some other cultures make more use of 'back-channelling', that is, responsive noises (like 'mm-hmm' or 'oh'), non-verbal communication, and 'supporting talk', as shown in the table in Box 5.2a. Explain that this activity is to help learners become sensitive to the level of interest that they are conveying to the people they're talking to.

2 Present an audio or video clip of people talking, showing how listeners support speakers through these signals. You should also indicate those facial expressions that indicate surprise, shock, sympathy, amusement and boredom. Introduce the supporting talk table in Box 5.2a to learners.

3 Call for two volunteer speakers. The class then chooses a topic for one of the speakers (Speaker A) to talk about. The topic should allow the speaker to tell a dramatic story (e.g. The day I had my bag stolen in the street!). Next, go through the scale of interest table (Box 5.2b) with the class, pointing out that there are various ways in which the second speaker (Speaker B) might respond. This will also depend on their culture.

4 Speaker B chooses a level of interest with which to respond to A's story, on a scale from 0 (very bored) to 5 (over-interested). Get Speaker B to hand you a piece of paper or card on which he or she has indicated the level of interest they will show. This card should not be visible to the class.

5 Speaker A tells the story to Speaker B, who responds with the level of interest appropriate to the level written on the card. The class guesses the level that Speaker B has chosen, based on his or her performance. If other learners have stories they want to tell, you could continue this activity.

Box 5.2a: Supporting talk

Table: Examples of supporting talk

Type of supporting talk	Example of supporting talk (in italics)
Ask for repetition of something misheard or misunderstood.	'I just wanted to run away.' *'You wanted to what?'*
Confirm that you have heard the right information.	'I just wanted to run away.' *'You did?'* or *'You didn't!'*
Ask for some additional information that might help you to understand the speaker.	'I just wanted to run away.' *'Why – were you scared or embarrassed?'*
Volunteer further, related information for confirmation.	'I just wanted to run away.' *'Yeah – dogs can be really frightening.'*
Show that you have understood and agree or disagree with the speaker.	'I just wanted to run away.' *'Absolutely!'* or *'Totally!'* or *'Surely not!'*

© Cambridge University Press 2010   PHOTOCOPIABLE

> **Box 5.2b: Supporting talk**
>
> **Table: Scale of interest 0–5**
>
> **0** – Very bored: Don't say anything. Look pained. Yawn. Check your watch.
> **1** – Quite bored: Respond, but minimally with expressions like 'mmm', 'oh' and 'yeah' only when given the chance. Keep your intonation flat.
> **2** – Slightly interested: Respond as in (1) but make sure you ask one or two clarifying or checking questions too.
> **3** – Interested: Try to use a range of supporting talk.
> **4** – Very interested: Use a range of supporting talk, as in (3), but also listen hard for emotional statements and sympathise with them. Say things like 'Wow, great!' or 'Ooooh, that's awful!'
> **5** – Over-interested: Interrupt the speaker with strong sympathetic statements. Ask lots and lots of checking and clarifying questions, and nod your head a lot. Use a very wide intonation range.
>
> © Cambridge University Press 2010   PHOTOCOPIABLE

5.3 Exploring non-verbal communication

Outline	Learners explore non-verbal communication in their community and report their findings to the class.
Focus	Describing non-verbal behaviour and its meanings.
Level	Intermediate and above
Time	20 minutes in the first lesson and 30 minutes plus in the second lesson
Preparation	For an example presentation, you may like to give learners copies of Box 5.3a. This activity should be spread over two lessons and involves learners, in their own time, going into the local community and observing non-verbal behaviour.

Procedure

1 Decide on a type of non-verbal communication that the class would like to investigate. Possible options might include:
   - how people greet each other
   - how couples display affection in public (Note that in some contexts, public displays of affection are considered inappropriate.)
   - styles of walking
   - behaviour in lifts
   - behaviour when people pass each other in the street

- shop assistants' hand gestures and body language
- lecturing styles in different college or university departments

2 Once the class has decided the type of communication to study, they devise a simple coding system to record the behaviour on an observation schedule. Learners should also decide how many people they will observe. For example, to record different styles of walking, learners might devise an observation schedule as follows:

Location:	Date and time of day:				
For each person observed, give their age (pre-teen, teens, 20s, 30s, 40s, 50s 60+), their dress code and comment on what behaviour you see.					
	Person 1	Person 2	Person 3	Person 4	Person 5
Age					
Dress code: smart/casual					
Hands in pockets					
Arms swinging: not at all / a little / a lot					
Posture: slouched/erect					
Type of step: skip / shuffle / smart step / jog / run					

3 In groups, learners pre-agree the locations they will observe so comparisons can be made later. Outside class time, learners go into the community and collect data, using the observation sheets devised in class.

4 In a following lesson, the groups prepare a presentation based on their data. The learners must:
   - summarise and present the information they have collected
   - identify patterns (e.g. age-related behaviour)
   - suggest meanings (e.g. What does slouching or erect posture mean to you?)

For an example, hand out the presentation on styles of walking in Box 5.3a.

Box 5.3a: Exploring non-verbal communication

Example presentation: Styles of walking

We did our observation on 6 June, between three and four o'clock in the afternoon. We watched 50 shoppers in the Shangri-La Shopping Mall. We watched 25 males and 25 females of different ages. The table shows our results.

Walking style	Pre-teens		Teens		20s+30s		40s+50s		60+	
	M	F	M	F	M	F	M	F	M	F
Hands in pockets	2	1	4	2	2	1	1	0	3	0
Big arm swing	3	0	0	0	1	0	2	0	1	1
Little or no arm swing	2	5	5	5	4	5	3	5	4	4
Upright	5	5	2	4	4	5	4	5	3	5
Slouched	0	0	3	1	1	0	1	0	2	0
Smart step	2	3	1	4	4	5	4	5	3	5
Shuffle	1	0	4	1	1	0	1	0	2	0
Skip	2	2	0	0	0	0	0	0	0	0
Jog	0	0	0	0	0	0	0	0	0	0
Run	0	0	0	0	0	0	0	0	0	0

Our results suggest the following:

- Generally, males have their hands in their pockets more than females.
- Some males swing their arms more, while females usually do not.
- Pre-teen boys seem to swing their arms more than older males.
- Teenagers tend to slouch more than other age groups.
- Teenage males tend to shuffle more than anyone else.
- Pre-teens tend to skip more than anyone else.
- Nobody jogged or ran.

PHOTOCOPIABLE

5 Learners present their findings and compare patterns of behaviour in different settings. For example, is behaviour in lifts different depending on where the lift is situated (in a residential block of flats, offices, a hotel, shopping centre, etc.)? If they have e-partners, the learners can share their findings online.

5.4 The eyes have it

Outline	Learners reflect on the function of eye contact in spoken communication.
Focus	Reading; role playing simple conversations.
Level	Intermediate and above
Time	40 minutes plus
Preparation	Copy the worksheets in Boxes 5.4a to 5.4c.

Procedure

1 Introduce the topic of eye contact, and ask the learners why they might wish to establish or avoid eye contact with someone. Possible answers follow.
   Reasons for establishing eye contact:
   • You want information from someone.
   • You want to show someone you are interested in them, or like them.
   • You want to check whether someone is sincere, or telling the truth.
   • You want to show that you are interested in what is being said.
   • You want to take part in a conversation, or take control of it.
   • You want to show your feelings about what someone is saying.
   • You want to attract someone's attention (e.g. a waiter).

   Reasons for avoiding eye contact:
   • You do not wish to be picked by the teacher to answer a question.
   • You are not telling the truth about something.
   • You do not wish to get into a conversation with someone.
   • You want to hide your feelings.
   • You are busy and do not wish to be interrupted.
   • To show respect.
2 Ask for a volunteer from the class and get them to tell you a story about his or her life (e.g. memories about the first day at school). Respond to the learner's story with a lot of eye contact. Then get the learner to repeat the story and respond with very little eye contact. Afterwards, the volunteer

reports how they felt about your eye contact in both the first and second demonstration. Which did they prefer? You can also ask the other class members how interested they think you were in both demonstrations, in the volunteer's story.

3   Choose a pair of learners, A and B, and ask them to act out the role play in Box 5.4a before the rest of the class. Tell the other class members that afterwards they must comment on the eye contact between A and B.

Box 5.4a: The eyes have it

Role play: Teacher and pupil

Speaker A: You are a teacher. You are annoyed with a teenage pupil, who has failed to hand in his or her homework on time.
Don't forget to decide whether to establish or avoid eye contact with the pupil.

 -

Speaker B: You are a teenage school pupil. You have forgotten to do the homework assignment that you were given last week. Your teacher has called you to a meeting. Decide how you are going to act. Are you going to (a) pretend you do not care, (b) say that you are sorry and promise never to forget your homework again, or (c) invent a really good excuse for not having your homework with you.
Don't forget to decide whether to establish or avoid eye contact with the teacher.

© Cambridge University Press 2010   PHOTOCOPIABLE

After the pair has completed the role play, they and the class consider how the eye contact between the two speakers affected the conversation. Did the teacher seem weak or authoritative? Did the student seem insulting, submissive, sincere or insincere?

4   Divide the class into groups of three or four and distribute the role play cards in Boxes 5.4b and 5.4c to each group. Two people in each group perform the role plays. The others in each group observe the speakers, and afterwards comment on their eye contact. Learners take it in turns so that they all get the opportunity to perform a role play and observe.

5 After the role plays have been completed, the learners report back to the class about how the eye contact affected the exchanges of dialogue.

Box 5.4b: The eyes have it

Role play: Two friends

> Speaker A: You have just come back from an adventure holiday in Africa. You went on a safari and took hundreds of photographs of animals in the wild: lions, zebras, elephants, giraffes and crocodiles. Tell your friend what a great holiday it was.
> Don't forget to think about the eye contact you will use.

 -

> Speaker B: Your friend has just come back from holiday and is telling you all about it. Show by your eye contact whether you find the stories interesting or boring.

© Cambridge University Press 2010 PHOTOCOPIABLE

Box 5.4c: The eyes have it

Role play: Employer and employee

> Speaker A: You are an employee in a big firm. You represent the other employees. The cost of living is rising fast, and, at a recent meeting, the employees instructed you to ask your employer for higher wages. You must ask the employer for more money for the employees.
> Don't forget to think about the eye contact you will use.

 -

> Speaker B: You own a large firm that employs many people. The economy is in a difficult state and you cannot afford to raise wages. You are going to meet a representative of the employees. Tell the representative that it is impossible to give the employees more money.
> Don't forget to think about the eye contact you will use.

© Cambridge University Press 2010 PHOTOCOPIABLE

5.5 Empathy and body language

Outline	Learners do a role play that is designed to draw their attention to the body language that indicates empathy and concern.
Focus	Personal narratives; the expression and denial of empathy through body language, back-channelling, etc.
Level	Intermediate and above
Time	40 minutes plus
Preparation	Two learners will need copies of the role play in Box 5.5a. All learners will need copies of the observation schedule in Box 5.5b and the role play in Box 5.5c.

Procedure

1 Write the word *empathy* on the board and either ask the class for a definition or give an explanation, e.g. 'the ability to see a situation from another person's point of view'. Give an illustration of this; for example, explain that a medical doctor needs to show empathy visibly, through his or her language, facial expressions and body language. You can mime two possible responses from a doctor to a patient who is telling the doctor about a problem: (a) a concerned facial expression, a slight leaning forward, and a reassuring phrase like, 'Oh, I'm sorry you're feeling unwell'; or (b) a folding of the arms, a raising of the eyes to the ceiling, and a slight grunt. Ask students which shows 'empathy'.

2 Choose a volunteer from the class and announce that you are going to tell the volunteer a story about a stressful time. But first, ask the class how the volunteer might respond to this story by showing empathy. The class's answers can be listed on the board or screen. The class might suggest that the volunteer does some of the following:
   * nods his or her head more visibly than usual
   * makes more eye contact than usual
   * adjusts his or her facial expression
   * makes reassuring noises (back-channelling), e.g. 'mm-hmm', 'oh no'
   * stands closer to you than usual, or leans towards you
   * touches you briefly and non-threateningly on the arm

3 Tell your story to the volunteer, who shows empathy in some of the ways discussed. A possible 'story about a stressful time' might be:
   Oh, I've had a really terrible day! I needed to arrive early at school to prepare for classes and so I set my alarm for six o'clock so that I could leave home before seven. But my alarm clock didn't go off, and I slept

in till 8.30. I missed out breakfast and rushed out the house. But when I got to my car, I saw that one of the tyres was flat! I had to change the tyre, and when I finished, I realised that all my clothes were black and filthy. I had to go back into the house, have a shower and change my clothes. I arrived at school at 10.15, too late for my first class, and totally unprepared! It's been very stressful!

With the class, discuss how appropriate the volunteer listener's responses were, and, from this discussion, you can summarise on the board some advice on 'good listenership', e.g. the listener should not interrupt the speaker too much, the listener's nods should not be too exaggerated, and any body contact (if it is appropriate at all) should be reassuring, not threatening. Mention that these features of communication are difficult to judge across cultures and across situations, so it is best not to be too extreme.

4   Choose two learners, A and B, to perform the role play in Box 5.5a. While learners A and B are studying their parts, explain to the rest of the class that the role play is between an airline passenger and someone who works at the airport check-in desk. The passenger has arrived five minutes too late to check in for a flight and must persuade the airline staff to allow him or her to check in. Tell learners that they are going to observe the role play and complete their evaluation of the interaction in the observation schedule.

Go through the observation schedule in Box 5.5b with them, making sure they understand how to fill in the schedule. Then, check that the two learners understand their role cards and are prepared to perform.

5   While learners A and B are performing their role play, the others in the class observe their exchange and complete the observation schedule.

6   After the role play is over, the class discusses how A invited sympathy, and how B showed empathy. They give advice on how A and B might have improved their performance.

7   In pairs, all the learners rehearse the role play in Box 5.5c.

8   Invite selected pairs to repeat their exchange in front of the whole class for them to observe and discuss. The observation schedule can be used again to give a focus for the class discussion.

Box 5.5a: Empathy and body language

Role play: At the airport

Speaker A: You are booked on a flight with a budget airline from a small airport. The check-in time at the airport desk is 19.00. Unfortunately, your taxi was delayed in a traffic jam, and you have arrived at the check-in desk at 19.05. You have no bags to check in, only hand luggage. You know that it only takes about ten minutes to pass through airport security. The plane will not be boarding until 19.30 and it will not depart until 20.00. There is plenty of time. Persuade the airline staff to allow you to check in late. If necessary, demand to see the manager.

Speaker B: You work for a budget airline at an airport check-in desk in a small airport. The check-in time for your airline's next flight was 19.00. It is now 19.05. You are changing the signs when a passenger arrives late. You know that for security reasons you cannot allow the passenger to check in. Be very sympathetic, but explain to the passenger that it is impossible to check in now. The passenger must stay the night in a hotel, and pay for a new ticket for another flight tomorrow.

If the passenger demands to see the manager, explain that the manager is very busy. If the passenger really insists, choose another learner from the class to be the manager, and let the passenger explain the situation to him or her!

© Cambridge University Press 2010   PHOTOCOPIABLE

Box 5.5b: Empathy and body language

Observation schedule: Observing body language

	Person 1:	Person 2:
Role of person:		
Signals of empathy:		
Eye contact	effective/could be better	effective/could be better
Use of gesture	effective/could be better	effective/could be better
Facial expression	effective/could be better	effective/could be better
Tone of voice	effective/could be better	effective/could be better
Back-channelling	effective/could be better	effective/could be better
Use of touch	effective/could be better	effective/could be better
Position of body	effective/could be better	effective/could be better
Overall appearance:	sympathetic/hostile	empathetic/hostile

© Cambridge University Press 2010   PHOTOCOPIABLE

Box 5.5c: Empathy and body language

Role play: Parent-child discussion

Speaker A: You are the parent of a 17-year-old child. He/She has just received excellent results in his/her school leaving examinations, and you hope that he/she will go to university next year. However, he/she wants to take a gap year and go back-packing around the world with some friends. You don't think this is a good idea.

Think of some good reasons why he/she should go to university and not take a gap year. For example, you know that it is difficult to start studying again after a long break. Then have a discussion about his/her future. Be sympathetic, but be firm.

Speaker B: You are 17 years old. You have worked hard at school, and you have achieved excellent grades in your leaving examinations. Your grades are good enough for a place at university. However, you have saved up enough money to travel, and you want to take a gap year first, and go back-packing around the world with some friends. You want to chill out on a beach in Thailand! Unfortunately, your parent wants you to go to university immediately after school. Think of some good reasons for not doing so. For example, you need a break from examinations, and you want to experience some of the world before beginning to study again. Then have a discussion with your parent about your future. Be sympathetic, but be firm.

PHOTOCOPIABLE

5.6 Gestures

Outline	Learners explore the gestures that the class uses to communicate particular meanings. Learners also investigate the meanings of particular gestures worldwide.
Focus	Meaningful gestures; rude gestures.
Level	Pre-intermediate and above
Time	30 minutes plus
Preparation	Half the class will need copies of the questionnaire in Box 5.6a and the other half will need copies of the questionnaire in Box 5.6b.

Procedure

1 Explain to the learners that they are going to look at the meanings of gestures in different cultures. Lead into this topic by asking the learners what gestures they would use to communicate the following meanings:

Meaning	Possible gestures
'Come here!'	Crooking a finger.
'OK!'	Thumbs up, or circling index finger and thumb.
'We share a secret.'	Tapping nose, or winking.
'I like you.'	A tap on the upper arm, or even a kiss.
'I agree!'	A nod of the head.
'I disagree!'	A shake of the head.
'This is delicious!'	Pursing lips and nodding head slightly.

2 Explain that different gestures mean different things in different cultures. Sometimes gestures and other forms of non-verbal communication can cause offence. One obvious example is to circle the index finger and thumb, while extending the other fingers. In some parts of the world this means 'OK!' but in other parts of the world (e.g. parts of South America) it can be very rude indeed.

3 Invite the class, in pairs or small groups, to devise a dialogue in which they use four of the gestures they identified in step 1. Allow the learners time to rehearse their dialogues and then invite selected learners to perform the dialogues to the whole class.

4 Divide the class into groups. Give half of the groups Questionnaire A and the other half Questionnaire B. Tell the group members to rate how rude they find the gestures listed in the questionnaires.

5 After completing the questionnaires, the groups report back to the class as a whole and compare their answers.

6 If they have e-partners, the learners can discuss their findings with them online.

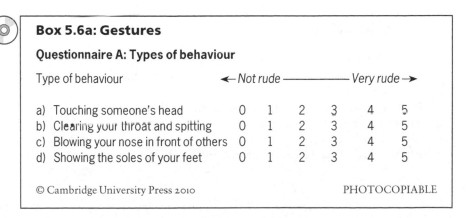

Box 5.6a: Gestures

Questionnaire A: Types of behaviour

Type of behaviour	← Not rude ———— Very rude →					
a) Touching someone's head	0	1	2	3	4	5
b) Clearing your throat and spitting	0	1	2	3	4	5
c) Blowing your nose in front of others	0	1	2	3	4	5
d) Showing the soles of your feet	0	1	2	3	4	5

PHOTOCOPIABLE

Box 5.6b: Gestures

Questionnaire B: Types of behaviour

Type of behaviour	← Not rude ———— Very rude →					
a) Looking someone directly in the eye	0	1	2	3	4	5
b) Passing food with the left hand	0	1	2	3	4	5
c) Winking at someone	0	1	2	3	4	5
d) Eating with your mouth open	0	1	2	3	4	5
e) Leaving food on your plate	0	1	2	3	4	5

© Cambridge University Press 2010   PHOTOCOPIABLE

Follow-up

1 If the learners are interested in this topic, encourage them to research and compare the meanings of gestures in different cultures. Some language coursebooks have information on this topic; another relatively accessible source is G.R. Wainwright's *Teach Yourself: Body Language* (see *Further reading and resources* on pp. 253–257). Accessible online sources on gesture and sign language include Wikipedia (http://en.wikipedia.org/wiki/Gesture) and A Nice Gesture (http://jeroenarendsen.nl). Learners can compile a visual 'dictionary' of gestures from different countries, with their meanings.

2 Some subcultures also have distinctive gestures. For example, some of the specific gestures used in the performance of hip-hop music are shown on the Flocabulary website: http://www.flocabulary.com/handgestures.html Again, more advanced learners, in their teens, can research this site, and then practise chanting some rhymes or song lyrics while using appropriate hip-hop gestures.

5.7 In the office

Outline	Through role plays in an office environment, learners consider messages managers and employees send each other through body language.
Focus	Requesting, reprimanding; describing and evaluating behaviour.
Level	Intermediate and above
Time	40 minutes plus
Preparation	Learners need copies of the role plays in Boxes 5.7a and 5.7b.

Procedure

1   Explain to the class that they are going to role play some common situations that take place in an office and discuss behaviour and body language.

2   Using the role play in Box 5.7a play the part of the manager, with a volunteer playing the part of the employee. The other class members observe, and afterwards discuss if the manager's behaviour was polite or unacceptable.

3   Next choose another volunteer and repeat the role play, this time with you taking the part of the employee. You might wish to vary the behaviour demonstrated in step 2; for example, if the learner has looked at the manager directly in the eyes when role playing the employee, you might wish not to look the manager directly in the eyes. Now the class discusses whether the employee's behaviour was acceptable or unacceptable.

4   Ask the class to give advice to the 'manager' and the 'employee' about how to modify their body language in order to be more or less polite.

5   Divide the class into groups of 'managers' and 'employees'. In pairs (one manager and one employee), the learners then perform the role play in Box 5.7a choosing which body language to adopt.

6   Next, explain to learners that they are now going to role play or observe a manager reprimanding an employee. Together, the class brainstorms ways in which a manager might begin to reprimand an employee, e.g.

   We need to discuss something.
   I'm afraid there's a bit of a problem.
   I've a bone to pick with you.
   We need to talk.
   I have some issues/concerns that we need to talk about.

7   Divide the class into three groups, 'managers', 'employees' and 'observers', and distribute the role cards for the role play in Box 5.7b. You should ensure that there are a roughly equal number of learners playing Manager A and B, and a roughly equal number of learners playing Employee A and B. While the learners study their cards in groups, circulate making sure all the learners understand their role.

8   Next, organise the managers and employees into pairs. One or two observers are assigned to each manager-employee pair. Tell learners

that the role play begins with the manager and employee standing some distance apart. Then, the managers should tell the employees to join them, and they rehearse the role play.

9   After the rehearsal ask the observers to report to the class on what they have observed. The observers should make recommendations on how the body language of the managers and employees might be improved.

10 Next ask the other learners how they felt about the body language they used as the manager and employee. How comfortable did they feel?

11 Finally, ask the class, in groups, to write down four or five rules of behaviour for 'the good manager' and four or five rules for 'the good employee'. If learners are involved in an online intercultural exchange, they can send their e-partners their rules for further discussion.

Box 5.7a: In the office

Role play: Requesting

Speaker A (Manager): Ask one of your employees to photocopy a document for you. You need the photocopied document immediately.
- Pick up the document and go to your employee's desk.
- Sit on the edge of the desk. Move the employee's stuff around a little. Use expressive hand gestures.
- Ask the employee to photocopy your document. Tell the employee that you need the photocopy immediately.

Speaker B (Employee): You are very busy at your desk. Your manager is going to ask you a question. Choose which body language to adopt while your manager is talking:
either:
a) Relax. Fold your arms, cross your legs and sit back. Look directly at your manager. Look in his/her eyes.
or:
b) Clasp your hands in your lap. Look down. Nod politely, but do not look directly at your manager.

© Cambridge University Press 2010   PHOTOCOPIABLE

Box 5.7b: In the office

Role play: Reprimanding

Manager A: One of your employees has done a bad job. An important client asked for information urgently, and the employee forgot to send it. As a result, your company might lose a valuable contract. Tell your employee that this kind of behaviour is unacceptable.

- Ask your employee to come to see you.
- Calmly explain to the employee what has happened.
- Tell him or her that this kind of behaviour is unacceptable.
- Tell the employee that you know he or she can do better.
- Ask your employee if he or she understands how serious the problem is.
- Touch him or her briefly on the upper arm or shoulder.
- Tell your employee that he or she can go now.

Manager B: One of your employees has done a bad job. An important client asked for information urgently, and the employee forgot to send it. The client is very angry and your company might lose a valuable contract. You have to tell your employee that this kind of behaviour is unacceptable.

- Tell your employee to come and see you. Use hand gestures to tell him or her to hurry up.
- Explain to the employee what has happened. Stand very close to him or her. Show that you are angry. Use lots of expressive gestures.
- Tell him or her that this behaviour is totally unacceptable.
- Tell your employee that he or she is very stupid.
- Tell your employee to get out of your sight.

Employee A: You've had problems at work. Your workload has been increasing and you forgot to send urgent information to an important client. Your boss is angry with you, and he or she wants to see you. When he or she calls you, do the following:

- Clasp your hands in front of you.
- Look downwards and do not make any eye contact with your boss at all.
- Keep your expression neutral.
- Say as little as possible in response to him or her, e.g. 'Yes', 'No' or 'I don't know'.

Employee B: You've had problems at work. Your workload has been increasing and you forgot to send urgent information to an important client. Your boss is angry with you, and he or she wants to see you. When he or she calls you, do the following:

continued

Box 5.7b: (*cont.*)

- Clasp your hands in front of you.
- Make eye contact with your boss.
- Occasionally nod.
- Apologise, but try to explain that you have got too much work.

 -

Observer:
- Describe each person's behaviour.
- Was the behaviour polite or unacceptable?
- Is there a difference between male and female behaviour?
- Should the manager or employee change his or her behaviour? If so, how?

© Cambridge University Press 2010   PHOTOCOPIABLE

5.8 Exploring informal language

Outline	Learners consider the kind of informal expressions that characterise face-to-face communication. Some of these informal, colloquial expressions are associated with particular 'in-groups' in a culture, whether these groups are defined by geography, age, gender, profession or another social variable. This activity invites learners to consider whether they have equivalents in their first language.
Focus	Words and phrases associated with informal speech or writing.
Level	Intermediate and above
Time	40 minutes plus
Preparation	Learners need to have access to freely available online corpora on the Internet. The websites they need to access are: http://corpus.byu.edu/bnc/ and http://www.americancorpus.org Learners also need copies of the worksheet in Box 5.8a and the table in Box 5.8b.

Procedure

1   Elicit from the learners whether they know the following words and phrases:

a) *chuffed*   f) *a hunk*

b) *to diss*   g) *grotty*

c) *thingummy*   h) *icky*

d) *naff*   i) *umpteen*

e) *cool*   j) *to go postal*

2 Ask the learners to match the words and phrases to the meanings below:

1) *excellent, fashionable*
2) *to lose control, go mad*
3) *pleased, gratified*
4) *a good-looking young man*
5) *lacking in style or taste*
6) *many, countless*
7) *to insult or show disrespect*
8) *dirty, disgusting* (two expressions)
9) *thing, person (used when you cannot remember the name of that thing or person)*

Answers: *a–3, b–7, c–9, d–5, e–1, f–4, g and h–8, i–6, j–2.*

3 Ask the class to classify these informal expressions under the headings: positive, negative or vague.

Suggested answers:

Positive expressions	Negative expressions	Vague expressions
cool	*naff*	*umpteen*
chuffed	*to diss*	*thingummy*
a hunk	*icky*	
	grotty	
	go postal	

4 If the learners have access to the Internet, instruct them to explore the uses of some of the informal words in British and American English using the freely available British National Corpus and Corpus of Contemporary American English online. You can introduce the class to the necessary steps, by taking the learners through Box 5.8a, using *naff* as an example.

5 After you have taken the learners through the procedure, ask them to repeat the steps for the other expressions and prepare to report back to the class. Remind learners to check the uses of the examples as well as their frequency. *Chuffed* can have several meanings, and the abbreviation 'diss.' in academic prose means something very different from the verb *diss* in informal speech!

6 Encourage the learners to reflect on the use of informal expressions in their own languages. The table in Box 5.8b invites them to think about equivalent informal words and phrases in their first language. If you are teaching a multicultural class, you can encourage the learners to teach their classmates three informal expressions in their own language. They will need to explain what the expressions mean and say when they are used. If they are taking part in an online intercultural exchange, they can teach the phrase to their e-partners – remembering to give advice on pronunciation.

A further possibility is for learners to ask older members of their family or older friends about informal expressions (like 'groovy') that were once popular but are no longer used. What do they mean and when were they used?

Follow-up

Encourage learners to compile their own 'Dictionary of Informal English' by adding to the table colloquial expressions they have learned from watching television or films, listening to popular music, or from their encounters with other speakers of English. At regular intervals, you can ask learners to share their additions to their dictionaries with the others in the class.

Box 5.8a: Exploring informal language

Worksheet: Exploring informal expressions in British and American English

- Look at the words and phrases below and guess which ones are more likely to be found in British English and which ones are more likely to be American English.

naff	*grotty*	*chuffed*
to go postal	*to diss*	*icky*

- Follow the steps below to test your predictions. *Naff* is used as an example.

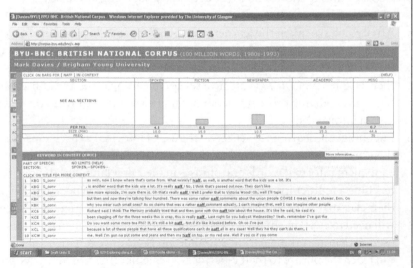

Figure 1: British National Corpus results for 'naff'

continued

Box 5.8a: *(cont.)*

a) Go to http://corpus.byu.edu/bnc/ and enter the British National Corpus.
b) In the 'Display' section, click on 'Chart'.
c) In the 'Word(s)' box, type *naff* and click on 'Search'. To see some examples of spoken uses, click on the 'SPOKEN' bar. The display in Figure 1 should be seen.

Now repeat the search, but this time look for *naff* in the Corpus of Contemporary American English (CCAE):

d) Go to http://www.americancorpus.org and enter the Corpus of Contemporary American English.
e) In the 'Display' section, click on 'Chart'.
f) In the 'Word(s)' box, type *naff* and click on 'Search'. The following display should be seen:

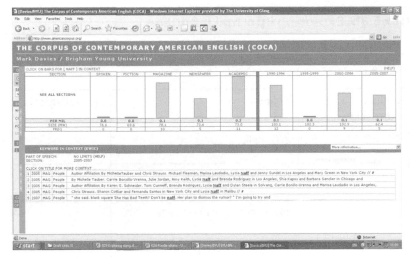

Figure 2: Corpus of Contemporary American English results for 'naff'

Note on *naff*

It is clear from Figure 1 that the most common uses of *naff* in British English are in speech (4.1 occurrences per million words), where the word means 'vulgar', or 'lacking in good taste'. We can see from the individual occurrences that *naff* is often preceded by a qualifying word or phrase, like *rather naff, really naff, a bit naff*. Although *naff* is occasionally found in writing, especially newspapers, it is mainly confined to speech.

continued

Box 5.8a: (*cont.*)

Figure 2 shows us that *naff* is much less frequent in American English. Indeed, most of the uses in the CCAE are in fact the surnames of people like Lycia Naff! However, if you click on the 'MAGAZINE' bar, you will see at least one example of the British meaning of *naff* – with reference to Victoria Beckham, the famous pop-star wife of an equally famous English footballer, David Beckham. The American magazine probably uses a British expression here because both David and Victoria Beckham's nationality is so obviously British.

© Cambridge University Press 2010   PHOTOCOPIABLE

Box 5.8b: Exploring informal language

Table: Comparing informal expressions

Complete the following table.

English expressions	Meaning	My equivalents
icky, grotty, gross	disgusting	
cool	excellent, fashionable	
naff	vulgar, lacking in good taste	
thingummy	used to refer to something whose proper name you cannot remember	

© Cambridge University Press 2010   PHOTOCOPIABLE

6 Interviewing

One way of finding out about people from another culture is to interview them. The skills involved in interviewing, however, involve more than simply devising and asking questions. Learners may have to tease information out of reluctant interviewees and interpret the answers they are given. Often the answers will not give information directly, and the interviewers will have to infer what the interviewees think and believe. The next few activities therefore break down some key interviewing skills into stages. *Developing interview questions* (6.1) focuses on devising questions for different kinds of interviewees from different cultural groups; *Following up interview questions* (6.2) helps learners elicit further information in interviews; and *Exploring assumptions* (6.3) considers how learners might interpret their interviewees' unspoken assumptions. *The interviewers from another planet* (6.4) invites learners to 'defamiliarise' their everyday lives and routines radically, by imagining that they come from an entirely different planet; while the final activity, *Preparing for an online interview* (6.5) guides learners in conducting an interview online, by email or through a chat room.

6.1 Developing interview questions

Outline	Learners develop questions for ethnographic interviews, that is, interviews with members of a particular cultural group, e.g. a youth subculture, an ethnic group, or a particular occupation.
Focus	Asking appropriate and polite questions; personal narratives.
Level	Intermediate and above
Time	40 minutes plus
Preparation	Learners need copies of the photographs (a punk rocker, a Muslim bride and groom, and a group of car factory workers on strike) in Box 6.1a on the CD-ROM for step 1 and copies of the role cards in Boxes 6.1b and 6.1c. Similar photographs of people from particular youth subcultures, ethnic backgrounds, religious cultures or occupations should be brought to the lesson – you can ask learners to look for these beforehand, or bring them yourself. These will be needed for step 5.

Procedure

1   Introduce the idea of exploring different kinds of cultural groups by interviewing its members. Show the three sample photographs (CD-ROM 6.1a) and ask what kinds of 'culture' they might illustrate. The answers might include:

   • youth culture (e.g. punks, rockers, mods, hippies, goths, etc.)
   • ethnic culture (e.g. African, Asian, Caucasian, etc.)
   • religious culture (e.g. Buddhist, Christian, Jewish, Muslim, etc.)
   • occupational (e.g. manual worker, street artist, clerical worker, entrepreneur, etc.)

2   Divide the class into groups, and ask each group to think of three questions that they would ask the punk rocker. Possible questions might be:

   • When did you become a punk rocker?
   • Why did you become a punk rocker?
   • What are your favourite bands/groups? *Or* What is your favourite music?
   • Does your appearance shock people? *Or* How do people react to your appearance?
   • Have you got a job? What does your manager think of your clothes?

Box 6.1a: Developing interview questions

Photos: Cultural groups

© Alamy/Jon Arnold Images Ltd

continued

Box 6.1a: (*cont.*)

© Scran

© Corbis/Bernard Bisson/Sygma

From *Intercultural Language Activities*
© Cambridge University Press 2010

PHOTOCOPIABLE

After they have come up with their questions, discuss polite ways in which interviewers might introduce their questions, for example:
> *Excuse me, would you mind answering one or two questions?*
> *I'm doing a project for my school. Or I'm writing an article for the school magazine.*

3 Take the role of a punk rocker (see the sample role card below). The groups take turns to ask you some of their questions and you respond using the role card.

Teacher's role card: Punk rocker

You got into punk rock through the music: Sex Pistols, Stranglers, Ramones, New York Dolls. For some people it's a weekend thing, but for you it's a way of life. You work in a trendy fashion store in town, and the manager doesn't mind if your hair is spiky, or if you wear leather and studs. Some people are shocked by your clothes and the make-up but, really, you get irritated when they jump to conclusions about your attitude or your beliefs. You just feel comfortable like this; it's a bit of fun. You never wanted to be a boring, middle-class, office-suit, nine-to-five kind of person.

4 Invite the class to reflect upon the questions they asked:
   * Did they get the information they wanted or expected?
   * What reaction did they get to the questions?
   * How might the questions be better phrased?
5 Divide the class into four groups, A, B, C and D. Groups B and D will play the part of interviewers. Groups A and C will play the interviewees. Distribute the role cards in Boxes 6.1b and 6.1c. Explain that the interviewees in Group A should prepare to be the Muslim bride or groom, while the interviewees in Group C will be one of the car factory workers. The interviewees should study their role cards, and try to anticipate the questions they will be asked. Instruct the interviewers to prepare five questions. Tell Group B they will be interviewing the Muslim bride/ groom and Group D will be interviewing the car factory worker.
6 After the preparation, organise learners into pairs and get them to rehearse their interviews. After this rehearsal stage is completed, select particular learners to re-enact their role play for the whole class. Again, the class reflects on the questions asked, and considers if they can be expanded or improved upon. Guide this reflection by asking the learners to think about the following questions:

- Which questions elicited the information the interviewers wanted?
- Which questions were less effective?
- Did any questions make the interviewees angry? Why?

7 Distribute the photographs you or your learners found showing people from particular youth subcultures, ethnic backgrounds, religious cultures or occupations. Each member of the class chooses a photograph and invents a history for the 'subject' shown in the picture. In pairs, learners prepare questions for each other's 'subjects' in the photographs and then interview each other.

Box 6.1b: Developing interview questions

Role cards: Muslim bride or groom and interviewer

Bride: My parents come from Pakistan, but I was born and brought up in Bradford, in England, where I went to school. My husband's parents also come from Pakistan, but he was born and went to school in Newcastle, in England. We both decided to have an arranged marriage. We met before the wedding, and decided that we would be happy as husband and wife. We plan to live in Newcastle, where my husband works in the family catering business. The photograph was taken on our wedding day, just after the formal ceremony, or 'nikah'.

Groom: My parents come from Pakistan, but I was born and brought up in Newcastle, in England, where I went to school. My wife's family comes from Pakistan, too, but she was born and went to school in Bradford, in England. We both decided to have an arranged marriage. We met before the wedding, and decided that we would be happy as husband and wife. We plan to live in Newcastle, where I help my father manage a catering firm that he started up. The photograph was taken on our wedding day, just after the formal ceremony, or 'nikah'.

Interviewer: You are going to interview the Muslim bride or groom shown in the photograph. Look at the photograph and think of five questions that you would like to ask him or her. Remember to be polite!

© Cambridge University Press 2010   PHOTOCOPIABLE

Box 6.1c: Developing interview questions

Role cards: Car factory worker and interviewer

> Car factory worker: This was me and my mates, ten years ago, when the bosses wanted to close the local factory. The workers went on strike and organised protests like this one. I had worked in the factory for years: first as an apprentice after leaving school, and then as a skilled worker. It was hard work but there was a sense of pride in seeing those shiny, new cars leaving the factory. The solidarity between the workers was strong – they were a great bunch of guys, always telling jokes. They're all gone now. The factory closed and I was unemployed for over a year, before I found work on the railways.

 -

> Interviewer: You are going to interview one of the car factory workers shown in the photograph. Look at the photograph and think of five questions that you would like to ask him. Remember to be polite!

© Cambridge University Press 2010   PHOTOCOPIABLE

6.2 Following up interview questions

Outline	Learners practise using follow-up questions and eliciting further information as not all interviewees give clear or extensive answers to interviewers' questions. This task follows on from *Developing interview questions* (6.1).
Focus	Eliciting information by asking follow-up questions.
Level	Intermediate and above
Time	40 minutes plus
Preparation	Learners need copies of the interview in Box 6.2a.

Procedure

1   Explain that this activity is going to develop learners' interviewing skills by practising with a 'difficult' interviewee. Many people who do research find that interviewees do not necessarily give full or helpful answers. Researchers therefore often have to use follow-up questions and request clarification.

2   Together, look at the sequence of questions and answers in Box 6.2a. Tell the learners that the interviewer here wishes to learn about the interviewee's time at school.

Box 6.2a: Following up interview questions

Dialogue: Interviewer and interviewee

Interviewer: So, can you tell me something about your school?
Interviewee: Well, what do you want to know?
Interviewer: Um, well, about where you went to school and what it was like.
Interviewee: Well, I just went to the local school.
Interviewer: Oh, right. And when did you leave school?
Interviewee: Oh, I was 18.

3   Ask the class how the interviewer could improve his or her interview technique. What follow-up questions could he or she ask? Discuss the fact that some questions can be answered with just *yes* or *no*, so there needs to be a follow-up question. For example:
   • How old were you when you started school?
   • Did you like your teachers?
   • What were your favourite subjects?
   • Were you ever punished for bad behaviour? If so, how?
   • Did you have lunch at school? What was the food like?
   • Do you remember playing any games between classes? What?
   • Did you enjoy sports at school? Which ones?
   • Can you tell me more about the classroom layout – how were the desks arranged, for example? Were there posters on the wall?
4   Tell the learners that they are now going to interview each other. The job of the interviewer is to obtain as much information as possible. However, the interviewee is not going to be very helpful. With the class, brainstorm some possible topics for the interviewer to ask about and list some on the board or screen. Possible topics might include:
   • everyday routines
   • best ever holidays
   • hobbies or leisure interests
   • favourite music or films, etc.
5   Instruct each class member to write down three or four main questions on one of the topics and two or three follow-up questions for each main question. For example:

- What is your favourite film?
  - How old were you when you first saw it?
  - Did you see it alone or with someone else?
  - Where did you first see this film?
- Can you tell me about your best ever holiday?
  - Where did you go?
  - Did you go alone, or with your family or friends?
  - What made it so memorable?

6 Ask learners for ideas of how an interviewer can encourage an interviewee to give more extensive answers, e.g. the interviewers should use encouraging body language and show an interest. Organise the class into pairs. The learners take it in turn to interview each other on the topics they have chosen. Before they begin, remind them that the interviewer should be friendly, smile and look interested in the answers. The interviewee meanwhile should not be very helpful.

7 After the interviews have been completed, the learners reflect in groups on how much information their questioning provided. Finally with the class produce a list of some good interview techniques, e.g.

- Follow general questions with more detailed questions.
- Vary closed (*yes/no*) questions with open (*wh-*) questions.
- Be polite and give encouraging back-channelling (e.g. nod and smile).
- Show interest through your body language and facial expressions.
- Avoid leading questions that make assumptions about the interviewee's beliefs or values (e.g. *'Aren't you proud to be . . .?'* or *'Doesn't modern society make you disgusted?'*).

6.3 Exploring assumptions

Outline	Learners reflect on issues that arise when people make different assumptions about why they are talking.
Focus	Asking questions; giving and requesting clarification.
Level	Intermediate and above
Time	40 minutes plus
Preparation	Learners need copies of the role cards in Box 6.3a.

Procedure

1   Explain that sometimes, when we ask questions, we make assumptions
    that lead to misunderstandings. Introduce the following situation:
    Jennifer is an English housewife who has moved with her husband
    and child to live in a new flat in Birmingham, England. The
    family has just arrived. While her husband is at work and her child is
    at play school, Jennifer has noticed a delicious cooking smell coming
    from her neighbour's flat. Jennifer and her husband love Asian food,
    and she enjoys cooking. She wonders if her Asian neighbour will
    share some of her recipes. So, one day, she knocks at her door.

2   Ask learners to suggest some different conversational openers Jennifer
    could use. Then read out the following:
    Mumtaz is a Pakistani housewife who has moved with her husband
    and three children to live in Birmingham, England. The family
    arrived two months ago, and they are living in a new flat in a large
    building. Mumtaz's husband is at work, and her children are at
    school. She likes living in Birmingham, but there has been one
    slight issue. She cooks spicy food for her family, and some of the
    neighbours have complained about the strong smell of her cooking.
    One day a neighbour knocks at her door.

3   Now that learners know the whole situation, ask them to choose
    the best conversational 'opener' for Jennifer and think about why
    they have chosen it: *'Hello, I'm your new neighbour. My name's*
    Jennifer. . .'
    a) *. . . I couldn't help noticing that you've been cooking.'*
    b) *. . . Does that lovely smell come from your flat?'*
    c) *. . . You know, I'm a great fan of Asian food.'*
    d) *. . . You must have been cooking all day!'*
    Discuss the fact that the first opener, (a), and the last one (d), are
    fairly neutral in tone, but they are both open to misinterpretation,
    and Mumtaz might think that Jennifer is complaining about the
    smell. Opener (b) is more positive, but it is still probably not polite
    to draw attention to the smell in a neighbour's flat! Opener (c)
    begins by explaining Jennifer's perspective and is probably the best.

4   In groups of three, learners role play a situation in which one person (A)
    asks another person (B) for information that could be sensitive. Person
    A needs to think about the best way to ask for information. While the
    interaction is taking place, a third person (C) observes the exchange,
    giving advice afterwards on how the interview might have been improved.

Box 6.3a: Exploring assumptions

Role play: Interviewing a goth

Speaker A: You are a learner doing research into different youth cultures. You are interested in goth styles. Young men and women dress in black clothes, and use pale make-up, with black eye-liner and black nail polish. You want to do some research into goth culture, so you approach someone who looks like a goth at a music concert. Find out what makes them a typical goth. For example, are they all pessimistic? Are they rejecting society?

Speaker B: You are a teenager who likes the goth image. You wear pale make-up, black eye-liner and black nail polish. You get angry when people think that all goths are the same – sad and gloomy! In fact, there are over 100 different types of goth. You are a cyber-goth: your clothes are black and white with lots of studs and zippers; you wear big, black boots; and you have bright orange hair. You are influenced by science fiction comics and films, and you listen to electronic dance music. It's cool being a goth.

Speaker C: You are going to observe an interview between a researcher and a goth. Listen carefully to the questions and answers and be prepared to give advice about the interview afterwards. For example:

- Did the interviewer begin by explaining the reason for the interview?
- Did the interviewer ask clear questions?
- Did the interviewer ask good follow-up questions?
- Did the interviewer vary his or her type of question?
- Did the interviewee cooperate?
- Did the interviewer and interviewee have positive body language? Did they smile, nod, and look interested in each other?

5 Before the role play starts, ask each person in the group (A, B and C) to study their role cards in Box 6.3a, and plan their questions and answers. Circulate amongst the groups and check learners' understanding of the task. The learners then perform the role play.

6 After the role play is over, and the groups have discussed the performances, with the class, list good interview techniques, e.g.

- Interviewers should explain the reason for the interview.
- Interviewers should ask clear, simple questions.

- Interviewers should ask follow-up questions.
- Interviewers should have sympathetic body language.
- Interviewers should listen to the answers and respond to them.

6.4 The interviewers from another planet

Outline	Learners reflect on the way questions relate to our own particular interests and concerns.
Focus	Questioning and answering; inferring someone's interests from his or her questions.
Level	Intermediate and above
Time	40 minutes plus
Preparation	For the follow-up, more advanced learners need copies of Craig Raine's poem *A Martian sends a postcard home* in Box 6.4a.

Procedure

1 Explain that the class is going to meet the first alien creatures to visit Earth from another planet. The aliens want to ask some questions about human culture. As representatives of the human race, the learners must answer the aliens' questions.
2 Depending on the class, you might wish to brainstorm the aliens' background, e.g.
   - Which planet do they come from?
   - What do they look like?
   - What do they want to know about us?
3 Divide the class into groups. One group (A) takes the role of the aliens. They devise six to eight questions to ask the 'humans'. While the learners in Group A are devising their questions, the learners in Group B devise six to eight questions that they want to ask the 'aliens'. The questions asked by each group, A and B, should indicate what topics they currently think are important – for example, food, the environment, what they feel about peace, hostility, etc.
4 Bring the groups together and get them to ask and answer each other's questions. They should use as much imagination as possible.
5 After the interviews, ask the groups to reflect on the following questions:
   - What did the aliens' questions suggest to you about life on the alien planet?
   - What did the humans' questions suggest to you about life on planet Earth?

Follow-up for more advanced learners
Get learners to read Craig Raine's poem *A Martian sends a postcard home* in Box 6.4a and discuss the way in which the poet defamiliarises the everyday through the alien's strange descriptions of commonplace things. Can learners guess what familiar, everyday things are being described?
Suggested answers: a book, a car, a watch and a telephone.

Box 6.4a: The interviewers from another planet

Reading text: A Martian on Earth

A Martian sends a postcard home
by Craig Raine

Caxtons are mechanical birds with many wings
and some are treasured for their markings –
they cause the eyes to melt
or the body to shriek without pain.

I have never seen one fly, but
sometimes they perch on the hand.

Mist is when the sky is tired of flight
and rests its soft machine on ground:

then the world is dim and bookish
like engravings under tissue paper.

Rain is when the earth is television.
It has the property of making colours darker.

Model T is a room with the lock inside –
a key is turned to free the world

for movement, so quick there is a film
to watch for anything missed.

But time is tied to the wrist
or kept in a box, ticking with impatience.

In homes, a haunted apparatus sleeps,
that snores when you pick it up.

If the ghost cries, they carry it
to their lips and soothe it to sleep

with sounds. And yet they wake it up
deliberately, by tickling with a finger.

continued

Box 6.4a: (*cont.*)

Only the young are allowed to suffer
openly. Adults go to a punishment room

with water but nothing to eat.
They lock the door and suffer the noises

alone. No one is exempt
and everyone's pain has a different smell.

At night when all the colours die,
they hide in pairs

and read about themselves –
in colour, with their eyelids shut.

© Craig Raine, 1979.
From *Intercultural Language Activities*
© Cambridge University Press 2010   PHOTOCOPIABLE

6.5 Preparing for an online interview

Outline	Learners prepare to interview someone from another culture online, by email or through a web-based chat room or discussion forum.
Focus	Asking questions and giving answers.
Level	Lower intermediate and above
Time	30 minutes plus
Preparation	Pieces of paper are needed for steps 2 to 7. You will need a computer and projector to display either the photo in Box 6.5a or the one in Box 6.5b. Learners also need copies of the discussion thread in Box 6.5c.

Procedure

1   Explain that this activity prepares learners to interview someone online. Show the class a photograph of an interesting person from another culture, e.g. either the image in Box 6.5a or the one in 6.5b, and tell them to imagine they are going to interview them.

  Get learners to think of topics they would like to ask about, e.g.
  * their job/school
  * free time

- food they like
- their home
- a typical day

Write the topics that you have elicited on the board or screen, and add a few more of your own if necessary.

2 Learners then work in pairs. Each learner takes a sheet of paper and chooses one topic and writes a question about it to ask their partner. The partners in each pair then exchange questions.

3 Each learner writes one or two sentences in response to the question, and they return the sheet of paper to their partner.

4 Choose one of the learners and ask them to read to the class the question they wrote and their partner's response, e.g. *Where do you live? I live in a small village in Switzerland.*
Ask the class to think of some follow-up questions that could now be asked, e.g. *What did you study at school? How many people were in your class? What was your favourite subject?* Write these up on the board as 'follow-up questions'.

5 The learners then write a follow-up question. Suggest that they write something encouraging before it, e.g. *That's really interesting! Now, can you tell me . . .* The learners exchange sheets of paper again. Then they answer their partner's follow-up question.

6 When they have finished answering the follow-up question, the learners exchange the sheet of paper again. They repeat the process with another follow-up question or two.

7 Now show the learners the sample exchange between Viviana and Wieke in Box 6.5c. They read the exchange and note down any expressions they find useful for asking and answering questions.

8 Ask the learners to change partners and begin another exchange with a new sheet of paper and a new question.

9 After this rehearsal, learners can go online and interview their e-partners or someone else from another culture via a chat room or discussion forum.

Box 6.5a: Preparing for an online interview

Photo: Person A

© Alamy/Blend Images

From *Intercultural Language Activities*
© Cambridge University Press 2010   PHOTOCOPIABLE

Box 6.5b: Preparing for an online interview

Photo: Person B

© Alamy/Blickwinkel

From *Intercultural Language Activities*
© Cambridge University Press 2010   PHOTOCOPIABLE

Box 6.5c: Preparing for an online interview

Discussion thread: Opening question, first answer, follow-up question and answer

From: Viviana

Hi!

I'm Viviana, from Argentina. I'm studying in La Plata but I come from San Nicolás, a city not so far away from here. I often go back to my home town during the winter and summer holidays. I can't afford anything else!! I'd like to know where you all spend your free time!!

Hope to hear from you soon!

Best wishes

Vivi

From: Wieke

Hi Viviana,

I'm Wieke from the Netherlands. I'll try to tell you something about Dutch people and their holidays!

In the Netherlands most people generally go on a three-week holiday either in the Netherlands or elsewhere in Europe. Many Dutch people love to go camping in France, sometimes to camps owned by Dutch people. There are so many Dutch people there they are really 'Dutch camps'! I never understand this though, because why would you go to France if you're not going to meet any French people? Quite a lot of people go on cycling holidays, taking a lightweight tent and cycling for hours every day to get to the next campsite.

I hope I have given you some insight into Dutch holidays!

Best

Wieke

continued

Box 6.5c (*cont.*)

From: Viviana

Hi Wieke

Thanks for the insight! That's really interesting. Do Dutch people like going to the beach too?

Vivi

From: Wieke

Hi Vivi

Yes, the Spanish coast is really popular with young people. Some of the villages over there seem like Dutch villages during the summer (i.e. Salou, Lloret de Mar). The goal of those holidays is mostly lying on the beach, going out all night, drinking, sleeping till noon and then lying on the beach again. Not really my kind of thing, but many people go there for a week with friends after their secondary school graduation.
Tell me about holidays in Argentina!

Wieke

PHOTOCOPIABLE

* The discussion threads contain some errors as they are written by students.

7   Interpretations

In this chapter, the emphasis shifts from face-to-face contact to the written word. The following activities involve learners in collecting and interpreting different kinds of visual and verbal cultural representations. The stimuli that learners explore vary from traditional sources of classroom activities, such as postcards and advertisements, to more recent digital resources, such as online newspapers, and online corpora of English language texts.

The first two activities, *Postcards* (7.1) and *Analysing advertisements* (7.2), help develop the learners' interpretive and critical skills, by asking them to collect and analyse postcards and advertisements, considering the impact of a local culture. The next activity, *Writing an online review* (7.3), encourages learners to engage actively in the international, intercultural discussion forums provided by book, music and film websites. The next two activities (7.4 and 7.5) make use of further internet resources, namely, large-scale digital corpora of English which are becoming freely available online. *Proverbs across cultures: using the TIME corpus* (7.4) allows learners to explore the meaning and usage of proverbial sayings in English while *Famous quotations in action* (7.5) allows learners to investigate the meaning and use of famous quotations. The final activity in this chapter, *Comparing newspapers around the world* (7.6), encourages learners to make use of the wealth of international English-language newspapers that are now easily available online in order to see how different countries report current events.

7.1 Postcards

Outline	Learners analyse postcard pictures of the community in which they are currently living, discuss the messages that these images are sending to people from other cultures, and whether these messages are accurate, adequate and desirable.
Focus	Describing and evaluating postcard images. This activity is a useful supplement to classes on describing places and landscapes.
Level	Intermediate and above
Time	30 minutes plus
Preparation	Bring to class a set of postcards showing different scenes of the community, preferably with a diversity of images and periods. Alternatively, ask learners to bring to class some postcards that they think do and do not represent the locality well. For the variation, learners may need digital cameras to take photographs of their community.

Procedure

1 Display the postcards and ask learners to consider them and choose one that they think is a good representation of the local community and one that they think is *not* a good representation of the local community.

2 The learners then write a brief description of the two postcards, and state why they think each image is – or is not – a good representation of the community in which they are currently living.

3 If the learners are participating in an online intercultural community, they can choose two postcards of their local area to send to their e-partners. They have to decide what to write on the card, and invite the e-partners to give *their* views of the cards once they receive them.

Variation

Some places do not have a tradition of producing postcards for the tourist trade. If the class is based in one of these places, you can show postcards from elsewhere. Then you can ask learners to identify local scenes that would – and would not – make good postcards of their local community. Learners with access to the Internet can use a search engine like Google™ Images to find suitable scenes, or they can take their own photographs and make their own postcards. They can then share these with their e-partners.

7.2 Analysing advertisements

Outline	Learners consider how advertisements are responsive to local cultures, and how multinational firms present their products to different audiences in different ways.
Focus	Describing advertisements and learning to read them critically.
Level	Intermediate and above
Time	10–15 minutes in the first lesson and 40 minutes plus in one or more follow-up lessons
Preparation	Learners need to collect examples of product advertising from magazines and/or websites aimed at different parts of the world. This activity will need to be spread over a few lessons and includes homework.

Procedure

1 Explain to the class that they are going to look at how products are advertised in different cultures. Ask the class to think of advertisements they have seen for popular international products, such as:
   - a soft drink
   - a fast-food restaurant
   - a car
   - a brand of cosmetics

   Brainstorm with the class the ways in which each product creates a distinctive image, for example by using:
   - particular groups of people (e.g. young people or families)
   - memorable slogans, possibly in another language
   - music and/or songs
   - particular locations (e.g. exotic or dramatic landscapes; architecturally well-designed interiors)
   - animation

   Then ask the learners to think of a product that is more regional in origin, e.g. a local drink, a local delicacy or a local craft. Is this product advertised in the press or on television? If so, how is its image created? If not, how would they design a television advertisement to promote it?

2 Choose one of the international products discussed and ask the learners for homework to collect advertisements for it from magazines, newspapers, websites, etc. If the product is advertised on television or radio, they can record or describe the TV or radio

commercials. Instruct learners to look on the Internet for examples of the product being advertised in different geographical areas, as well as in the national or local press.

3   Once the learners have collected the advertisements put them in groups, and get them to discuss how the product is presented. Each group should consider the following questions:
   • What visual images are used?
   • What languages are used?
   • What kind of audience is targeted?
   • Are the consumers shown in the advertisements? If so, what is their ethnicity, gender, etc.?
   • Is the product represented as a luxury or an everyday item?
   • Does the representation of the audience change across the regions where the product is advertised?
   • Do different advertisements for the product use different languages – or is the product always associated with one particular language?

4   Finally, ask the learners, in their groups, to choose a product that they wish to design an advertisement for. They should consider the following points:
   • What visual images will they use to promote the product? (Groups with access to the Internet might use a search engine like Google™ Images to find suitable images.)
   • How will they promote the product to a local audience?
   • Will they change the product image to promote the product to markets in another region, e.g. in Europe, North or South America, the Middle East, Africa, Asia, Australasia?
   • Will they change the product image to promote the product to different parts of the same country, e.g. the major cities, coastal towns or country villages?

5   In the next lesson, the groups present their marketing campaign to the rest of the class, and they explain how and why their advertising strategies for different markets would vary.

7.3 Writing an online review

Outline	Learners practise writing evaluations of work (e.g. films, books or music) from their own culture and that of others.
Focus	Writing a description and evaluation of films, books or music which have been previously watched, read or listened to.
Level	Intermediate and above
Time	30 minutes in the first lesson and 30 minutes plus in the second lesson
Preparation	You might like to find a recent example of a review from a website such as www.amazon.com or www.rottentomatoes.com which can be used as a potential model for the learners' own submissions. You may like to give learners copies of the reviews in Boxes 7.3a and 7.3b. This activity should be spread over two lessons and includes homework.

Procedure

1 Brainstorm with the class a list of things to review, i.e. books that they have read, films they have watched and music they have listened to (from their own or another culture). Write a list on the board.
   Note: This activity works particularly well when the books, music or films have a strong regional flavour or feature a particular social group.

2 Ask learners to choose a book, a film or some music and explain that they will be writing an online review of it in a following lesson.

3 Show the class one or two sample reviews of recent films, books or music from the websites above. For example, see the reviews of the prize-winning film *Slumdog Millionaire* (released in 2008) in Boxes 7.3a and 7.3b. Reviews like this can be used to illustrate the structure of a review, and as a source of vocabulary for positive and negative evaluations. Instruct the learners to identify and list some positive and negative expressions in each review. Then ask them to ask and answer questions about recent films they have seen, using some of the expressions from the reviews, e.g.

   What did you think of . . . ? I thought it was so lame!

   Have you seen . . . yet? I loved it. I nearly fell off my chair, it was so tense.

Box 7.3a: Writing an online review

Film review A: *Slumdog Millionaire*

Set in India, *Slumdog Millionaire* follows a kid from the poorest slums through the city of Mumbai. Eventually he lands on the set of a television game-show that could change his life. . .

OK, the plot seems lame, but in fact this is a classic, old-fashioned romance at heart. It's also full of life, energy and honest emotion. *Slumdog Millionaire* really does capture Indian culture today. Through a child's eyes we see the country grow and transform into a modern economic superpower. But it goes deeper than that. India is a country that is busy, lively and emotional, and this movie is full of the same qualities. It was shot in the real slums, with real kids and the camera captures everything. As a result, the film is full of energy, chaos, love and colour.

The climax was so tense I actually fell off my chair. And the ending had me in tears. Tears of joy.

Adapted from a review by Marc Fennell
http://www.abc.net.au/triplej/review/film/s2451606.htm

From *Intercultural Language Activities*
© Cambridge University Press 2010   PHOTOCOPIABLE

Box 7.3b: Writing an online review

Film review B: *Slumdog Millionaire*

Slumdog Millionaire will be praised in some circles, but the pieces do not form a believable or satisfying whole. The film is beautifully shot by Anthony Dod Mantle (2003's *Dogville*), and its use of music is entirely successful. The rest of the movie, unfortunately, is neither entertaining nor emotionally sound. The plot shamelessly manipulates your emotions. *Slumdog Millionaire* wants to send the viewer out singing a happy tune, tidily sweeping the sinister side of the story under the rug. It feels dishonest.

Based on a review by Dustin Putman
http://www.themovieboy.com/reviews/s/08_slumdog.htm

From *Intercultural Language Activities*
© Cambridge University Press 2010   PHOTOCOPIABLE

4 Tell the learners that, after class, they should explore an online
discussion forum such as those found on the Amazon or Rotten
Tomatoes websites, and list some more useful expressions with
which to summarise a film and then give an opinion about it. Some
examples are:

> Summarising: *The basic storyline is the following* . . .
> Indicating key characteristics: *The thing that struck me most about
> this book/film/music is*. . .
> Giving a personal view: . . . *as far as I can tell.*
> Giving a positive evaluation: *I loved the idea of* . . .
> Giving a negative evaluation: *On the downside,* . . .

Learners should also pay attention to the style of the reviews: for example
do the reviewers adopt formal or informal language? Which reviews are
rated as helpful, and which are not helpful?

5 In the next lesson, the learners bring their lists of useful expressions and
share them in groups.

6 Individually, the learners then write a draft review of the work they
selected in the previous lesson. If the work being reviewed is from
another culture, they must explain what they found strange or familiar
about it. If the work is from their own culture, they must imagine what
audiences elsewhere might find strange, and provide them with an
explanation.

7 The learners share their reviews with three others in the class, who rate
it as *Very Helpful, Helpful* or *Not Helpful.* If the review is rated *Not
Helpful,* the person rating it should recommend changes to improve it.
The reviewer can then re-draft the review.

8 The final drafts of the reviews can be posted on the Amazon or
Rotten Tomatoes websites, and the learners can check periodically for
responses.

7.4 Proverbs across cultures: using the *TIME* corpus

Outline	Learners explore the meaning and use of proverbial sayings in English through the *TIME* corpus.
Focus	Looking at how the literal and figurative meanings of proverbs compare across cultures, and exploring the use of English proverbs in journalism.
Level	Intermediate and above
Time	40 minutes plus
Preparation	Learners need a table like the one in Box 7.4a, with some English proverbial expressions written on it. They will also need access to a computer to explore the free *TIME* corpus at http://corpus.byu.edu/time/ You will need to bring some newspapers and magazines to the lesson for step 7.

Procedure

1   Ask the learners if they can explain the meaning of some common English proverbial expressions, for example:

Every cloud has a silver lining = every bad situation can have an unexpected good side or consequence.

Too many cooks spoil the broth = if too many people are trying to do the same thing at the same time, they will do it badly.

To be born with a silver spoon in your mouth = to be born into a wealthy or privileged family.

Next, brainstorm some other proverbial expressions and write them on the board. You might include some proverbs that are certain to have interesting results. A few are given below (with the likeliest search phrase underlined):

Don't put all your <u>eggs in one basket</u>.

A chain is no stronger than its <u>weakest link</u>.

There are plenty more <u>fish in the sea</u>.

<u>A stitch in time</u> saves nine.

<u>Actions speak</u> louder than words.

2   Ask the learners if these proverbial expressions have equivalents in their own language. Are the expressions literal translations of the English proverbs, or are they different? Bear in mind that there might not be an equivalent proverb in the mother tongue.

3   The learners then complete a table such as the one in Box 7.4a with the proverbs they discussed in step 1. In the sample answers on p. 139, Brazilian Portuguese equivalents are given in italics.

4 Discuss together how proverbial expressions are used in speech and
   writing. For example:
   • Do people drop entire proverbial expressions into their conversation,
     essays or articles?
   • What kind of people use proverbial expressions – and when do they
     use them?
5 Give each learner *one* of the proverbial expressions to explore using
   the *TIME* corpus. Using the corpus, the learners should explore the
   following issues:
   • How is the expression used? As a whole or in part?
   • Has the frequency of its use changed over the decades since the
     1920s?

Box 7.4a: Proverbs across cultures: using the *TIME* corpus

Table: English proverbs

English proverb	Literal translation into mother tongue	Equivalent proverb	Translation into English
Every cloud has a silver lining.			
Too many cooks spoil the broth.			
To sup with the devil, you need a long spoon.			
He was born with a silver spoon in his mouth.			
Don't judge a book by its cover.			

© Cambridge University Press 2010   PHOTOCOPIABLE

138

Sample answers:
Brazilian Portuguese equivalents (where available)

English proverb	Literal translation into mother tongue	Equivalent proverb	Translation into English
Every cloud has a silver lining.	*Toda nuvem tem um forro prateado.*	*Tudo tem o seu lado bom.*	Everything has its good side.
Too many cooks spoil the broth.	*Muitos cozinheiros estragam o caldo.*	No equivalent	
To sup with the devil, you need a long spoon.	*Para comer com o diabo, é preciso usar uma colher comprida.*	*É melhor não cutucar onça com vara curta.*	It's better not to poke a jaguar with a short stick.
He was born with a silver spoon in his mouth.	*Ele nasceu com uma colher de prata na boca.*	*Ele nasceu em berço de ouro.*	He was born in a golden cradle.
Don't judge a book by its cover.	*Não julge um livro pela sua capa.*	*Quem vê cara não vê coração.*	Whoever sees the face does not see the heart.

6 If necessary, demonstrate how to use the *TIME* corpus as follows. To investigate the expression *born with a silver spoon in his/her mouth* you do the following:
   • Log onto http://corpus.byu.edu/time/ and enter the *TIME* corpus.
   • In the 'Display' section, click on the option to show 'Chart'.
   • Type in the proverb to find out if it is in the corpus. Note that the proverb will often appear in part, or in a variation, so you might need to type in a few searches, like *silver spoon* and *spoon in his mouth, spoon in her mouth, spoon in their mouths*, etc.
   • When the results are displayed, you can click on the bars in the graph to see the results for each decade.
   As can be seen from the screengrab on p. 140, most results for *silver spoon* occur in the 1940s, though when you click on the bar you can see that some examples actually refer to silver spoons, not the proverbial use.

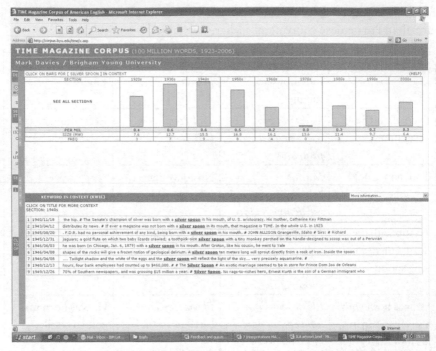

Result of a corpus search for 'silver spoon'

There is a definite dip in the 1970s, but the expression revives in the 1980s. When you click on *spoon in his mouth*, the general pattern across the decades is similar – but the search also picks up creative variations such as *iron spoon in his mouth* and *silver-plated spoon in his mouth*.

7 Finally, tell the learners that many headlines draw upon variations in proverbs as headlines for their stories. Divide the learners into groups and ask them to look at the topics in the newspapers that you have brought to the lesson. Then elicit from the groups one or two topics and ask them to think of a *variation* of a proverb that might be used as a headline for the story, e.g.

- Actions speak *softer* than words
- Born with a *wooden* spoon in his/her mouth
- *No* silver lining for unlucky workers/contestants/demonstrators . . .

7.5 Famous quotations in action

Outline	Learners explore the meaning and use of famous quotations in English. First they find famous quotations, and then they use the *TIME* corpus to explore how these quotations have been used in *TIME* magazine over the last hundred years.
Focus	Looking at how famous quotations are used explicitly and indirectly in journalism.
Level	Upper-intermediate and above
Time	40 minutes plus
Preparation	Learners will need access to a computer to explore an online dictionary of quotations such as http://www.bartleby.com/ or http://www.online-literature.com/ and also to explore the free *TIME* corpus at http://corpus.byu.edu/time/ Alternatively, a published dictionary of quotations might be used for the first stage.

Procedure

1   Together brainstorm the names of some famous writers, historical figures, songwriters and actors from the English-speaking world, e.g. Jane Austen, Charles Dickens, Arthur Conan Doyle, Martin Luther King, William Shakespeare, George Orwell, Groucho Marx, Al Pacino, etc.

2   Ask the learners if they know any phrases or sayings by these people that are still frequently quoted. Possible examples might be:

- *It is a truth universally acknowledged, that a single man in possession of a good fortune, must be in want of a wife.* (Jane Austen, *Pride and Prejudice*, 1813)
- *The law is an ass – an idiot.* (Charles Dickens, *Oliver Twist*, 1838)
- *Elementary, my dear Watson.* (Sir Arthur Conan Doyle – actually this phrase only ever appears in Sherlock Holmes films, based on the books and stories by Conan Doyle. Holmes does say 'Elementary' in the 1893 short story *The Crooked Man*.)
- *I have a dream.* (Martin Luther King, speech given in Washington DC in 1963)
- *Parting is such sweet sorrow.* (William Shakespeare, *Romeo and Juliet*, 1594/5)
- *Big Brother is watching you.* (George Orwell, *Nineteen Eighty-Four*, 1949)
- PLEASE ACCEPT MY RESIGNATION. I DON'T WANT TO BELONG TO ANY CLUB THAT WILL ACCEPT ME AS A MEMBER (Telegram written by

Groucho Marx, as related in his autobiography, *Groucho and Me*, 1959)

- *Keep your friends close, but your enemies closer.* (Al Pacino in the film *The Godfather, Part II*, 1974)

3   Demonstrate how to search for a quotation in the *TIME* corpus:

- Log onto http://corpus.byu.edu/time/ and enter the *TIME* corpus.
- In the 'Display' section, click on the option to show 'Chart'.
- Type in the quotation in the 'Word(s)' box to find out if it is used in the corpus.
- Often only parts of quotations or variations will be found and sometimes phrases are misquoted, so you and the learners will need to type in searches such as *sweet sorrow, a truth universally acknowledged, the law is an ass,* etc.

4   Instruct the learners to pay attention to the following information in the display of results:

- How frequently was the quotation used?
- Was it used more or less frequently over time? In which decade was it used most frequently?
- Was the quotation used in its original form or was it changed? If it was changed, how was it changed?
- Was the original source of the quotation mentioned? Do you think the journalist intended the audience to recognise the source?

For example, as can be seen on p. 143, a search for the phrase *sweet sorrow* indicates that it has been used fairly regularly since the 1920s, with a peak occurring in the 1940s. When actual instances are examined, the phrase *sweet sorrow* often appears by itself, often as the headline of an amusing article in which someone loses something. This activity gives learners an insight into the way in which phrases taken from literature or written by historical figures are constantly recycled in new contexts.

5   After your demonstration, the learners can search for some of the quotations listed earlier or they can log on to an online dictionary of literary quotations, such as http://www.bartleby.com/ or http://www.online-literature.com/ Alternatively, learners can consult a dictionary or a website of quotations to find examples they like from different sources, such as literature, film and song.

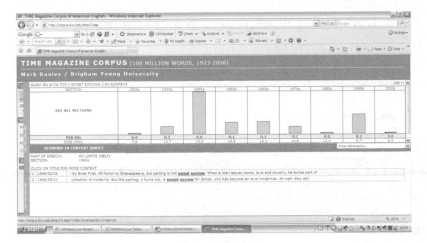

Results of a corpus search for 'sweet sorrow'

6　In groups, the learners search for five quotations that strike them as interesting. They identify the author, the original context, and the meaning of the quotation, e.g.

　　George Orwell – *Big Brother is watching you* – From *Nineteen Eighty-Four* = The authorities can see everything you do.

7　The learners then log onto http://corpus.byu.edu/time/ and check if the quotation, or a variation of it has been used by writers of *TIME* magazine. They answer the questions in step 4. (Note that, of course, not all examples of 'big brother' will be quotations of Orwell!)

8　Finally, the groups report their findings to the class.

Follow-up 1

The learners can extend their searches to other corpora, e.g. the British National Corpus and the Corpus of Contemporary American English, both of which are available at http://corpus.byu.edu or the Scottish Corpus of Texts and Speech, available at http://www.scottishcorpus.ac.uk By extending the search to more general corpora, the learners can see how the quotations are used beyond *TIME* magazine.

Follow-up 2

If learners are interested in making cross-cultural comparisons, and if there are available corpora in their first language, they can repeat the steps of the above activity using quotations in their mother tongue. Online corpora for Spanish and Portuguese are also available at http://corpus.byu.edu/

7.6 Comparing newspapers around the world

Outline	Learners explore how online newspapers from different countries report current events.
Focus	Reading and reporting current events from a range of online newspapers.
Level	Intermediate and above
Time	40 minutes plus
Preparation	You need a computer with an Internet connection and a projector. Learners browse online newspapers from around the world to identify major news stories. Learners need a copy of the summary template in Box 7.6a.

Procedure

1   Introduce the learners to sources of online newspapers from around the world, e.g. www.world-newspapers.com, www.onlinenewspapers.com, www.ipl.org/div/news/
    You could project the home pages from these websites onto the board.

2   Tell learners that (individually or in groups) they are going to compare news coverage from around the world for a particular day. Then they are going to choose a news report to share with the class.

3   The learners (individually or in groups) log onto one of the sources of online newspapers and complete the summary in Box 7.6a.

4   The learners report back to the class on their findings. They can also speculate *why* some countries give more space to international events than others, *which* international events they choose to report, *how* they report them, and so on. If two sets of learners have covered the same story from different international perspectives, find out if the point of view was similar or different.

5   Ask the class to find out if and how newspapers in different countries report events from the learners' own home country. Ask learners to report back to the class.

Box 7.6a: Comparing newspapers around the world

Summary: Exploring newspapers

Name of newspaper:
Date of publication: Language(s) used:
Country of origin: Daily/Weekly/Monthly?
Topics of three top news stories:

1

2

3

Headline of chosen story:

What is the story about?

Is this a local or an international story?

Who was involved?

What were the main events?

What is the newspaper's point of view?

8 Childhood

One powerful way of exploring culture is to invite learners
to recall and reflect upon their childhood. Childhood will be closer
to some learners than to others, and remembering it might trigger a
number of emotions, such as pleasure and nostalgia, but also, depending
on circumstances, embarrassment or loss. In the following activities,
be sensitive, as ever, to the potentially painful memories as well as the
pleasurable memories that this topic may evoke. 'The past,' wrote the
novelist L.P. Hartley in *The Go-Between*, 'is another country'. As society
changes over time, the ways in which children behave also change.
Children's games (8.1) deals with traditional and contemporary games
across different cultures and generations. *Children's toys* (8.2) looks at toys
which are often the centre of children's lives; *Classrooms from culture to
culture* (8.3) asks learners to reflect upon the organisation and structure
of their schools and compare experiences with those elsewhere; and *The
language we bring to school* (8.4) considers how formal education changes
the very language we speak. Finally, *Childhood's end* (8.5) focuses on the
milestones that indicate, in different countries, that childhood has come to
an end.

8.1 Children's games

Outline	Learners explore the different kinds of games that they used to play and compare the games played by different generations and different cultures.
Focus	Language of different kinds of game, simple and habitual past (*we played, we used to*); instructions for playing.
Level	Lower intermediate and above
Time	40 minutes plus
Preparation	Learners need copies of the reading text in Box 8.1a. This activity should be spread over two lessons and includes homework.

Procedure

1 Begin by finding out from the learners whether they are familiar with any
of the following kinds of traditional children's games:

- *Hopscotch*: played by drawing grids on the pavement and hopping or jumping from one to another.
- *Skipping games*: played by jumping over a rope or knotted rubber bands.
- *Marbles*: played with small, glass or metal balls.
- *Tag*: played by chasing and touching other players.
- *Ball games*: various kinds, played with different sizes of ball. For example, in 'Dodge ball' a player tries to hit a part of another player's body with the ball, sending the other player out of the game. Sometimes the ball has to be thrown against a wall before it touches the other player.
- *Circle games*: various kinds, played in a circle of up to 30 children. For example, in 'Pass the parcel' players pass something that has been wrapped up in several layers of paper while music plays. When the music stops, the player with the parcel must unwrap one layer. This continues until the last player unwraps the object, which he or she keeps as a prize. In 'Stations' all but one of the players sit in a circle. These players are all given the name of a station (e.g. Aberdeen, Swansea, York). One player (the station master) sits in the centre of the circle, with all the station names on pieces of card – plus one card that says 'All Change'. The station master shuffles the name cards and calls out the names of two or three stations. The players who have those station names then have to jump up and exchange positions. As they do so, the station master has to try to take one of their places. The player who is left without a seat is the new station master. When the station master calls out 'All change!' everyone has to change position.

2 Organise the class into groups. Give them Box 8.1a as an example and tell them they are going to describe the rules of one of the games they remember playing. Suggest they answer these questions about their game:
   - When did you play?
   - Who did you play with?
   - Where did you play?
   - How did the game start? What did you have to do?
   - How did someone win?
   - Did you enjoy the game?
   - Would you like to play the game again?

3 Each group tells the class about the game they remember. Then the learners do some research, either with their e-partners or with people

of the generation above or below them to compare different childhood games. Get learners to brainstorm some possible questions that they could ask. Possible questions are:

- How international are traditional children's games?
- Do the rules differ from country to country?
- What games did parents play that their children no longer play?
- What games are today's children playing?

Note: Different questions may be needed for e-partners and for people of a different generation.

4   In a following lesson, learners report back to the class.

Box 8.1a: Children's games

Reading text: Peirilia (a Cypriot form of marbles)

Sometimes, when I'm alone and trying to relax, I remember things I did when I was a child. As a kid, I used to play a lot of games with my friends, especially in the summer when the weather was good and we had a lot of time because we didn't have school. Late in the afternoon when the sun was down and the climate not too hot, every kid in my neighbourhood used to play a game. One of the best games we used to play is marbles. As I remember, we had a lot of fun playing that game.

How we played the game

Every player had to bring six marbles. Then we drew a triangle in the middle of the yard. We put the marbles in the middle of the triangle with two centimetres space between each one. Then we made a line. The game started.

To decide who would play first, we all stood next to the triangle and took turns to throw a marble as near the line as we could. The player whose marble was nearest to the line played first. His or her goal was to throw a marble and knock some other marbles out of the triangle. Each player collected the marbles they knocked out of the triangle.

The winner of the game was the player who took all the marbles from the other players. I would like to play that game again. I would like to feel like a kid again, but I think I can't.

By Yiannis Tziortzis from Cyprus

From *Intercultural Language Activities*

© Cambridge University Press 2010

PHOTOCOPIABLE

8.2 Children's toys

Outline	Learners explore the different kinds of toys that children from different cultures play with, and the toys different generations used to play with.
Focus	Describing toys and activities; discussing changing trends.
Level	Lower intermediate and above
Time	40 minutes plus
Preparation	Learners need copies of the questions in Box 8.2a and the reading text in Box 8.2b.

Procedure

1   Ask the class, in pairs or small groups, to say what their favourite toys were when they were children. Then ask the class if anyone owned or played with the following:
    - rag dolls or teddy bears
    - wooden toys, such as pirate ships or wooden puppets
    - action figures, such as soldiers or monsters
    - dolls' houses, fire stations or toy garages
    - train sets, racing cars or model aeroplanes

2   Explain to the class that favourite toys change from place to place, and from generation to generation, across cultures and that they are going to read part of a short article from an online magazine, about the changing nature of toys in Vietnam. Tell learners that the article is about the mid-autumn festival of Tet Trung Thu, which is held on the fifteenth day of the eighth lunar month each year. Children are the focus of the festival. The celebrations include giving toys, playing traditional games, and eating special food such as 'mooncakes'. Circulate copies of the reading text in Box 8.2b and get learners to answer the questions in Box 8.2a. (Note that the questions are designed to stimulate discussion as much as to check information.)

3   After learners have completed the activity, as a class, discuss their answers.

Box 8.2a: Children's toys

Questions: *Child at Heart*

a) What does this article say about the way toys in Vietnam are changing?

b) Do you agree with Pham Van Manh's views? Do you think the Vietnamese children would agree with him?

c) Is there an equivalent festival in your country? If so, compare your festival with Tet Trung Thu. What kind of gifts are given? What kind of food is eaten?

d) Think about the toys that you played with as a child. Were they traditional or modern? Were they produced locally or imported? Were they educational or not? Were they similar to the toys mentioned by Pham Van Manh?

Box 8.2b: Children's toys

Reading text: *Child at Heart*

Toys and mooncakes remain the focus of the mid-autumn festival even today. Hang Ma street is the traditional trading centre for Tet Trung Thu toys at this time of year.

Masks, crowns, puppets and paper lanterns are sold by the box-load on this street in the week leading up to the big day, creating a unique festive atmosphere that you won't see at any other time of year.

However, the traditional toys are gradually being replaced by modern ones. The general public is slowly deserting shops on Hang Ma street, choosing instead to buy the year's most fashionable toys from shops on Luong Van Can street. Jeeps, helicopters, plastic lanterns and toy guns now dominate the marketplace.

'I think it's time for the government to minimise the importation of toys into Vietnam,' said Pham Van Manh, a 65-year-old man on Hang Bong street. 'I am afraid that Vietnamese children will forget all about tradition and end up with modern toys. It's particularly sad because toys such as masks, puppets and lanterns are cheaper, more educational and more traditional.'

Extract from 'Child at Heart', an article from the Vietnamese online journal *Timeout*

From *Intercultural Language Activities*

4   If the learners have got e-partners, they can go online and ask them the
    following questions:
    •   Do you have festivals where children receive toys as gifts?
    •   What kind of toys do children play with now?
    •   Are children's toys nowadays traditional, modern, or a combination of
        both?
    •   Where are children's toys produced?
5   After they have received replies, learners can report back to the class on
    their findings.

Variation
If the learners have not got e-partners, then they can talk to older relatives
and ask similar questions in their mother tongue. For step 4 instead, they can
then write a short text, in English, about 'Toys – Now and Then'.

8.3 Classrooms from culture to culture

Outline	Learners think critically about the organisation, structure, layout and resources of their school classroom. They compare their experiences with those elsewhere, as described in images, and by classmates from different cultures, as well as their e-partners.
Focus	Describing, contrasting, comparing and evaluating physical space.
Level	Intermediate and above
Time	40 minutes plus
Preparation	Learners need copies of the form in Box 8.3b. Learners also need access to a computer with an internet connection. If this is not available, you can use the photos in Box 8.3a on the CD-ROM, or, before the lesson collect photographs of school classrooms, past and present, and if possible, in different cultures. A model answer is provided in Box 8.3c. For lower-level learners you could make copies of the template in Box 8.3e. Learners will also need copies of the template timetable in Box 8.3d.

Procedure
1   Inform the learners that they are going to compare different kinds of
    school classroom. They will then get a chance to design their ideal course.
2   Ask the learners to complete the form in Box 8.3b, describing their own
    classroom.

Box 8.3a: Classrooms from culture to culture

Photos: Classrooms

© Alamy/Chad Ehlers

© Alamy/Andrew Rodriguez

© Alamy/Phovoir/FCM Graphic

From *Intercultural Language Activities*
© Cambridge University Press 2010   PHOTOCOPIABLE

Box 8.3b: Classrooms from culture to culture

Form: Classroom design

Number of learners:
Age(s) of learners (primary, secondary, college or university, mixed-age?):
Number of teachers/assistants:
Organisation of desks (in rows, in a U-shape, in a circle?):
Resources available (whiteboard, interactive whiteboard, overhead projector, computer, etc?):

© Cambridge University Press 2010   PHOTOCOPIABLE

3   Next, ask the learners to log onto an image bank such as Google™ Images (http://images.google.com/) and type in 'Photographs from classrooms'. Alternatively, you can show the selection of photographs of different kinds of classroom you found or use the images on the CD-ROM in Box 8.3a. The learners choose one of the classroom photographs that is very different from their own and complete a similar form for the classroom in the photograph.

4   The learners then use the two forms to write a brief comparison of the two classrooms, their own and the one in the photograph. They should note the advantages and disadvantages of each classroom, and which one they prefer. For example, they might write something like the model in Box 8.3c. This model can be used as the basis of a template for less advanced learners (see the Variation on p. 155).

Box 8.3c: Classrooms from culture to culture

Model: Classroom comparison

This is a comparison of our classroom with a classroom in Y. Our classroom has desks for 15 pupils, in a horse-shoe shape, whereas the classroom in Y has more than 30 pupils, all in rows. One advantage of the horse-shoe is that it is informal and friendly, but a disadvantage is that you can't hide from the teacher! Our classroom has an overhead projector, an interactive whiteboard, and a computer with an internet connection, whereas the classroom in Y has only got a chalkboard. On the whole, I prefer our classroom. It is less formal and better equipped.

© Cambridge University Press 2010   PHOTOCOPIABLE

5 Invite the learners to consider the content of their curriculum. Ask them who decides what they learn – the government education department, the institution or the teachers? Would they like the opportunity to decide what they learn?

6 Divide the class into groups, and get them to discuss how they would organise their ideal course. They should discuss the following:
  • topics of lessons
  • time of lessons
  • How would the activities be organised: individual work, pairwork, groupwork, whole-class activities?
  • Would there be formal assessment? By coursework or final exam?

7 The groups report to the class on their decisions. Their ideal courses can be shared and discussed online with their e-partners.

Box 8.3d: Classrooms from culture to culture

Worksheet: My ideal timetable

1) List the subjects you would like to study:

2) Fill in the timetable with the subjects you have chosen and the days and times you would like to study them.

Times	Day 1	Day 2	Day 3	Day 4	Day 5
			Assembly		
			Break		
			Lunch		

© Cambridge University Press 2010   PHOTOCOPIABLE

8 Next, ask learners to design their ideal timetable. Hand out copies of the template timetable in Box 8.3d to learners and ask them to list the subjects they would like to study, e.g. Geography, History, Languages (Arabic, English, Latin, Spanish?), Mathematics, Physics, Chemistry, Citizenship, Physical Education (PE), Computing, Philosophy, Engineering, Cookery, Media Studies, etc. Learners should then fill in the timetable, showing the selection of courses they have chosen and the days and times they would like to study them. Finally, get learners to compare their ideal timetable with another learner or e-partner.

Variation for lower-level learners

In step 4, you can give a template for learners' writing. For example, the learners can be asked to complete a version of the following text, which you can adapt, depending on the circumstances of their own schools and the classroom photos they will compare.

Box 8.3e: Classrooms from culture to culture

Template: Classroom comparison

A comparison of our classroom with a classroom in _____

Our classroom has desks for _____ pupils, whereas the classroom in _____ has enough desks for _____. Our desks are arranged in _____
_____.
One advantage of this arrangement is that _____
but a disadvantage is that _____.
The desks in the classroom in _____ are arranged in _____
_____. Our classroom is equipped with _____
_____, whereas the classroom in _____
is equipped with _____. On the whole, I prefer
_____ because _____.

© Cambridge University Press 2010   PHOTOCOPIABLE

8.4 The language we bring to school

Outline	Learners use a poem to explore attitudes to the dialect of the home and the standard language of the school, and the impact of those attitudes on the individual.
Focus	Reading a past narrative; discussing the uses and attitudes towards dialect.
Level	Upper-intermediate and above
Time	40 minutes plus
Preparation	Learners need copies of the pre-reading questions in Box 8.4a and the poem in Box 8.4b. If possible, try to get a recording of the poem.

Procedure

1 Explain that the class is going to explore the relationship between language and education.

2 Ask learners to close their eyes and recall their first day at school. The learners open their eyes and share their memories in pairs.

3 Next, ask the learners to compare the language of their school with the language of their home. The following specific topics can be discussed:

- Was the language used in the community, home and playground the same as the language of the classroom?
- If there was a difference, was it a difference of language, dialect, or accent?
- Were the learners taught at school to speak differently from their parents?
- If there was a difference between the language of the school/home/ playground ask the learners to give examples.

4 Explain that the learners are going to read a poem by a Scottish writer, Liz Lochhead, which imagines a child's first day at school in Scotland, in winter. Put learners into pairs, and in their pairs ask them to discuss the questions in Box 8.4a and make a note of their answers. Hand out copies of the questions and make sure the learners understand them.

5 Now hand out copies of the poem in Box 8.4b. Explain that the first part is written in the language of the child's home. Tell learners, in their pairs, to try reading it aloud all the way through. Or, if you have a recording of the poem play it to learners. With their partners, they should check their understanding of the first 12 lines.

6 Get learners to compare the description in the poem with their notes. How accurate were their predictions?

Box 8.4a: The language we bring to school

Questions: Kidspoem/Bairnsang

1 Can you imagine the weather in Scotland in winter? Describe it to your partner.

2 Imagine a five-year-old girl, going outside on a winter morning in Scotland. Describe to your partner what she is wearing on her head, around her neck and on her hands.

3 Imagine that you are one of the five-year-old girl's parents. What do you say to your daughter before she goes to school for the first time? Tell your partner.

© Cambridge University Press 2010   PHOTOCOPIABLE

Box 8.4b: The language we bring to school

Reading text: Kidspoem/Bairnsang

It wis January
and a gey dreich day
the first day Ah went to the school
so ma Mum happed me up in ma
good navy-blue napp coat wi the rid tartan hood   5
birled a scarf aroon ma neck
pu'd oan ma pixie and ma pawkies
it wis that bitter
said *noo ye'll no starve*
gie'd me a wee kiss and a kid-oan skelp oan the bum   10
and sent me aff across the playground
tae the place Ah'd learn to say
it was January
and a really dismal day
the first day I went to school   15
so my mother wrapped me up in my
best navy-blue top coat with the red tartan hood
twirled a scarf around my neck
pulled on my bobble-hat and mittens
it was so bitterly cold   20
said *now you'll not freeze to death*

continued

Box 8.4b: (*cont.*)

gave me a little kiss and a pretend slap on the bottom
and sent me across the playground
to the place I'd learn to forget to say
it wis January   25
and a gey dreich day
the first day Ah went to the school
so ma Mum happed me up in ma
good navy-blue napp coat wi the rid tartan hood
birled a scarf aroon ma neck   30
pu'd oan ma pixie and ma pawkies
it wis that bitter.

Oh saying it was one thing
but when it came to writing it
in black and white   35
the way it had to be said
was as if you were posh, grown-up, male, English and dead.

Liz Lochhead, 'Kidspoem/Bairnsang' from *The Colour of Black and White: Poems*
1984–2003 Edinburgh: Birlinn pp. 19–20 [www.birlinn.co.uk]

From *Intercultural Language Activities*
© Cambridge University Press 2010   PHOTOCOPIABLE

7 Get the learners, in pairs, to use the poem to devise a brief phrase book
   that helps to translate 'the language of the home' into 'the language of the
   school', e.g.

The language of the home	The language of the school
It wis that bitter	*It was so bitterly cold*

8 Next, get learners to look again at line 24. With their partners, they
   should explain why school can be a place where we 'learn to *forget* to say
   things'. What kind of language do we *forget* to use in schools? Why? Ask
   some pairs to feed back their answers to the class.

9 Direct learners to look at lines 33–37. According to the poem, what kind
   of people use 'the language of the school'? Why did the child feel like
   this? As a class, discuss whether you agree with the poem.

10 With their partners, learners should devise a brief guide explaining the
   language rules that they remember from their own schooldays. They

should be prepared to explain the differences to an English-speaker. For example, the girl in the poem might give the following rule and explanation:

Don't say...	Do say...	Explanation...
starve	*freeze to death*	*'starve'* is dialect/ old-fashioned

11 Ask learners to look at their rules again and ask them if they still obey these rules today. If so, do learners agree that they are now 'posh, grown-up, male ... and dead'?

8.5 Childhood's end

Outline	Learners consider the ages at which individuals in the UK and in other cultures begin to assume certain adult rights and responsibilities. When, in other words, does childhood end?
Focus	Numbers (ages) and the language of rights and responsibilities; language of debate – expressing opinions, justifying arguments, opposing and (partially) accepting.
Level	Intermediate and above
Time	30 minutes plus; optional 20 minutes plus in a follow-up debate
Preparation	Learners need copies of the tables in Box 8.5a and the conventions of a debate in Box 8.5b on the CD-ROM or on p. 196 (Box 10.6b).

Procedure

1 As a warm-up, find out from the class their knowledge of the following:
   - At what age can they legally leave school?
   - At what age can they legally join the army?
   - At what age can they legally get married, with or without their parents' consent?
   - At what age do they think they legally stop being a child?

2 Hand out copies of the tables in Box 8.5a. Ask learners to complete the second column in class, from their knowledge of their home culture, or after class, by researching internet sites. After class, they should also complete a third column by asking their e-partners or researching another country online. Also ask them to complete the fourth column by entering what they think the legal age *should* be.

Box 8.5a: Childhood's end

Tables: Legal ages

At what age are you considered ...	In the United Kingdom	In	In	In my opinion
a child?	Under 14			
a young person?	14–17			
an adult?	18 and over			
At what age can you ...	**In the United Kingdom**	**In . . . .**	**In . . . .**	**In my opinion**
leave school?	Currently 16, but it is due to be raised.			
make a will?	18			
drive a car or van?	17			
play an adult computer game?	18			
join the army?	16			
get married with parents' consent?	16			
get married without parents' consent?	18			
be left home unattended?	No official minimum age, but child must not be at risk.			
buy alcohol and cigarettes?	18			
gamble online?	18			

© Cambridge University Press 2010   PHOTOCOPIABLE

3   In a future lesson, once they have completed the tables, the learners
    prepare, in groups, to debate issues such as:
    • At what age should people have the right to buy alcohol or cigarettes?
    • At what age should people have the right to marry without parents'
      consent?
    • At what age should people have the right to gamble online?
    You may like to brainstorm or model some language of debate, e.g.

Making a case	Asking questions
I think/feel/believe that. . .	*What do you think/feel*
	about. . .?
I'm sure/certain that. . .	*Can you be sure/certain that. . .?*
I think that X is a good idea because. . .	*Why do you think X is a good idea?*
What I'm saying is. . .	*What are you really saying here?*

Agreeing	Disagreeing
Yes, absolutely.	*Absolutely not!*
That's a good point.	*That's not the point/issue.*
Where I agree with you is. . .	*Where I disagree with you is. . .*

The debate can be more or less formal. If the class wishes to have a
formal debate, you can go through the conventions in Box 8.5b on the
CD-ROM (or on p. 196 in Box 10.6b) with learners.

9   Icons

Most people know the names of national and international 'icons', that is, figures whose characteristics seem to symbolise or represent people in the country as a whole, or figures whose qualities demand national, or even international, respect and admiration. Because these individuals usually embody qualities that are admired by a group, nation or the broader international community, they offer scope for intercultural exploration. This chapter focuses on different local, national and international icons and considers what makes them admirable or famous. The first activity, *Five most famous . . .* (9.1) invites learners to share their knowledge of five famous people from their own country and five from another culture. A follow-up option involves some learners choosing one of these people to role play in a 'balloon debate'. *Founding figures* (9.2) focuses on those national icons who are considered the 'founding figures' of the nations to which the learners belong. Learners are asked to reflect on the qualities that these founders are considered to have, and how well they reflect the core values of the nation. The third activity, *National bards* (9.3), discusses poets that different countries have adopted as 'national bards'. Again, learners are invited to think about how these 'bards' and their work represent qualities that the nation as a whole is expected to find admirable. The next activity, *International heroes* (9.4), moves from the national to the international arena, and asks learners to reflect on the qualities that have made certain people icons across nations and cultures. Finally, *Someone I admire* (9.5) focuses on the personal, and invites learners to share their own stories of 'unsung heroes' who are not famous, but whom they admire.

9.1 Five most famous . . .

Outline	Learners explore varying perceptions of the five most famous people in their own country (past and present) and their perceptions of the five most famous people from another country. This activity is best done with a multicultural class, or with a class that has access to e-partners. When learners from different countries compare their perceptions, they often find that their choices vary, which is a useful basis for discussion.
Focus	Language of personal characteristics and achievements.
Level	Lower intermediate and above
Time	30 minutes plus
Preparation	Learners need copies of the tables in Box 9.1a.

Procedure

1   Ask the class to write down the names of the five most famous people in their home country – past and present – and a brief reason why they have chosen these people.

2   Elicit some names from the class, and write them on the board or project them onscreen. Group the names by the activities or reasons for which the person is famous, e.g. sport, politics, literature, military achievements, member of a royal family, etc. Probe how the learners came to know about these famous people – was it through education, the media, family stories, etc.?

3   Match learners up with individuals in the class from another culture or ask them to contact their e-partners. The learners from both cultures complete the tables in Box 9.1a listing famous people from their own culture and people who they think are famous in their partner's culture. They then compare their notes.

4   The learners discuss the similarities and differences in their choice of names, the reasons they have given, and the source of information about these famous people. For example, have the learners chosen figures from the world of politics, sport, entertainment or public service? Did they find out about these figures from the media, from school, or from their own reading? Get class feedback on the similarities and differences learners found.

Box 9.1a: Five most famous . . .

Tables: Famous people

My culture: _____

Famous person	Why is s/he famous?	Source of information
1		
2		
3		
4		
5		

Other culture: _____

Famous person	Why is s/he famous?	Source of information
1		
2		
3		
4		
5		

PHOTOCOPIABLE

Follow-up

This activity can be followed by a 'balloon debate'. For example:

1   Divide the class into three to five groups. Each group must choose one
    of the famous figures discussed. Ensure each group selects a different
    person.
2   Explain that these figures are in an aeroplane that is going to crash.
    Unfortunately, there is only one parachute. Each group must think
    of reasons why their famous figure deserves to get the parachute. If
    necessary, you can brainstorm with the class some possible reasons that
    different figures might give for having the parachute, e.g.

    *I deserve the parachute because I am . . . generous/brave/entertaining/
        needed . . . etc.*

*For instance, look at ... the money I have donated to charity / the
people I have saved / the music I have composed / the people who
voted for me ... etc.*

3 Each group then selects one learner to represent their chosen figure in the
debate. The representatives, in turn, take the role of the famous figures
and give their reasons why they should receive the parachute.
4 After the representatives have all had their turn, the class votes for the
figure who should be allowed to use the parachute.

9.2 Founding figures

Outline	Learners focus on the description and discussion of figures who are considered 'founders' of the nations to which they belong.
Focus	Describing qualities and past narrative of achievements.
Level	Lower intermediate and above
Time	15–20 minutes in the first lesson; 20 minutes plus in the second lesson
Preparation	Learners need to be able to do some research on the Internet or at a local library either during or after the lesson. Learners also need copies of the worksheet in Box 9.2a.

Procedure

1 Elicit from the class one or two people who might be considered
'founding figures' of their home nations. Explain that they can be
historical, mythical or a mixture of both, e.g.
- Chile: *Bernardo O'Higgins, José Miguel Carrera*
- China: *Sun Yat-sen, Mao Tse-Tung*
- England: *Britannia, Boudica, King Alfred*
- Egypt: *Ahmed Oraby, Gamal Abdel Nasser*
- India: *Mahatma Ghandi*
- Ireland: *Charles Parnell, Michael Collins*
- South Africa: *Nelson Mandela*
- Turkey: *Mustafa Kemal Atatürk*
- USA: *George Washington, John Adams, Thomas Jefferson*
- Venezuela: *Simón Bolívar*
2 Elicit what the learners know about the people they have named.
3 Ask the class to describe the characteristics and achievements necessary
to be considered the founding figure of a nation, e.g. physical and/or
mental strength, courage, stamina, perseverance and national pride.

4   Ask the learners to do some research on their founding figures in a library or on the Internet to find out about his or her story. In a monocultural class, learners choose the founding figure of their own nation and a founding figure from a different nation. Ask learners to complete the worksheet in Box 9.2a.

Box 9.2a: Founding figures

Worksheet: Writing about a founding figure

1   Identify a 'founding figure' for your home nation and, if you are in a monolingual group, choose a founding figure from a different nation as well.

2   Write a brief description of his or her story, including as much of the following information as you can find, e.g.
   • place and date of birth
   • upbringing
   • difficulties faced
   • achievements
   • personal qualities
   • if no longer alive, the circumstances of his or her death
   • how he or she is remembered in the nation (e.g. on banknotes, by statues, by buildings or places named after him or her)

3   Decide if this person reflects the core values of the nation.

Note the sources of your information after the description you have written.

© Cambridge University Press 2010   PHOTOCOPIABLE

---

5   After the learners have researched their founding figures, divide the class into groups, and ask them to share the stories of the figures they researched. You can ask the learners to look for similarities between the stories told, e.g.
   • humble origins
   • early indications of greatness
   • hardship endured
   • opposition faced
   • triumph against the odds
If the class is participating in an online exchange, they can share their stories with their e-partners too.

9.3 National bards

Outline	Learners research and discuss some of the writers whose work is widely considered to represent their nation or community.
Focus	Researching and reporting on personal biographies, identifying and quoting from literary works.
Level	Upper-intermediate and above
Time	30 minutes plus in the first lesson; 30 minutes plus in the second lesson
Preparation	You will need a computer and projector to display the photographs of bards in step 2; these images are available on the CD-ROM in Box 9.3a. Learners need copies of the worksheet in Box 9.3b. Learners also need to research different figures on the Internet, or by asking e-partners or consulting reference books in a library. This activity should be spread over two lessons and involves homework.

Procedure

1 Explain the concept of a 'national bard' – that is, a poet, dramatist or possibly a novelist whose work is thought to represent their nation or community. Ask the class who they would consider their own national bard to be, and find out if the learners can give a quote linked to them. You can write a list of names and quotations on the board.

2 Ask the class for the name of the national bard of England. There might be some disagreement even amongst English people about the choice. Shakespeare is probably the first choice, but others, such as Byron or Wordsworth, might also be chosen by some. Alternatively, ask learners if they can identify the portraits of 'national bards' in Box 9.3a.
   Answers: Top left–Robert Burns (Scotland); top right–William Shakespeare (England); bottom left–Pablo Neruda (Chile); bottom right–Chinua Achebe (Nigeria)

3 Circulate the worksheet in Box 9.3b. The class, in groups, match up the names of different national bards with their nations, and a famous quotation (translated where necessary into English). Do the first one with learners.
   Answers:
   a 4–v, b–3–ii, c–5–iv, d–2–iii, e–1–i

Box 9.3a: National bards

Photos: Bards

© Getty Images/Hulton Archive

© Getty Images/Hulton Archive

© Alamy/RIA Novosti

© Getty Images/AFP

From *Intercultural Language Activities*
© Cambridge University Press 2010

PHOTOCOPIABLE

Box 9.3b: National bards

Worksheet: Matching nations, bards and quotations

Nations   *Bards*

a) USA   1) Kazi Nazrul Islam

b) Russia   2) Dante Alighieri

c) Germany   3) Alexander Pushkin

d) Italy   4) Walt Whitman

e) Bangladesh   5) Johann Wolfgang von Goethe

Quotations

i)   I am the eternal rebel
     I raise my head beyond this world
     High, ever erect and alone!

ii) The clock of doom had struck as fated;
     The poet, without a sound,
     Let fall his pistol on the ground.

iii) In the middle of the journey of our life
     I found myself in a dark wood
     Where the straight way was lost.

iv) The most original authors are not so because they advance what is new, but
     because they put what they have to say as if it had never been said before.

v)   I dream'd in a dream, I saw a city invincible to the attacks of the whole of the rest
     of the earth;
     I dream'd that was the new City of Friends;
     Nothing was greater there than the quality of robust love – it led the rest;
     It was seen every hour in the actions of the men of that city,
     And in all their looks and words.

4 After this activity is finished, go through the answers and tell the class
that, in groups, they will choose a nation and do some research after class
on its national bard. Together, spend time preparing for this research.
First, suggest some of the following bards for learners to research:

Albania – Naim Frashëri	Nicaragua – Rubén Darío
Philippines – Francisco Balagtas	Turkey – Mehmet Akif Ersoy
Spain – Miguel de Cervantes	Vietnam – Nguyễn Du
Hungary – Sándor Petőfi	Wales – Dylan Thomas
Ireland – W.B. Yeats	

Alternatively, learners might like to select their own. Next, with the
class, identify sources of information (e.g. the Internet, e-partners and
reference books in a local library), and identify the kind of information to
be gathered, e.g.

- a brief biography of the bard
- a list of some of the major works
- some quotations from the works (in English)
- why they are a national figure
- what people today think of the bard and his or her work.

Tell learners that each member of the group should choose one aspect of
the bard to research.

5 In a following lesson, allow the groups time to discuss their findings
before they make a presentation to the class on the bard of their choice.

9.4 International heroes

Outline	Learners consider what qualities and achievements make someone an international hero, known and admired across cultures.
Focus	Describing qualities and past narrative of achievements.
Level	Lower intermediate and above
Time	15–20 minutes in the first lesson; 30 minutes plus in the second lesson
Preparation	This activity should be spread over two lessons and involves learners, for homework, researching international heroes on the Internet or consulting reference books in a library.

Procedure

1 Together, brainstorm some names of people who might be considered
international heroes. The names might be from the worlds of
entertainment, the arts, fashion or sport, charity, politics or business.

2 Elicit as much as the learners know about one or two of the people they have named, e.g. Bill Gates had a vision that everyone should have access to a personal computer. He founded the Microsoft company and became, for a while, the richest man in the world. He retired to devote his time to good causes.

3 Ask the class to describe the characteristics and achievements necessary to be considered an international hero in one or two fields, e.g. music, charity, politics, business, literature, sport and entertainment. For example, the learners might suggest that such a person needs artistic talent, physical beauty, ability to endure difficult times, physical strength and skill.

4 Ask the learners to choose someone who they would consider an international hero (or, alternatively, someone whom they might criticise) and, for homework, do some research in a library or on the Internet. They should do the following:

Write a brief description of his or her story, including as much of the following information as they can find:

- place and date of birth
- early life
- when his or her special qualities first became obvious
- difficulties faced
- main achievements
- some reasons why his or her popularity or fame goes beyond local or national boundaries

Learners should also note the sources of their information after the description they have written.

5 After the learners have researched their international heroes (or villains), divide the class into groups to discuss their findings. Are there any similarities or differences in their heroes' stories, e.g.

- Did they have a poor or wealthy childhood?
- Did they have a good education?
- Did something special happen to change their life at some point?

If the class is participating in an online exchange, they can share their findings with their e-partners too.

9.5 Someone I admire

Outline	This activity invites learners to share with others the qualities and achievements learners admire in someone who is not necessarily famous.
Focus	Describing qualities and past narrative of achievements.
Level	Intermediate and above
Time	20 minutes plus
Preparation	Learners need copies of the discussion thread in Box 9.5a.

Procedure

1 Show learners the email discussion starter, and the responses to it in Box 9.5a.
2 Elicit from the class the names of some people who are not famous, but whom they admire. Also ask the learners to state some reasons for their choices.
3 Next, on the board, with the class, model their own variation of the discussion starter and the first response. Include one example of a 'local hero' in the response.
4 The learners then compose their own individual responses to the discussion starter. If the class is participating in an online intercultural exchange, they can post their discussion starter and responses, and discuss their choices with their e-partners.

Variation
Instead of step 3 above, you could ask the class to imagine that there is a competition to put the portrait of a local hero on a postage stamp. The local hero is not nationally famous, but is someone who has done good things for the local community. In groups, the learners identify one candidate for the title of 'local hero'. One person from each group then justifies the group's choice of candidate to the class as a whole, and, finally, the class members vote for the worthiest person to put onto the postage stamp.

Box 9.5a: Someone I admire

Discussion thread: Discussion starter and two responses

From: Vanessa

Hi everyone,

I have been thinking about the relationship between cultures and the individual – and in particular how we identify with people we admire.

I would just like to know who you would say you see or have seen as a role model. Or simply, who are the people you have the most respect and admiration for?

From: Laura

I most respect and admire people who have had a positive impact on society. I really respect people who work with animals, and the people who have left work all over the world to go and help search for those missing in disasters. I don't respect many people who hold a great deal of power in society (the Queen, Prime Minister). It is difficult to pick a role model ... but if I was to choose someone ... they would be 'down to earth' and have a passion for helping others.

From: Fernando

I respect people who make a difference in society, especially the people who often go unnoticed - like local people, who work hard for charity, or who work all the hours of the day and night for little money. These people are admirable when they still manage to run a household, bring up children and help others. Other people are local heroes who are reported in the newspapers. A policeman in my area was nominated for a local award, as he has done some amazing charity work. He has been on numerous treks, cycling journeys and arranged many raffles and charity nights. There are so many people who deserve our respect.

10 Sport

Participation in sport, whether as a player or as a spectator, cuts across national and cultural boundaries. Some sports, like football, athletics, tennis and swimming, are global phenomena. Other sports, such as baseball and cricket, are popular particularly in those places where the USA or Britain, respectively, have had historic influence. Yet other sports, like ice hockey, lacrosse and polo, have a following that is more geographically or socially limited. Whatever the sport and wherever it is played, it can incite passion in the hearts of its players and supporters, although, of course, some will always be immune to its charms. In this chapter, learners are introduced to sports that are mainly played in particular regions of the world and they explore three unusual games in *Local sports* (10.1); they are encouraged to reflect on their knowledge of global and local team sports in *Team sports: cultural associations* (10.2); they consider the language used to support and criticise teams in *The language of fandom* (10.3). In *Cheerleading* (10.4) learners explore the history and status of cheerleaders. *Attending a sports event* (10.5) is a fieldwork project where learners observe and describe a live sports event; and they formally debate a topic that divides communities and cultures, specifically whether it is acceptable for a society to allow its members to pursue blood sports in *Debate on blood sports* (10.6).

10.1 Local sports

Outline	Learners are introduced to the general language of sport by focusing initially on three unusual games that are played in different parts of the world: horseball, shinty and dragon boat racing.
Focus	Basic language of sports, e.g. *player, ball, score, game*.
Level	Lower intermediate and above
Time	40 minutes plus
Preparation	The basic information about these games is provided; however, you may like to do further research and download some more photographs of the games for use in class. You will need a computer and projector to show the images in Box 10.1a and 10.1e and the information on horseball in Box 10.1b. The learners need copies of the reading texts in Boxes 10.1c and 10.1d.

Procedure

1 Tell the learners that they are going to find out about three unusual sports. Write these sports on the board or project them onscreen: *horseball, shinty, dragon boat racing.*

2 Tell the class that you are going to mime the rules of horseball. You then mime the following information:

> *The players ride on horses.*
> *The players pick up a ball.*
> *The players pass the ball to each other, by hand, three times.*
> *To score, a player throws the ball through a net (like a basketball net).*

As you mime the game, the learners call out a description of what you are doing. After the mime is over, write the rules of horseball on the board or project them onscreen from Box 10.1b and show the learners the photograph on the CD-ROM in Box 10.1a. For further information, see www.trymysport.co.uk/horseball.htm

---

Box 10.1a: Local sports

Photo: Horseball

© Alamy/Jordi Salas

From *Intercultural Language Activities*
© Cambridge University Press 2010   PHOTOCOPIABLE

Box 10.1b: Local sports

Reading text: Horseball

Horseball is a young sport, compared to football or rugby. In the 1970s, the Depons brothers from Castillion, near Bordeaux in France invented the sport. Its rules are based loosely on rugby and basketball – but on horseback! Each game of horseball lasts for 20 minutes; two ten-minute halves with a three-minute interval. In the game there are four players on each side.

The players must gain possession of a small football, with leather handles, and pass it at least three times, as they gallop towards a goal. No player can keep the ball for more than ten seconds. Passes may go forwards or backwards. Players can be physically tackled and dispossessed of the ball. If the ball is dropped, the players must sweep it up without getting off their horse.

Players score a goal by shooting the ball through a hoop, 1 metre wide, that stands on poles 3.5 metres above the ground. The team with the higher number of goals wins, and most games have about 15 goals in total.

Horseball quickly became popular in France and its popularity has spread to other European and South American countries. The British Horseball Association began in the 1990s. There is now a junior and senior league in England, with over 200 members.

© Cambridge University Press 2010   PHOTOCOPIABLE

---

3   Next, tell the learners that they are going to read about two more unusual sports in Boxes 10.1c and 10.1d. For each sport, they must identify the following information:
   • In which country is the sport played?
   • How many players/people are there in a team?
   • What do the players/people use?
   • What do the players/people do?
   • How does one team win?

Box 10.1c: Local sports

Reading text: Shinty

Shinty is one of the oldest games in the world. It is an exciting team sport, played mainly in Scotland. There are two teams of 12 players each. The players each have a curved stick. They use the stick to hit and carry a small ball, like a tennis ball. The players can also use their feet to kick the ball. To score a goal, the players must hit the ball into a net, past a goalkeeper, who is allowed to use his or her hands to stop the ball. A game of shinty lasts 90 minutes. The team that scores most goals wins the game.

© Cambridge University Press 2010   PHOTOCOPIABLE

Box 10.1d: Local sports

Reading text: Dragon boat racing

All across China, and among Chinese communities overseas, on the fifth day of the fifth month, there is the annual Dragon Boat Festival, which often includes a race. Teams carve and paint their boats to look like dragons, with a big, fiery mouth at the front and a long tail at the end. The boats can be from 20–30 metres long, and can carry a crew of between 20 and 80 people. A drummer and flag-catcher sit at the front of the boat. Pulling on their paddles, the crew rows to the sound of the drum. An oar is used to steer the boat. Dragon boat races can have many boats competing. The winning team catches a flag at the end of the course. Dragon boat racing is becoming more popular every year.

© Cambridge University Press 2010   PHOTOCOPIABLE

Go through the answers with learners and show them the photographs of the sports in Box 10.1e.

Answers:

Shinty

- *In which country is the sport played?* Mainly in Scotland
- *How many people are there in a team?* 12
- *What do the people use?* A curved stick and a small ball
- *What do the people do?* Hit and kick the ball into a net
- *How does one team win?* It scores more goals than the other team.

Box 10.1e: Local sports

Photos: Shinty and Dragon Boat Racing

© Alamy/John MacTavish

© Getty Images/AFP

From *Intercultural Language Activities*
© Cambridge University Press 2010   PHOTOCOPIABLE

Dragon Boat Racing

- *In which country is the sport played?* In China and among Chinese communities overseas
- *How many people are there in a team?* Between 20 and 80
- *What do the people use?* Oars, a drum
- *What do the people do?* Row the boat to the sound of a drum.
- *How does one team win?* A crew member catches a flag at the end of the course.

4 With the class, brainstorm a vocabulary list that is useful for describing sports, e.g.

People:	*player*	*team*	*referee*	*goalkeeper*
Equipment:	*ball*	*stick*	*racket*	*bat*
Actions:	*throw*	*row*	*ride*	*kick*
Places:	*pitch*	*course*	*track*	*court*

5 Ask the class to describe a sport of their own choice that they are familiar with, either a universally popular sport like football or tennis, or a sport that is more popular locally, like ice hockey, water polo or camel racing. To organise their descriptions, the learners can answer the five questions given in step 3. Afterwards, ask some learners to read out their descriptions.

6 If the class is participating in an online intercultural exchange, the learners can post their descriptions of sports to their e-partners, and ask for descriptions in return. Together, work out a model 'discussion opener' in class beforehand, e.g.

Hi! I'd like to find out your favourite sport. I like basketball. This is a team game with five or six players . . . What is your favourite sport? How do you play it? I look forward to hearing from you!

The learners then post their discussion openers to their e-partners.

7 When learners have heard back from their e-partners, they can bring the descriptions to a following lesson to read out. Learners may like to ask their e-partners further questions about the sport, particularly if it is only played locally.

10.2 Team sports: cultural associations

Outline	Learners do this project-based activity to check their basic knowledge of some familiar – and less familiar – team sports played around the world.
Focus	Researching and reading about different kinds of sport in a library or online, and summarising information in a table.
Level	Intermediate and above
Time	20 minutes in the first lesson and 30 minutes plus in a follow-up lesson
Preparation	Learners should have access to a library or online resource with information about team sports played around the world. Learners also need copies of the table in Box 10.2a and the debate conventions in Box 10.2b on the CD-ROM or on p. 196 (Box 10.6b). This activity should be spread over two lessons and includes research in a library during class time, or for homework.

Procedure

1 Inform learners that they are going to research the topic of team sports that are played around the world. As a warm-up, ask the learners if any of them regularly play or watch a team sport – if so, which?

2 Write several of the suggested team games on the board or project them onscreen, and ask the learners to give some further information about them, e.g.
   • How long does the game last?
   • What do the players wear?
   • Where did the game originate?

3 Next distribute the table in Box 10.2a. Elicit from the class some basic information about football, and, with this information, the learners complete the first column of the table.

4 Together identify possible sources of information about the other sports in the table, e.g. internet sites, encyclopaedias in libraries, e-partners.

5 Divide the class into groups. Each group is assigned the task of researching a particular team sport. This can be done in the school library or after class.

6 In a following lesson, after the learners have completed their research, they prepare to present their findings to the class as a whole, using the table as a basis. If possible, they can illustrate the talk with pictures and props.

Follow-up

Ask learners to identify sports that are popular locally, but that are not
Olympic sports. For example, sports that are currently *not* official Olympic
sports include darts, karate, paintball, skateboarding and squash. Other
non-Olympic sports can be found at www.non-olympic.org

Once learners have identified some popular local sports, ask the class to
choose one. Divide the learners into two groups with one arguing for its
inclusion and the other group against its inclusion in the Olympic Games.
If necessary, learners should spend some time researching their argument.
Learners should then have a class debate following the conventions in Box
10.2b on the CD-ROM (or on p. 196 in Box 10.6b).

Box 10.2a: Team sports: cultural associations

Table: Exploring team sports

	Football	Volleyball	Basketball	Hockey	Cricket	Tennis
Number in each team						
Length of game						
Object of game						
Dress of players						
What makes contact with the ball?						
Country of origin?						

© Cambridge University Press 2010   PHOTOCOPIABLE

Answers:

	Football	Volleyball	Basketball	Hockey	Cricket	Tennis
Number in each team	11	6	5	11	11	1 or 2
Length of game	90 minutes	Varies; teams usually have to win three out of five sets.	Varies; 40–50 minutes.	70 minutes	Varies – can be up to five days, though shorter versions are now common.	Varies; players usually have to win three out of five sets (men) or two out of three sets (women).
Object of game	To score goals.	To score points. The first team to win 25 points wins a set.	To shoot a ball through the opposing team's basket.	To score goals.	To score runs and bowl out the opposition.	To score points: from 0 ('love') you go to 15, 30, 40 and then you win the game. If you win six games you usually win a set.
Dress of players	Uniform shirt and shorts; long socks and boots.	Uniform shirt and shorts; volleyball shoes.	Uniform shirt and shorts; basketball shoes.	Uniform shirt, shorts or short skirt, gloves, protective padding, hockey shoes.	White shirt, white trousers, and spiked shoes; a helmet when batting.	Traditionally white shirt and shorts, or short skirt; tennis shoes.
What makes contact with the ball?	Any part of the body except arms and hands. Unless they are the goalkeeper.	Hands and arms	Hands	Stick	A wooden bat	Racket
Country of origin?	United Kingdom	USA	Canada/USA	United Kingdom (though similar games exist elsewhere)	United Kingdom	Difficult to say. Some argue Egypt, others France.

10.3 The language of fandom

Outline	Learners explore the language used to support their own team and criticise rival teams.
Focus	Language of qualified and unqualified praise and criticism.
Level	Intermediate and above
Time	30 minutes plus in the first lesson and 10–20 minutes in a follow-up lesson
Preparation	Learners need copies of the worksheet in Box 10.3a, the role play cards in Box 10.3b and the table in Box 10.3c. This activity is enhanced if learners have out-of-class access to sports discussion sites on the Internet. It should be spread over two lessons and includes homework.

Procedure

1 Ask the class to identify two local, rival sports teams. Then brainstorm with the class some expressions that might be used in the following contexts:
   * to praise the players and/or management of one's own team
   * to criticise the players and/or management of one's own team
   * to praise the players and/or management of the rival team
   * to criticise the players and/or management of the rival team

2 Next, hand out copies of the worksheet in Box 10.3a. Ask the learners to put the phrases into the appropriate column in the table. The expressions were taken from football discussion forums. Some refer to players, others to the manager or coach and some expressions might go in more than one box. Some phrases express unqualified praise (usually for one's own team) or criticism (usually for the rival team). One's own team can also be criticised, of course, sometimes intensely, but criticism of the rival team tends to be more extreme, e.g. *There's no creativity* (own team); *The tactics are mind-numbingly boring* (rival team). Praise for the rival team is usually restrained.

There is no absolutely 'correct' allocation of phrases in this exercise, but the expressions were originally used in the contexts shown on the next page.

Suggested answers:

	Own team	Rival team
Language of praise	*He's got us out of a mess.* *He's done an excellent job.* *He's magic.*	*They strung a few nice moves together.* *It's a decent team.* *The team deserves our respect.*
Language of criticism	*OK, we're not the team we were.* *The last game was a very low point.* *There's no creativity.* *No wonder attendances are down.* *It was a totally amateur performance.*	*The tactics are mind-numbingly boring.* *The style of play is soulless.* *The team is overrated garbage.*

Box 10.3a: The language of fandom

Worksheet: The language of praise and criticism

He's got us out of a mess.	*OK, we're not the team we were.*
The style of play is soulless.	*The tactics are mind-numbingly boring.*
They strung a few nice moves together.	*The last game was a very low point.*
The team is overrated garbage.	*He's magic.*
It's a decent team.	*No wonder attendances are down.*
It was a totally amateur performance.	*There's no creativity.*
The team deserves our respect.	*He's done an excellent job.*

	Own team	Rival team
Language of praise		
Language of criticism		

PHOTOCOPIABLE

3   After they have familiarised themselves with the expressions of praise
    and criticism, the learners can role play a radio sports programme
    phone-in, using the role cards in Box 10.3b. This role play can be done
    initially in groups of four, with one learner taking the role of broadcaster
    (Speaker A), and the others taking the part of members of the audience
    (Speaker B) who are phoning in. They can use expressions from the
    worksheet if they wish. Before starting, establish what they will be
    discussing, e.g. a football match where the home team won 5-0. The
    role play can then be repeated with the whole class, where one learner
    plays the part of the broadcaster, and nominates other learners to be
    participating audience members.

Box 10.3b: The language of fandom

Role cards: Sports phone-in

Speaker A: You are a sports broadcaster and the host of a local phone-in
show. You are going to discuss a recent match between two rival teams with
members of the audience.
*   Introduce the topic.
*   Invite members of the audience to phone in with their comments.
*   Nominate other members of the group or class to contribute (e.g. by
    saying 'Caller one, what point do you wish to make?' or 'Caller two, you're
    live on air.').
*   Follow up or challenge the caller's points, e.g. by asking for clarification or
    questioning their comment.
*   Close the discussion down when you think the caller has had enough time.

Speaker B: You are listening to a local sports phone-in show. The
broadcaster has announced the topic (a recent match between two rival
teams) and you are trying to phone the show with your comment. If or when
you are picked, you must:
*   Praise or criticise the teams involved.
*   Be prepared to clarify or defend your comments.
*   Be as emotional and persuasive as you can be.
*   Speak for as long as possible.

© Cambridge University Press 2010   PHOTOCOPIABLE

4   After class, if learners have access to sports websites on the Internet, they can be invited to visit sports discussion forums to collect further expressions of praise and criticism. Different groups can be sent to different websites to discover if the language used to praise and criticise teams is similar or different across sports and across countries. Learners should list at least 12 more expressions that fans use to *praise* and *criticise* their own and rival teams. Suggested websites are:

> http://news.bbc.co.uk/sport2/hi/606/default.stm [Various]
> http://forum.football.co.uk/ [UK football]
> http://www.footballworldsgame.com/forum/ [World football]
> http://www.baseballforum.com/ [Baseball]
> http://www.worldcricketforum.com/ [Cricket]
> http://forum.planet-rugby.com/index.php [Rugby]
> http://www.bigfooty.com/forum/ [Australian Rules Football]
> http://www.gogirlworld.org [A website resource to encourage girls of 8–18 into sports]
> http://www.netballonline.com [Netball]
> http://www.volleyballforums.com/ [Volleyball]

Learners should then complete the table in Box 10.3c.

5   In a following lesson, after having collected their own language examples, the class can perform the sports programme phone-in again, if they wish, using the new vocabulary they have learnt. Learners should also discuss whether the language used to praise and criticise teams is similar or different across sports and countries.

Box 10.3c: The language of fandom

Table: Exploring the language of praise and criticism online

Team sport chosen: Website visited: Date accessed:		
	Fans' own team	Rival teams
Language of praise		
Language of criticism		
Other useful expressions		

10.4 Cheerleading

Outline	Learners explore cheerleading, its history and current status. Learners are encouraged to reflect on whether audience participation in sports is encouraged in their own culture, and if it is, how.
Focus	Practising and inventing cheerleading 'chants'.
Level	Intermediate and above
Time	40 minutes plus
Preparation	You need a computer and projector to display the photographs of the cheerleaders on the CD-ROM in Box 10.4a. Learners need copies of the questions in Box 10.4b, the reading text in Box 10.4c and the worksheet in Box 10.4d. If possible, ask learners to watch clips of cheerleaders on www.youtube.com or, if you can, watch together in the lesson.

Procedure

1 Show some pictures of cheerleaders from the CD-ROM in Box 10.4a and if possible, watch some performances on www.youtube.com

---

Box 10.4a: Cheerleading

Photos: Cheerleaders

© Getty Images   © Alamy/H Mark Weidman

From *Intercultural Language Activities*
© Cambridge University Press 2010   PHOTOCOPIABLE

---

2 Ask the class what they know about *cheerleading*, e.g.
   • What kind of people usually become cheerleaders?
     Mainly girls and young women, though some boys and young men participate.

- What do cheerleaders do?
  They chant team slogans, wave pom-poms (fluffy balls of decorated fabric) or batons, jump, perform acrobatic routines, etc. They encourage spectators to give vocal support to their team during a game, and entertain the crowds before the game starts and during intervals in play.
- Which games do you associate with cheerleading?
  American football, baseball, etc. Cheerleading is now itself a competitive sport in the USA.
- What kind of clothes do cheerleaders wear?
  The girls usually wear bright tops and shorts or short skirts, usually in the colours of the teams they support.
  Learners discuss whether they have cheerleaders/audience participation in their countries. If so, what do they say? What do they do? What language is used?

3 Tell the learners that they are going to read a text about the history of cheerleading and that they will then answer questions on it. Guide the learners through the questions in Box 10.4b and then ask them to read the text in Box 10.4c and discuss it with a partner.

4 Afterwards, get learners to feed back their opinions/answers to the rest of the class.

5 Next, in the same pairs, get learners to make up a dialogue in which they are arguing about whether or not cheerleading is a 'real' sport. Then choose some pairs to demonstrate their dialogue before the class.

Box 10.4b: Cheerleading

Questions: Cheerleading

a) Describe your image of a 'typical cheerleader'.

b) Is there anything in the text that contradicts your image?

c) Imagine that you were talking to someone who said cheerleading was not a serious sport and art. What evidence from the text would you choose to support or challenge that opinion?

d) Does organised cheerleading add excitement to a sports event, or is it too rehearsed and 'unnatural'?

© Cambridge University Press 2010   PHOTOCOPIABLE

Box 10.4c: Cheerleading

Reading text: Cheerleading

Cheerleading began in the United States of America in the 1880s. The original cheerleaders were men who wanted to encourage supporters to cheer university athletes. The first organised cheer took place at Princeton University in 1884, and by the end of the century a Princeton graduate had introduced cheerleading to University of Minnesota football games. It was a Minnesota man, Johnny Campbell, who became the first widely known 'cheerleader' in 1898. Only later, in 1923, did women start cheerleading. Now most American high schools and universities have cheerleading teams.

Cheerleading slowly became a competitive sport itself. The National Cheerleaders Association was started in the USA in 1948, and as well as chanting their support, cheerleaders began attempting more and more ambitious routines, involving jumping, stunts, gymnastic formations, throws, tumbles and pyramids.

Although cheerleading is not always officially recognised as a sport or an art, it attracts participants across the globe, in countries such as Australia, China, Denmark and the United Kingdom. The routines can be dangerous, and cheerleaders now need to be athletes. Their training can take up to eight hours per week. The All-Star Cheerleading World Championships are held each year in the USA. Famous people who have been cheerleaders in the past include film and pop stars like Halle Berry, Cameron Diaz, Tom Hanks, Steve Martin, Madonna and Rihanna, as well as ex-presidents Ronald Reagan and George W. Bush!

Cheerleading can be a serious business. At the 2008 Beijing Olympic Games, there were reports that 800,000 students had been recruited to act as cheerleaders for the Chinese teams. They were given discount tickets and in return they had to learn a four-part chant. It started with a double clap and a chant of 'Olympics', moved on to a thumbs up with arms pointing skywards and a chant of 'Let's go!', then another double clap and a chant of 'China', and finally fists were punched in the air to another shout of 'Let's go!' While some commentators criticised the 'official cheerleaders' as being too forced and orchestrated, others admitted that the chanting created a great atmosphere for the spectators and athletes.

PHOTOCOPIABLE

Box 10.4d: Cheerleading

Worksheet: Cheerleading chants

Chant 1
Two, four, six, eight,
Who do we appreciate?
[Spell out the name of the team you have chosen, e.g. *H-o-y-a-s*]
[Shout out the name of the team you have chosen: *Hoyas!*]
Go! Go! Go!

Chant 2
One, two, three, four,
Who's the team we all adore?
[Spell out the name of the team you have chosen, e.g. *H-o-y-a-s*]
Go, [team's name, e.g. *Hoyas*]! Go, [team's name, e.g. *Hoyas*]! Go! Go! Go!

Chant 3
Six-foot two, eyes of blue,
Big [player's name, e.g. *Greg Mitchell*] is after you!
Nice one, [player's name, e.g. *Greg*]
Nice one, son!
Nice one, [player's name, e.g. *Greg*]
Let's score another one!

Move 1
Jump straight up and down, stretching your arms out in a T motion.

Move 2
Jump up and down. This time, as you stretch your arms out, stretch your legs apart too, so that you form an X.

Move 3
Stand with your arms by your side. Then, as you stretch one arm out to the side, bend the leg opposite, e.g. as you stretch out your right arm, bend your left leg. Then do the same with the opposite arm and leg. Repeat.

Move 4
Stand with your legs slightly apart. Lean over and with your right hand touch as far down your left leg as you can. Then repeat with your left hand and your right leg.

PHOTOCOPIABLE

Follow-up for teenagers

Learners practise some cheerleading chants and moves. First, divide the class into groups of between four and eight members, and tell each group to look at the worksheet in Box 10.4d. Next, instruct the groups to choose a team to support and one of the chants (which they can adapt). They should study the cheerleading moves and invent a routine to accompany their chant. If learners wish, they can create their own moves and chants rather than using the ones suggested in the worksheet. After the groups have practised they present their chants to the others.

10.5 Attending a sports event

Outline	Learners observe and describe a live spectator sports event, from a school team sport to a professional competitive event.
Focus	Describing physical surroundings, physical activities, etc.
Level	Intermediate and above
Time	30 minutes plus in the first lesson and 30 minutes plus across one or more follow-up lessons
Preparation	If the class is participating in an online intercultural exchange, digital photographs might be taken for a class report that can be shared with the learners' e-partners. Learners need copies of the questions in Box 10.5a. This activity should be spread over two lessons and includes learners, outside class, observing a sports event.

Procedure

1   Ask the learners if they have attended a live sports event of any kind. Choose one learner who has, and go through the questions in Box 10.5a with him or her.

2   Organise the class into groups, each of which should contain at least one person who has attended a live sports event. Give each group the list of questions in Box 10.5a, and the learners share their experiences of attending a sports event. If the groups only have one person who has attended a sports event, learners should ask this person about their experience. They should then discuss what event, if any, they would like to attend themselves.

3   Ask the learners, in groups, to do some fieldwork in which they will attend and observe a sports event of their choice. They should attend different events of the same sport, and then, between lessons, they should meet and prepare a group report that covers some of the questions in Box 10.5a. If possible, the learners should take photographs of the event.

Box 10.5a: Attending a sports event

Questions: Describing a sports event

- What kind of event was it? (e.g. school sports event, professional event, etc?)
- Where and when did the event take place?
- How much did admission cost (if anything)?
- How many spectators were there? (roughly – dozens, hundreds, thousands?)
- What did the spectators wear? (e.g. sports clothes in team colours?)
- How did the spectators behave? (e.g. cheering, shouting, chanting, singing?)
- How long did the event last?
- Was there any other entertainment provided apart from the sporting event itself? (e.g. music, cheerleaders, competitions?)
- Was food or drink available – if so, what was provided and who provided it? (e.g. hot dog stalls, drinks from vendors?)

© Cambridge University Press 2010   PHOTOCOPIABLE

Note: There are usually informal sports events, e.g. in the school or in local clubs, that learners will be able to attend and report on. However, if it is difficult to find a sports event for learners to attend, they can be encouraged to watch a sports event on television or online – possibly in a public place like a bar or a club. If the learners are restricted to watching the sports event at home, they can still look at the questions and consider what aspects of the experience are *not* available to the home viewer (e.g. the additional entertainment, the hot dog vendors, etc.). They can then contrast the experience of being a spectator at a live event with being a television viewer.

4   In a following lesson, the groups report back to the class their observations and show their photographs. Learners can also say what they liked and disliked about the event and their experience. If the learners are participating in an online intercultural exchange, they can create written reports and share them and the photographs with their e-partners. They can then compare how attending sports events differs between countries.

5   Finally, ask learners to use the group reports to compare two different kinds of sports event, e.g. a major championship and a school event; or a basketball game and a snooker match. You can model a comparative report on the board, such as the one in p. 193, and introduce some useful expressions in advance, e.g. *while* (contrast), *both* (comparison), *although* (qualification).

Basketball versus snooker

Basketball is a team sport, with five players on each side. *In contrast*, snooker is a game played by individuals. A basketball game lasts 40 minutes, *whereas* a game of snooker can last hours, or even days. In basketball, the aim is to score by shooting a ball into the opposing team's basket. In snooker, the object is to 'pot' a number of coloured balls into holes arranged around a table, using a wooden cue. *While* basketball players wear a vest or jersey, and shorts, snooker players are often smartly dressed in a waistcoat, trousers, shirt and bow-tie. *Both* sports demand skill – and a good eye!

10.6 Debate on blood sports

Outline	Learners research and debate the issue of whether society should or should not allow blood sports. While learners may well hold firm beliefs, for or against the abolition of blood sports, they are required to improve their persuasive skills by researching and understanding the values held by those who disagree.
Focus	The language and conventions of formal debate.
Level	Upper-intermediate and above
Time	20–30 minutes in the first lesson and 30 minutes plus in a follow-up lesson
Preparation	For their research, learners will need access to information on certain blood sports such as fox-hunting, bull-fighting, cock-fighting, etc. They might find this on the Internet, from e-partners, or from local library and leisure resources. Some possible websites are suggested in step 4. Learners need copies of the worksheets in Boxes 10.6a and 10.6b. They also need the debate score card in Box 10.6c. This activity should be spread over two lessons and includes learners, outside class, researching their argument.

Procedure

1 Elicit learners' knowledge of blood sports that are or were enjoyed in different parts of the world, e.g.
   - *fox-hunting* or *fox-chasing* (now illegal in the UK, but practised in some countries)
   - *bull-fighting* (particularly popular in Spain, Portugal and southern France)
   - *cock-fighting* (illegal in some countries, but still practised in others)

2 Divide the class into groups and ask each group to come up with the reasons *in favour of* and *against* the abolition of blood sports, e.g.
   - *pro-abolition:* cruelty to animals; desensitises spectators to violence, etc.
   - *anti-abolition:* blood sports are a traditional part of national or local cultures; the question of civil liberties; the abolition of some sports would adversely affect the tourist economy, etc.
3 Tell the learners that in a following lesson they are going to have a formal debate on the motion that *This class believes that the abolition of blood sports is a denial of civil liberties*. Explain to learners that those selected to argue in the debate for and against the motion do not necessarily need to believe the arguments that they are going to make. The class will judge them on how well they make their case.
4 Divide the class equally, and tell the learners in Group A that they must prepare to research the arguments *in favour* of the proposition, and the learners in Group B that they must research the arguments *against* the proposition. Hand out copies of the worksheet in Box 10.6a to groups A and B. Stress that the members of the groups need not necessarily believe the case that they are researching. The learners read the worksheet and discuss what they need to do. Websites that they may find useful are:
   http://en.wikipedia.org/wiki/Blood_sports
   http://en.wikipedia.org/wiki/Civil_liberties
   http://www.bullfightschool.com/
   http://www.banbloodsports.com/
   http://www.league.org.uk/
5 During the first lesson, explain the conventions of a debate by going through the worksheet in Box 10.6b. Explain that in the next lesson, each group will choose two speakers to represent them in the debate.
6 After class, learners should carry out their research online, in a library, or with their e-partners. They should then write a paragraph or two summarising their argument before the next lesson.
7 During the next lesson, the learners in each group discuss what they found out, what arguments they will put forward and what questions they might want to ask the opposition. Each group advises its speakers on how to make a good case.
8 When the groups are ready, the class follows the procedure on the worksheet in Box 10.6b. The speakers debate the proposition in front of the class who then vote as to whether it accepts or rejects the motion. To enable the class to decide, hand out copies of the score card in Box

10.6c to learners and explain that their decision should be based on the performance of the proposers and opposers.

9   Together discuss the issues that arose from the debate, e.g.
   •   How might the speakers improve their presentation and arguments?
   •   How easy or difficult is it to make an argument for something you do not believe in?

Box 10.6a: Debate on blood sports

Worksheet: Preparing an argument

Group A (for the motion): You must look for evidence in support of the argument that people who wish to ban blood sports are attacking the civil liberties of human beings. You need to construct a strong argument that human civil liberties are more important than the suffering and possibly even the death of animals. You might also point to the long tradition of sports involving living creatures, from fishing to bull-fighting – can you construct an argument that shows that these kinds of sport are economically and culturally vital to certain communities?

In your groups, think of possible sources of information about
   •   the practice of blood sports in different countries and communities
   •   the issue of civil liberties in those countries

Group B (against the motion): You must look for evidence against the argument that people who wish to ban blood sports are attacking the civil liberties of human beings. You need to construct a strong argument that preventing the suffering and possibly even the death of animals is more important than human civil liberties. You need to be aware of the long tradition of sports involving living creatures, from fishing to bull-fighting – what arguments can you produce against sports that have a long tradition and which are important to the economy of many local and national communities?

In your groups, think of possible sources of information about
   •   the practice of blood sports in different countries and communities
   •   the issue of civil liberties in those countries

© Cambridge University Press 2010   PHOTOCOPIABLE

Box 10.6b: Debate on blood sports

Worksheet: Holding a debate

a) The first proposer makes an argument for up to five minutes, in favour of the motion.

b) The two opposers can then ask the first proposer two questions about weak points in his or her argument.

c) The first opposer makes an argument for up to five minutes, against the motion.

d) The two proposers can then ask the first opposer two questions about weak points in his or her argument.

e) The second proposer speaks for up to five minutes, making further arguments in favour of the motion.

f) The second opposer speaks for up to five minutes, making further arguments against the motion.

g) The class then asks the proposers and opposers questions about their arguments.

h) The class votes in favour of, or against the motion, *based on the performance of the proposers and opposers.*

© Cambridge University Press 2010   PHOTOCOPIABLE

Box 10.6c: Debate on blood sports

Debate score card: 1 = weak; 5 = excellent

	Proposer 1	Proposer 2	Opposer 1	Opposer 2
Strength of argument				
Ability to deal with questions				
Entertainment value				
Style				
Total score				

© Cambridge University Press 2010   PHOTOCOPIABLE

11 Food

It is often said that we are what we eat and one of the most distinctive characteristics of any community is the food that it has adopted. In fact, food can become emblematic of a community, such as American burgers, Indian curries, Italian pasta, German sausages, Irish stew, Japanese sushi, Scandinavian smorgasbord, Scottish haggis, Spanish paella, Turkish kebabs, and so on. In many of today's cities and towns, local and regional restaurants and food stores exist side-by-side with places catering to those who desire more exotic or 'fusion' cuisine. The following activities take food as their topic: *National dishes: cultural associations* (11.1) explores the associations of the 'national' dish in different countries; and the range of ethnic and 'fusion' cuisines available in the community is explored in *Regional and ethnic cuisine* (11.2). *International food* (11.3) looks at the constraints on those who have to devise an 'international' menu that is acceptable to all passengers on long-haul flights. *Food idioms: using the British National Corpus* (11.4) highlights the enormous number of idioms found in the English language that relate to food. *Shopping lists* (11.5) invites learners to compare what is and isn't on their shopping lists and what individuals consider to be essentials, and the final activity, *Supermarket psychology* (11.6) returns to fieldwork, with the investigation of the organisation and contents of local supermarkets.

11.1 National dishes: cultural associations

Outline	Learners identify a national dish that they associate with their home culture or a culture that is familiar to them, and research the national dishes of other cultures.
Focus	Describing food, ingredients and associations.
Level	Lower intermediate and above
Time	30 minutes in the first lesson and 20 minutes in a follow-up lesson
Preparation	Learners need copies of the table in Box 11.1a. They also need access to the Internet to carry out research. Alternatively, they can ask classmates, e-partners, or consult recipe books in a local library. This activity should be spread over two lessons and includes homework.

Procedure

1 Explain that the class is going to explore the meaning that
particular meals have for different cultures. If you are working in
a multicultural classroom, get learners to call out their national
dish, that is, one meal that has a special significance for the learners'
home culture, and write them on the board. If you are working in
a monocultural classroom, ask learners if they know, and agree on,
what their national dish is.

2 Next, elicit the associations that go with the national dish. If it is a
multicultural group, get learners to select one of the dishes on the board
and discuss its associations. When eliciting the associations of the dish
you can ask learners the following:
   • What are its ingredients?
   • Is it a full meal or just a snack?
   • Where and when is it eaten (every day or on special occasions)?
   • What is it accompanied by?
   • What are its origins? For example, was it originally eaten by
     poorer people or the rich? Did it start in a particular ethnic
     community?
   • What do people do after eating it?

3 Distribute the table in Box 11.1a, and project it onscreen. Fill in the
first column using the information elicited in step 2. Next, brainstorm
together 'national dishes' from other countries, or if the learners are not
aware of any such dishes, you can provide a list, such as: *Feijoada* from
Brazil (black bean stew, made with beef and pork), *Haggis* from Scotland
(the insides of lamb, cooked in a sheep's stomach), *Fondue* from
Switzerland (a communal meal, where pieces of food, often bits of bread,
are dipped into melted cheese or sometimes chocolate), *Borscht* from
Eastern Europe (vegetable soup, often made with beetroot), *Goulash*
from Hungary (beef stew), *Dim sum* from China (a meal consisting of a
range of light dishes, like dumplings, rice noodles, seafood, dessert and
fruit), *Poronkäristys* from Finland (sautéed reindeer), *Kebab* from, e.g.
Turkey/Greece (grilled meat, served on a skewer or stick), *Bacalhau* from
Portugal (salted cod), *Kabsa* from Saudi Arabia (rice dish, made of meat
and vegetables), *Paella* from Spain (rice dish, made in a large pan, with
seafood and/or meat), *Hot dogs* from the USA, and *Fish and chips* from
the UK. Put learners into pairs and ask each pair to choose a dish or a
country. Ideally they should choose different ones. They must research
the national dish and complete the first column in the table. If you feel it

is necessary to help learners further, complete the second column in Box 11.1a using one of the suggested answers on p. 200 as an example.

4 Discuss with the learners potential sources of information – the Internet, local restaurants, classmates, e-partners, and recipe books in libraries.

5 For homework, the pairs research their chosen national dish, and present their findings in the following lesson. If learners have e-partners in an online intercultural exchange, they can share their findings with them.

Follow-up

In a multicultural class, learners can be invited to bring in to a future lesson a small snack typical of their home country. They then 'show and tell' about it before offering it to the other learners to taste. (Please be aware that some learners will not eat certain kinds of food for religious or other reasons.) In monocultural classes, learners can be encouraged to research recipes from other countries, and to prepare a simple dish at home, to bring in and share with others. (Again, be aware that some learners will not make dishes with certain ingredients.)

Box 11.1a: National dishes: cultural associations

Table: National dishes

Name of national dish	Your national dish:	Another national dish:
Which country/countries?		
Ingredients?		
Meal or snack?		
Where and when is it eaten?		
What is it accompanied by?		
What are its origins?		
What do people do after eating it?		

PHOTOCOPIABLE

Suggested answers:

Name of national dish	haggis	feijoada	hot dogs
Which country/ countries?	Scotland	Brazil	USA and Canada
Ingredients?	sheep's stomach, heart, liver, lungs and windpipe; onions, suet, oatmeal, salt and herbs	salt pork, pork sausage, ham, salted tongue, pig's knuckle and trotters, black beans, onion, parsley, tomatoes and garlic	Frankfurter sausages (beef or beef and pork); long oval-shaped buns
Meal or snack?	meal	meal	snack
Where and when is it eaten?	usually around 25 January, the birthday of Robert Burns, Scotland's national poet	Wednesdays and Saturdays, often in restaurants	often at sports games
What is it accompanied by?	mashed potatoes ('tatties') and turnips ('neeps')	rice, mandioca flour, sliced kale, sliced orange, hot pepper sauce	optional mustard, ketchup, pickles
What are its origins?	peasant food, later celebrated in a poem by Burns, *To a Haggis*	peasant food, originally on slave plantations	convenience food at sports games
What do people do after eating it?	at a Burns Supper, they dance, listen to speeches, songs and poems	lie down, doze, chat sleepily . . .	continue watching the game

11.2 Regional and ethnic cuisine

Outline	Learners reflect on the different kinds of food that they are familiar with, and the different kinds of restaurant that offer these foods locally. The follow-up activity invites learners to explore the availability of different types of restaurant in the community.
Focus	Describing food and restaurant decor; language used in restaurants.
Level	Intermediate and above
Time	40 minutes plus
Preparation	Learners need copies of the worksheet in Box 11.2b, the model dialogue in Box 11.2c and the descriptions of ethnic foods in Box 11.2d. Learners also need copies of Box 11.2e for the follow-up activity. You will need a computer and projector to display the photograph in Box 11.2a. For the follow-up learners, outside class, look at the different restaurants available in the community.

Procedure

1   Explain that in this activity, the learners will be comparing different kinds of food from different cultures. As a warm-up activity, ask them if they like the following kinds of food, or if they have tried them: Chinese, French, Japanese, Korean, Indian, Mexican, Spanish.

2   If you wish, show the photograph of a restaurant in Box 11.2a and ask learners to guess what kinds of food they serve. Talk about the food from different parts of the world and ask what kinds of food the learners would expect to eat in different restaurants, e.g. Japanese, Indian, Mexican, Spanish and Chinese. For example, the learners might identify *sushi, curries, nachos, tapas, stir-fry or noodles*, etc.

3   Next, circulate the worksheet in Box 11.2b and ask the learners, in pairs, to match the restaurant names with the kinds of food that they would expect to eat there and the kind of decor/atmosphere they might find in each of the restaurants. After completing the matching activity, ask some pairs to report back to the rest of the class and ask learners if they think the food/decor is typical of each type of restaurant, or whether it is a stereotype.
   Answers: a–iv–2, b–iii–1, c–v–4, d–vi–5, e–ii–3, f–i–6

Box 11.2a: Regional and ethnic cuisine

Photo: Restaurant

© Getty Images/Peter Poulides

From *Intercultural Language Activities*
© Cambridge University Press 2010   PHOTOCOPIABLE

Box 11.2b: Regional and ethnic cuisine

Worksheet: Matching restaurants, food, decor and atmosphere

Restaurant	*Food*
a) La Trattoria di Dino	i) a selection of tapas
b) Rawalpindi	ii) hamburgers
c) Pancho Villa	iii) curries and tandoories
d) Bangkok Palace	iv) pasta and ice cream
e) Sam's Diner	v) enchiladas and burritos
f) Café Andaluz	vi) king prawn and cashew nuts

Decor and atmosphere

1) highly patterned wallpaper and sitar music
2) red and white checked tablecloths
3) a 1950s jukebox
4) ranch-style furniture and sombreros
5) carved Buddha figures and wall murals of elephants
6) white-washed walls with ceramic tile decoration

© Cambridge University Press 2010   PHOTOCOPIABLE

4   Brainstorm with the class some useful language that they might use in a
    restaurant to ask about unfamiliar food, e.g.

    Can you tell me something about . . . ?
    Does it contain meat?
    Is it spicy / very salty / tasty?
    Is it a starter or a main course?
    Does it come with anything (on the side)?

5   Tell learners they are going to practise, in pairs, a dialogue in a
    restaurant. Give out Box 11.2c.

Box 11.2c: Regional and ethnic cuisine

Model dialogue: Restaurant conversation

CUSTOMER: Excuse me, can you tell me what a biryani is?
WAITER: A biryani? Um, it's roasted in different kinds of spices – you
                    know? Spices like cardamom and cinnamon. It's very tasty.
CUSTOMER: Is it hot?
WAITER: No, it's pretty mild, actually.
CUSTOMER: That's good, because I'm not too keen on hot food. Erm . . .
                    I don't know, I'm still not sure. Does it contain meat?
WAITER: You can have it with meat, or with vegetables only.
CUSTOMER: You can have it without meat? Because I'm a vegetarian.
WAITER: Oh yes, you can have a vegetable biryani. It's very good.
CUSTOMER: Okay, I'll take the vegetable biryani.

---

6   Now ask the learners to make up their own dialogues between a
    customer and a waiter, using the expressions they brainstormed in step
    4. Give them Box 11.2d containing descriptions of ethnic foods. They can
    use these or think of their own examples to ask about. Each learner plays
    the customer twice, asking about different food. After this rehearsal
    stage, selected learners perform their dialogue to the whole class.

Box 11.2d: Regional and ethnic cuisine

Reading text: Descriptions of ethnic foods

tapas – In Spain a *tapa* was originally an appetiser, like olives, cheese or fried baby squid. In European and American restaurants, an entire meal can consist of small plates of tapas, including dishes such as chorizo sausage and tortilla (a potato omelette).

sushi – In Japan *sushi* originally meant a dish of vinegared rice, topped by raw fish. Outside Japan, *sushi* has come to mean dishes consisting of raw fish, such as tuna or squid. Dishes consisting of sliced raw fish alone are called *sashimi*.

dim sum – This is a Chinese meal consisting of a number of light dishes served with Chinese tea. *Dim sum* may be 'salty' (when the light dishes involve meat, seafood or vegetables such as shrimp or pork dumplings, with mushrooms) or 'sweet' (when the dishes involve desserts and fruit, such as sweet tofu or mango pudding).

biryani – This refers to a family of South Asian rice dishes, popular in Bangladesh, India and Pakistan. The dishes use a distinctive range of spices such as cardamom, cinnamon, coriander and mint. The name *biryani* originally meant 'roasted', and a variety of vegetables, lamb or chicken are roasted in the selection of spices, and then served with rice.

a full English breakfast – This is usually a morning meal, often offered in hotels and guest houses. The essential ingredients are bacon and eggs, accompanied by a selection of sausages, tomatoes, fried bread or fried potato, mushrooms and baked beans. Some cafés offer an 'all day breakfast' at any time.

© Cambridge University Press 2010   PHOTOCOPIABLE

Follow-up

As a follow-up activity, invite the learners to undertake fieldwork on restaurants in their own community. Which ones are distinguished by a national cuisine? Using the worksheet in Box 11.2e, the learners, in pairs or small groups, explore the range of food cultures in their community. They should identify restaurants in the community that specialise in a particular kind of food, e.g. American, Argentinian, Chinese, Creole, French, Greek, Italian, Japanese, Mexican, Middle Eastern, Mongolian, Thai, Turkish, etc. Learners should then visit one of the restaurants even if only to look at the menu in the window.

In the next lesson, learners compare the restaurants they have visited. What kind of restaurant was most expensive? If the learners are participating in an online intercultural exchange, they can write a few paragraphs describing the restaurant and then share their findings with their e-partners.

Box 11.2e: Regional and ethnic cuisine

Worksheet: Food cultures in the community

- Name of restaurant:
- Briefly describe the restaurant (furnishings, decor, etc.):
- Type of food served:
- Typical dish (and price):
- Chef's 'specials' (and prices):
- Are any 'local' dishes offered? If so, what is a typical 'local' dish?
- Is there any entertainment offered (e.g. music/dancing)? If so, describe it.
- Are any of the dishes unfamiliar to you? If so, choose one and find out what the ingredients are and how it is prepared.
- Do you think the restaurant is expensive? How much will an average meal cost?

© Cambridge University Press 2010   PHOTOCOPIABLE

11.3 International food

Outline	Learners reflect on how chefs for airline companies arrange their menus so that they will be acceptable to as many international passengers as possible.
Focus	Describing food; making recommendations.
Level	Intermediate and above
Time	40 minutes plus
Preparation	Learners need copies of the questions in Box 11.3a and copies of the reading text in Box 11.3b.

Procedure

1   Ask the learners how many of them have flown in an aeroplane. Follow up by asking those who have flown to describe and evaluate the airline food they were served. Was it attractively presented, tasty, nourishing?

2   Invite the learners to consider the challenges facing airline catering
    managers and chefs – how do they produce a menu that will appeal to
    the many different people who travel on international flights? Then
    distribute the questions in Box 11.3a. Put learners in pairs and explain
    that they are going to be a catering manager and head chef of a major
    airline. Tell them they have to think about the kind of food they will
    serve on international flights, and ask them to discuss the challenges
    and decisions in the box. When the pairs have finished discussing their
    answers to these questions, select two or three pairs to report their
    decisions to the class.

Box 11.3a: International food

Questions: Devising a menu for international flights

- What special requests will some passengers have?
- What kind of ingredients will you use and what will you avoid?
- Will you bake, boil, grill or microwave the food?
- What will the food look like?
- Will you match the food to the destination of the flight (e.g. will you serve *sushi* on flights to Japan)?
- Will you serve different food to economy and first-class passengers?

© Cambridge University Press 2010   PHOTOCOPIABLE

---

3   Next, tell the learners that they are going to read a text about the
    challenge of finding acceptable food for international airline passengers.
    The learners, in their pairs, should compare their own discussions
    and decisions in step 2 with the suggested solutions offered in the text.
    Distribute the text in Box 11.3b.

4   After the learners have discussed the suggested solutions in the text,
    invite the pairs of learners to devise their own menu for an international
    flight, e.g. from Sydney to Seoul. Select a few pairs to explain their
    choices to the class. Which menu do the other learners prefer, and
    why? Learners can visit www.airlinemeals.net, a website devoted to airline
    food, and look at some of the photographs posted there. They can
    report back to class on photographs of meals they found attractive, and
    unattractive.

Box 11.3b: International food

Reading text: A guide to airline cuisine

Airline chefs have a difficult job – how do you serve food that will be acceptable, tasty, and interesting to many different passengers from many different countries? Here are some tips for preparing menus for passengers in economy class:

- Choose familiar recipes for meat, fish and vegetables, and food like rice or potatoes to go with them. Avoid 'exotic' food like octopus.
- Avoid dishes with a strong taste. If you are going to choose a curry, don't make it too spicy!
- Choose familiar ways of cooking the dish. For example, do not boil your meat; roast it or casserole it instead.
- The appearance of your food is very important, probably more important than its taste! The main job of an airline menu is to entertain the passengers, so make your food look pretty.
- You can add a little something to remind your passengers of their destination, e.g. a little mint with the fruit salad if you are going to the Middle East. But make sure it does not upset any passengers!
- If a dish has a religious name, call it something non-religious. For example, you can call 'Christmas cake', 'Festival cake'.

Adapted from Jeremy MacClancy's *Consuming Culture* (London: Chapmans, 1992), p. 207.

From *Intercultural Language Activities*
© Cambridge University Press 2010   PHOTOCOPIABLE

11.4 Food idioms: using the British National Corpus

Outline Learners explore the freely available British National Corpus (BNC) online to look at food idioms. This online corpus, made available by Mark Davies of Brigham Young University, contains 100 million words of contemporary spoken and written British English.

Focus Learners explore set phrases and idioms related to food – and they report back on issues such as the contexts in which they are used, and their frequency of usage.

Level Intermediate and above

Time 30 minutes in the first lesson and if required, 20 minutes in a follow-up lesson

Preparation You need a computer, Internet access and a projector. Learners also need access to a computer and the Internet to explore the free BNC corpus at http://corpus.byu.edu/bnc/ This activity could be spread over two lessons and for homework learners could work in pairs to explore the BNC.

Procedure

1   Explain that learners will explore an online corpus of current British
    English to identify how various food idioms are actually used in
    contemporary speech and writing. Explain that many people use idioms
    that refer to food, and some of these phrases can be quite strange. One
    example is 'kettle of fish'. Explain that a fish kettle is literally a long, thin
    pan used to poach fish. Then show the learners the following example
    (adapted from one example in the British National Corpus) and ask them
    to guess what 'kettle of fish' might mean in context:

> *Two envelopes lay on the unpolished table top. Cornelius sat down
> and regarded the envelopes with suspicion. One envelope looked safe
> enough. Cornelius recognised the untidy handwriting. He tucked
> this, unopened, into a dressing gown pocket. Two weeks' holiday
> money, he thought. The other envelope, however, was a different
> <u>kettle of fish</u>. This one was big and smart and official looking.*

[Adapted from Rankin, Robert, *The Book of Ultimate Truths.* (1993) London:
Doubleday, pp. 43–4]

   Ask the learners to guess the meaning of the phrase in context, i.e.
   'something very different indeed'.

2   Present the results from BNC searches on the phrase *kettle of fish*. The
    results are shown by following the search procedure below:
    • Log onto http://corpus.byu.edu/bnc/ and enter the corpus.
    • In the 'Display' section, click on the option to show 'Chart'.
    • In the 'Word(s)' box, type *kettle of fish* and click on 'Search'. The
      display in Figure 1 on p. 209 should be seen.

    As the display shows, the expression occurs 38 times, most commonly
    in speech and fictional prose. It is very uncommon in academic texts.
    Ask learners to make up a new context in which the idiom is used
    appropriately. An example would be: '*Now that Katie has taken over as
    director, things will change a lot. She's a completely different kettle of fish
    from Jim!*'

3   Tell the learners that they can do a slightly different search to find out
    more about the uses of the phrase *kettle of fish*.
    • Go back to the 'Search' page.
    • This time, in the 'Display' section, click on 'List'.
    • In the 'Word(s)' box, type *[aj*] kettle of fish*. (Note that in
      other corpora, like the *TIME* corpus, the symbol for 'adjective'
      is [j*].)

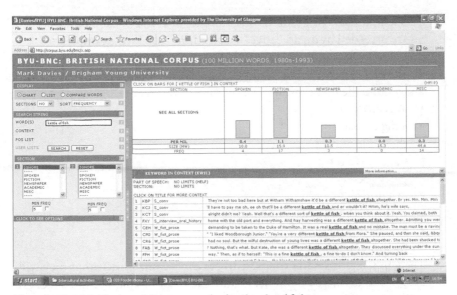

Figure 1: British National Corpus results for 'kettle of fish'

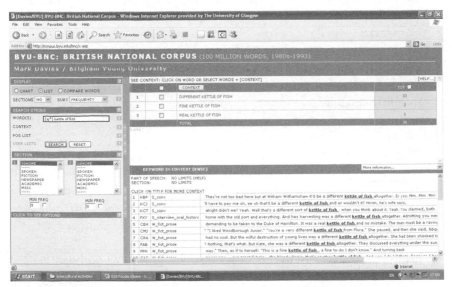

Figure 2: British National Corpus results for 'adjective + kettle of fish'

This search will list the occurrences of *kettle of fish* preceded by an adjective. The most frequent are listed first. This can be seen in Figure 2.

This search shows that, of the 38 examples of *kettle of fish* in the BNC, 36 are preceded by an adjective, usually *different*. Two examples are preceded by *fine* and one is preceded by the intensifier *real*.

4   Together, brainstorm other idioms that involve food. Check learners understand the literal meaning. Some possibilities are:
* as cool as a cucumber
* a big cheese
* the apple of his/her/my eye
* finger(s) in the pie
* pie in the sky
* in a nutshell
* with a pinch of salt
* a piece of cake
* not my cup of tea

5   Then, in pairs or small groups, learners choose one phrase that they will explore using the BNC online. Ensure each pair or small group chooses a different idiom. The learners might try guessing the frequency in advance – how many times would they expect the phrase to be used in 100 million words of English? Would they expect the idiom to be spoken or written?

6   After they have explored the BNC online for their idiom, get the pairs or groups to report their findings back to the class, discussing the literal and the idiomatic meanings of these phrases. Are there equivalent idioms in their first language?

Variations

1   Obviously, a large online corpus such as the BNC can be used to explore other idioms that have some feature in common, like idioms involving items of clothing, for example, *bright as a button, the cat's pyjamas, bee in your bonnet, heart on his/her/my/your sleeve, lose your shirt, pull up your socks,* etc. Get learners to repeat the activity using another such group of idioms.

2   Instead of focusing on the BNC, get different groups to explore different corpora to see if the results differ. A brief list of suggestions is given in the *Further reading and resources* section on p. 257.

11.5 Shopping lists

Outline	Learners compare what is and isn't on their regular shopping lists. This activity works particularly well in a multicultural classroom.
Focus	Food vocabulary; comparison across different food cultures.
Level	Elementary
Time	20 minutes plus
Preparation	Prepare a shopping list, or bring a bag of food from different ethnic cultures, e.g. pasta, curry, tacos, into class. Some of the food should be in packets, tins, jars or bottles.

Procedure

1   Tell the learners that they are going to look at foods in different cultures. Hold up the shopping list or the unopened bag of groceries, and ask the learners to guess what is on the list, or in the bag, e.g.

Have you got any . . . on your list / in the bag?

You answer either *yes* or *no*, and write any useful vocabulary on the board or project it onscreen in the form of a shopping list.

2   Introduce the items on your list or in the bag, writing on the board or projecting onscreen any items that the learners have not guessed, e.g.

a packet of	*tacos*	*a jar of*	*curry sauce*
	pasta		*sun-dried tomatoes*
	biscuits		*honey*
a tin of	*tuna*	*a bottle of*	*mineral water*
	soup		*wine*

3   Ask the learners to write a shopping list of eight things that they or their parents usually buy when they shop for food. While the learners are writing their list, circulate and help with necessary vocabulary.

4   Organise the learners into pairs and ask them to guess what is on their partner's list. Again, they can ask: *Have you got any . . . on your list?*

5   Then ask learners to look at their lists with their partners, and put an asterisk (*) beside anything that is *essential*, e.g. is ice cream or rice an 'essential' buy?

6   If the learners are participating in an online intercultural exchange, they can find out what kind of food their e-partners usually buy. Model a discussion opener, e.g.

Hi! I would like to know more about the food that you usually eat. When I go shopping, I buy . . . For me, . . . is essential! What do you buy when you go to the shops? What is essential, in your opinion? I look forward to hearing from you!

11.6 Supermarket psychology

Outline	Learners reflect upon how and why supermarkets are organised as they are.
Focus	Describing the form and function of physical space in a commercial context.
Level	Intermediate and above
Time	30 minutes in the first lesson and 30 minutes plus across one or more follow-up lessons
Preparation	Learners need copies of the worksheet in Box 11.6a, the reading text in Box 11.6b and the observation schedule in Box 11.6c. This activity should be spread over two lessons and includes learners visiting a local supermarket in their own time.

Procedure

1 Explain that this activity invites the learners to reflect on the organisation of a public space – a supermarket. Discuss if there are different kinds of supermarkets in the learners' home country and what they sell.

2 Distribute the worksheet in Box 11.6a, to learners. Put them in pairs and tell them that they have the job of designing a supermarket and deciding where to place the products. To do this they need to consider the questions in the worksheet. When they have finished, nominate several pairs to report their decisions to the class. The other learners say if they agree or disagree with the pairs who have been nominated.

3 Next, hand out the reading text in Box 11.6b. After the class has read it, get them to discuss whether or not they agree with the rules. The learners should compare their own rules, from step 2, with those given in Box 11.6b.

4 After class, learners visit a local supermarket in pairs. While they are there, they complete the observation schedule in Box 11.6c and see how closely the supermarket follows the ten rules in the reading text.

5 In a following lesson, the learners present their descriptions of a local supermarket, and explain to the class if it does or does not follow the ten rules.

6 If learners are taking part in an online intercultural exchange, after they have presented their report to the class, get them to write a few paragraphs about the local supermarket and share it with their e-partners.

Follow-up

This activity can be adapted to encourage learners to look at other kinds of retailer, for example a bookshop, electrical store, pharmacy or a large department store and report back to class on the following topics:

- Are products piled high or is there a lot of space?
- Is the decoration elaborate or simple?
- How are the products grouped in the retail space? How does the shopper navigate the products?
- Is customer service available? Are the assistants friendly, knowledgeable, insistent?
- How does the customer pay for the products?
- Does the shop contain a seating area, café or restaurant?
- Is the shopping experience designed to be friendly, relaxed and a pleasant experience – or is it simply a chore?

Box 11.6a: Supermarket psychology

Worksheet: Supermarket design

1) You can redecorate your supermarket. What colour do you choose, and why?

2) Where in your supermarket do you put the flowers, vegetables and fruit?

3) Where do you put food that people buy regularly, like tea, coffee, bread, etc.?

4) Do you put items with a low profit margin (e.g. low-cost, everyday groceries, such as tinned vegetables) in narrow or wide aisles?

5) Do you put items with a high profit margin (e.g. expensive electrical goods, such as plasma screen TVs) in narrow or wide aisles?

6) At what height do you place items that you really want to sell?

7) Where do you put items that are near their sell-by date, or that are slightly damaged (e.g. tins that are dented)?

8) Where do you put confectionery, like sweets?

9) Where do you put magazines?

10) What can you do to make your supermarket *really* attractive to shoppers?

© Cambridge University Press 2010   PHOTOCOPIABLE

Box 11.6b: Supermarket psychology

Reading text: Ten rules for supermarket designers

1) Paint the supermarket green. It is restful on the eye, and suggests freshness, healthy living and environmental concern.

2) Place fruit, vegetables, flowers and houseplants immediately after the entrance. That way you create an impression of freshness, healthy living, and natural growth, while masking the fact that most of the food in the supermarket is frozen, tinned or preserved.

3) Hide basic items that people buy regularly (like tea, coffee, bread, etc.) at the back of the supermarket so that people have to pass through aisles stacked high with other tempting items before they find them.

4) Put items with a low profit margin in uncomfortable, narrow aisles so that more people pass through quickly, without stopping.

5) Put items with a high profit margin (like electrical goods) in nice, wide aisles where people are more inclined to linger . . . and buy.

6) Put items that you really want to sell at eye level, where people can see them easily. You can even charge suppliers more if you promise to put their products at eye level. Remember: 'eye level is buy level'. Another good place is at the end of an aisle – the first place shoppers see when they turn a corner.

7) Put items that are near their sell-by date, or slightly damaged, in dump bins at the end of an aisle. Again, they are sure to attract attention there, especially from bargain hunters!

8) Put confectionery at the checkout till, at the eye level of young children.

9) Put magazines at the checkout till, at the eye level of adults.

10) Keep your store clean and tidy. Keep its shelves stocked full so that it gives the impression of abundance. If you do this well, the supermarket can even become an unofficial meeting place for unattached males and females. Is it every tired female shopper's dream to have a tall, dark stranger push his trolley next to hers and say, 'Excuse me, but do you know what the difference is between cider vinegar and balsamic vinegar?'

Adapted from Jeremy MacClancy's *Consuming Culture* (London: Chapmans, 1992), pp 215–16.

Box 11.6c: Supermarket psychology

Observation schedule: Supermarket observation

Name of supermarket: Date and time of visit:
Opening hours of supermarket:

What colour is the supermarket painted?

Where are the flowers, fruit and vegetables situated?

What kind of products are positioned furthest from the entrance?

What kind of products are placed in narrow aisles? In wide aisles?

What kind of products are placed at eye level?

Where are damaged items or items near their sell-by date placed?

What can you find at the checkout tills?

Spend some time observing the customers and their behaviour. Describe the shoppers and discuss their interactions (if any).

12 Politics

Much of our everyday lives is influenced by the people who govern us. Political systems vary from country to country and culture to culture. In some countries the adult population elects politicians to make decisions on its behalf. In others, elite groups make decisions on behalf of the majority. In most countries, however, those who govern try to persuade the general public that they have its best interests at heart, and that their policies will make everyone wealthier, happier and more secure. The following activities explore general ways in which political groups attempt to communicate with the population. The first activity, *Political symbols* (12.1) asks learners to reflect on symbols used internationally to signify particular types of political belief or activism, such as anarchism, communism, monarchism and environmentalism, before explaining the beliefs conveyed by the symbols of more local political groups. *Politicians' body language* (12.2) focuses on the body language adopted by politicians, who function here as an example of public speakers who need to inspire confidence in their authority and ability. Finally, *Political debate* (12.3) returns to the format of a formal debate, and explores the issue of who should have the right to vote. While the activities suggested here can stand alone, there are obvious opportunities to link them to other courses the learners might be taking in politics, history, citizenship, the social sciences or modern studies.

Warning: politics and religion can be sensitive topics for open discussion, and may not be suitable for all learners, teachers or teaching situations. Please be aware of how comfortable learners, school authorities and parents are with the classroom discussion of these issues.

12.1 Political symbols

Outline	Learners explore the symbolism used by political groups to identify themselves and to communicate their core values and beliefs.
Focus	Describing symbols, logos and slogans.
Level	Intermediate and above
Time	30 minutes in the first lesson and 20 minutes in one or more follow-up lessons
Preparation	Learners may need to have access to the Internet for information on political symbols from different countries. They will also need copies of the worksheet in Box 12.1a. This activity may need to be spread over two lessons and includes homework.

Procedure

1   As a warm-up, ask the class to match the political symbols with the names of the political beliefs in Box 12.1a.

Box 12.1a: Political symbols

Worksheet: Matching political symbols and beliefs

Symbol   *Political belief*

a)   1) environmentalism

b)   2) communism

c)   3) monarchism

d)   4) social democracy

e)   5) anarchism

© Cambridge University Press 2010   PHOTOCOPIABLE

Answers:

(a)–(5) Anarchism, which, loosely, believes that formal government is a form of oppression and argues that it should be abolished.

(b)–(2) Communism, which believes that workers (e.g. factory workers and farmers) should have common possession and control of the resources they produce. Ideally, all the people in the community should contribute according to their abilities and receive according to their needs.

(c)–(1) *Environmentalism*, which believes that political policies should focus on the conservation and maintenance of natural resources. Some environmental, or green, parties use the sunflower as a symbol; others use an image of the earth taken from space.

(d)–(3) *Monarchism*, which believes in government by hereditary kings and queens.

(e)–(4) *Social democracy*, which believes in a welfare state that combines some socialist and capitalist policies, e.g. the regulation of a market economy in order to influence unemployment rates.

2   Ask the learners, either during the lesson or for homework, to identify (or research) the symbols used by the main political parties in their country, or if they are in a monocultural class, learners can research another country. If possible, ensure that learners choose different countries so they can compare the political symbols later. Particular questions they can ask are:

   • What symbols do the political parties use, e.g. a flower, a torch, a bird, an animal, a crown, etc? What does each emblem mean?
   • What colours do they use, e.g. red, blue, yellow, orange, green? What meanings are associated with the colours?
   • What slogans do they use? If the slogans are not in English, how are they translated?

3   In a following lesson, after learners have completed their research, they feed back their findings to the class. As a class they then compare the symbols. Learners can then be put into groups and they can design posters to display in class, showing the symbols used by different parties in different countries. If the learners are participating in an online intercultural exchange, the learners then write a report on the political party they researched and post it to their e-partners.

Follow-up

After researching some symbols used by actual political parties, the learners, in groups, devise their own political party. Each group should consider:

• the main policies their party will promote
• what symbol they will use, and explain why they have adopted it
• what colour they will use, and explain what they associate it with
• a slogan, in English

They then design a poster and present it to the rest of the class.

Warning: politics and religion can be sensitive topics for open discussion.

12.2 Politicians' body language

Outline	Learners consider the kind of body language that is used by politicians and other people in authority, to encourage listeners to have confidence in them.
Focus	Language of persuasion and body language.
Level	Intermediate and above
Time	40 minutes plus
Preparation	You should record interviews, speeches or party political broadcasts featuring different politicians, ideally from different countries. They do not need to be speaking in English. Alternatively, websites such as www.youtube.com can be searched for clips of political speeches and interviews. Learners will need copies of the checklist in Box 12.2a and the observation schedule in Box 12.2b.

Procedure

1 Explain that the class will consider how people in authority, like politicians, use their body language to win the trust of listeners. To warm up, show the class clips of accomplished politicians, giving an interview or speaking to a large audience, but with the volume turned down. Ask the learners to complete the checklist in Box 12.2a. They should make a note of how many times the politician does each action.

Box 12.2a: Politicians' body language

Checklist: Body language

smiles
nods
leans forward
leans backward
points or wags a finger
folds his or her arms
opens his or her arms
raises one or both arms
punches the air
shrugs his or her shoulders

© Cambridge University Press 2010   PHOTOCOPIABLE

---

2   Organise the class in pairs. The learners compare their answers and discuss *why* they think the politicians use the body language they do. What overall impression do the politicians give? After a period of discussion in pairs, you can discuss some possible answers with the class, e.g.
    • Politicians lean forward to indicate a willingness to cooperate with an interviewer.
    • Politicians smile frequently to reassure the audience.
    • In interviews, politicians often use lots of eye contact to suggest personal authority, and also to control the discussion.
    • In interviews and discussions, politicians like to have the last word, because this is the message that is often remembered.
    • At rallies, politicians often use exaggerated gestures like chopping the hand, shrugging, punching the air, raising arms to the skies and pointing forcefully to emphasise a point.
    • Keeping your arms open suggests a more open personality; politicians avoid folding their arms, which suggests reserve and distance.
    • At rallies, politicians like to pause for applause, but a good speaker often starts talking just before the applause dies down again.

3   Tell the learners that they are going to watch one more clip of a politician speaking, this time with the volume turned up, and that they are going to fill in an observation schedule in Box 12.2b. Check the learners' understanding of the observation schedule by reciting the following extract from a speech two or three times, and changing your gestures accordingly.
    The first time, look directly at the learners and use exaggerated gestures, e.g.
    • raise your right arm high on 'So understand this'
    • raise your right index finger and wave it from side to side when you say 'this election is not between'
    • then bring your right fist down on your left palm on each key word 'regions', religions', 'genders', 'rich', 'poor', 'young' and 'old'
    • raise your hand high and chop the air when you say the key words 'past' and 'future'
    Then, the second time you read the extract, look up at the ceiling or down at the ground, and keep your gestures small, e.g.
    • simply shrug your shoulders slightly when you say 'So understand this'
    • relax your wrists and wave your right hand limply from side to side when you say 'this election is not between'
    • keep your wrists relaxed and wave both hands about in no particular

direction when you say the key words 'regions', 'religions', 'genders', 'rich', 'poor', 'young' and 'old'
* put your hands in your pockets or at your side when you say 'past' and 'future'

So understand this. The choice in this election is not between regions or religions or genders. It's not about rich versus poor, young versus old. And it is not about black versus white. This election is about the past versus the future.

[Adapted from an election speech given by Barack Obama in South Carolina, in 2008 (see http://www.cnn.com/2008/POLITICS/01/26/obama.transcript/index.html)]

After you have finished reading the extract, ask the learners to check each other's observation schedules and then ask them what they have observed. Once you are confident that the learners understand the observation schedule, play the video clip, or you can show the speech by Barack Obama on which this extract is based, and observe his body language using the observation schedule.

4   In pairs, the learners compare their results. How effective did they find the politician's body language? Note that views may vary!

Show again the clips of politicians from step 1 but this time with the volume up and ask learners to fill in the observation schedule for them. Alternatively, if you have shown clips of politicians from different countries, do learners notice any difference in the body language used?

Box 12.2b: Politicians' body language

Observation schedule: Political body language

Name of politician:
Use of eye contact: too much / the right amount / too little
Posture: upright / leaning forward / leaning backward
Gestures: exaggerated / forceful / limp
Smiles: too many / the right amount / too few
Pauses: at the right places / at the wrong places

© Cambridge University Press 2010   PHOTOCOPIABLE

Follow-up for advanced learners

1 Tell the learners that they are going to listen to a politician speaking, and then rehearse appropriate body language. Ask them to turn away from the screen, and listen to a politician giving a speech. They must not watch the clip at this point. Play the speech again, and this time, the learners should mime the speech, using appropriate body language. Then they can turn towards the screen and compare their own body language with that of the politician.

2 Next, ask the learners to prepare a short, two-minute, political speech of their own. Explain that the speech should do four things:

   a) Introduce a new political policy. You might like to brainstorm a few possibilities with the class at this point, e.g. introduce a new policy for recycling household waste; introduce a new national holiday; abolish school examinations, etc.

   b) Say why the policy is important. Some useful expressions for this phase are:
      This policy is crucial/vital/essential/necessary because . . .
      If we do not act now, then . . .
      Brainstorm with the learners possible ways of completing these sentences.

   c) Attack the policies of the political opponents as inadequate, e.g.
      Our opponents have failed to realise that . . .
      Our opponents continue to neglect . . .
      Brainstorm with the learners possible ways of completing these sentences.

   d) Encourage the audience to support the new policy, e.g.
      My friends, I urge you to join us in . . .
      Ladies and gentlemen, together we can . . .
      Brainstorm with the learners possible ways of completing these sentences.

3 The learners write a short speech and then rehearse their speeches in groups of three. The listeners in each group give the speakers, in turn, some advice to improve their performance, paying particular attention to gesture and body language.

4 Select some learners to perform their speech in front of the class. The class rates the learners, if appropriate, using the observation schedule in Box 12.2b and gives each of the speakers feedback on his or her performance.

12.3 Political debate

Outline	Learners research and debate a political issue. While they may well hold firm beliefs, for or against the issue being debated, they are required to improve their persuasive skills by researching and understanding the values held by those who disagree.
Focus	The language and conventions of formal debate.
Level	Upper-intermediate and above
Time	30 minutes in the first lesson; 20 minutes preparation in the second lesson; and 30 minutes plus in the third lesson
Preparation	For their research, learners need access to information on a classic political issue such as universal suffrage, or some relevant contemporary issue that concerns them, or that is relevant to the culture being studied. They might find this on the Internet, from e-partners, or from local library and leisure resources. This activity should be spread over a few lessons, with the debate taking place in the third lesson. Reading material on women's suffrage is supplied in Box 12.3a; however, you may wish to research and find your own reading material for step 2. Learners also need copies of the worksheet in Box 12.3b and the conventions of debate in Box 12.3c on the CD-ROM or on p. 196 (Box 10.6b).

Procedure

1 Explain that the class is going to debate a political topic. Ask learners about political issues that could be debated (see suggestions below), then ask them to choose one and elicit what they know about the topic.
   • Universal suffrage (the right to vote regardless of gender, race, religion, etc.)
   • The abolition of slavery (when did this occur in different countries?)
   • A common currency for the world
2 Next, focus on one particular example of a historical political issue, such as women's suffrage (votes for women). At this point, hand out the reading text in Box 12.3a, get learners to read this and summarise the information for practice.
3 Tell learners to now research the topic themselves, either during the rest of the lesson, or for homework. Before they do this, give advice on sources, e.g. library books, the Internet, e-partners. Suggested websites

where the learners can find supplementary information on women's suffrage are:

> http://en.wikipedia.org/ See 'Women's suffrage in the United Kingdom'
> http://www.bl.uk/learning/histcitizen/21cc/struggle/struggle.html This British Library website has a number of useful source documents.
> http://womenshistory.about.com/lr/women_s_suffrage/250078/2/

4 After learners have completed their own research, put them into groups and instruct them to prepare for a parliamentary debate on this or a similar motion. The learners can recreate a debate from a historical period, such as Britain in the 1920s, and argue that, *'This house supports the right of women to vote'*. Alternatively, the class might choose to apply their reading and research to a slightly different topic, such as *'This house supports the right of children above the age of 14 to vote'*. The latter option is taken on p. 226.

5 Divide the class equally, and tell the learners in one group that they must prepare arguments in favour of the motion, and the learners in the other group that they must prepare to argue against the motion. Hand out copies of the worksheet in Box 12.3b to learners. Remind the class that the members of the groups need not necessarily believe the case that they are debating. The learners may prepare their argument in class and complete it after class.

6 Explain, if necessary, the conventions of a debate by going through Box 12.3c on the CD-ROM (or on p. 196 in Box 10.6b) with learners. Explain that in the next lesson, each group will choose two speakers and advise them on how to make a strong argument for or against the proposition. Then the speakers will make their case, and the class will judge which speakers were the most effective persuaders.

7 In the next lesson, after the groups have finalised their arguments, each group should advise its speakers, who then debate the proposition. The class then votes whether it accepts or rejects the motion based on the performance of the speakers.

8 Finally, with the learners, reflect on the issues that arose from the debate.
Warning: politics and religion can be sensitive topics for open discussion.

Box 12.3a: Political debate

Reading text: Women's suffrage

The debate about women's suffrage in Britain dates from 1832, when women were, for the first time, explicitly excluded from voting by law. The reasons for excluding women from voting were various. Some people (including many women) felt that adult females were biologically and psychologically incapable of taking part in public affairs, and that their sphere of influence should be restricted to the home and family. Others feared the political power of women, especially at a time when women voters might outnumber male voters. Others simply feared change and the political instability that it might cause.

Even so, the demand for 'votes for women' increased towards the end of the 19th century, and several national movements were established to promote women's rights. Some women became increasingly militant in their demands and 'suffragettes' became associated with acts of violence and subversion – they broke windows, chained themselves to railings, burned down houses and vandalised works of art. In one famous incident, Emily Davison died attempting to disrupt the Epsom Derby (a famous horse-racing event) in 1913. She was killed by throwing herself under the King's horse.

The 1914–1918 war changed social attitudes towards women's social roles, and in 1918 an Act of Parliament gave women the right to vote, but only if they were over 30 years of age. Especially after the war, there was a fear that women might outnumber men and so women between the ages of 21 and 30 were still denied the right to vote. Only in 1928 did British women gain the right to vote on equal terms with men.

PHOTOCOPIABLE

Box 12.3b: Political debate

Worksheet: Preparing the debate

You are going to prepare an argument in favour of or against the motion that

'This house supports the right of children above the age of 14 to vote.'

Group A (for the motion): You must look for evidence in support of the argument that older children should be entitled to vote. To do this effectively, you need to consider the following questions:

- Why have older children been denied the vote?
- In whose interest is it to exclude older children from voting?
- Why might older children want the right to vote?
- Why might some older children not wish to have the right to vote?
- Can you use some of the arguments that were used in favour of women's suffrage to help you to argue the case for older children's right to vote?

You are going to prepare an argument in favour of or against the motion that

'This house supports the right of children above the age of 14 to vote.'

Group B (against the motion): You must look for evidence against the argument that older children should be entitled to vote. You might consider the following questions:

- Why have older children been denied the vote?
- In whose interest is it to exclude older children from voting?
- Why might older children want the right to vote?
- Why might some older children not wish to have the right to vote?
- Can you use some of the arguments that were used against women's suffrage to help you to argue the case against older children's right to vote?

13   Religion

Since intercultural language education engages explicitly with behaviour, values and beliefs, it often addresses a number of potentially controversial issues; topics that are often avoided in the language classroom. Given the nature of many people's strong and sincere commitment to religious beliefs that many others do not share, religion is one topic that teachers still may not wish to raise in the classroom. In addition, the direct and possibly critical engagement with religious authority might be less acceptable in some educational contexts than others. In such circumstances the teacher would be well advised to obtain written permission from his or her educational superiors before attempting this kind of activity.

Nevertheless, when a class is positively disposed to the discussion of religious ideas, and when the educational context is liberal enough to encourage such discussion, religion is clearly a rich resource for intercultural exploration. The Council of Europe's *Common European Framework* (2001: 102–103) refers to the sociocultural knowledge that learners might bring to the classroom. The authors note that some aspect of this knowledge 'is likely to lie outside the learner's previous experience and may well be distorted by stereotypes' (2001: 102). Religion is mentioned in this context, in passing, under values, beliefs, attitudes and ritual behaviour such as 'religious observances and rites; birth, marriage and death; audience and spectator behaviour at public performances and ceremonies' (2001: 103). Given the potential for sensitivity, the activities suggested here focus on non-judgemental, comparative observation and description of religious practices and beliefs, and you are encouraged to promote a non-evaluative, empathic response to different types of religious belief and ritual. In this spirit, *Religions: cultural associations* (13.1) gets learners to compare key features of several global and more localised religious beliefs; *Being accepted into a religion* (13.2) explores the ceremonies by which believers are welcomed into particular beliefs; and *Religious services* (13.3) encourages learners to do fieldwork that involves observing and describing a religious ceremony. These activities are intended to foster a sense of exploration and discovery. However, given that the comparison and discussion of religious beliefs can lead to disagreement which could be interpreted as criticism, sensitivity and care should obviously be taken when undertaking them.

Warning: politics and religion can be sensitive topics for open discussion, and may not be suitable for all learners, teachers or teaching situations. Please be aware of how comfortable learners, school authorities and parents are to the classroom discussion of these issues.

13.1 Religions: cultural associations

Outline	Learners research and describe key features of different kinds of religion, familiar and possibly unfamiliar. The main objective is to complete an 'association chart' that compares the key features across religious groupings.
Focus	The basic language of ritual and belief; generalisations and qualifications.
Level	Upper-intermediate and above
Time	20–30 minutes in the first lesson and 20 minutes in a follow-up lesson
Preparation	Learners will need copies of the table in Box 13.1a. This activity should be spread over two lessons and includes homework.

Procedure

1   Explain that this activity will compare key features of some religious beliefs, including major world religions such as Buddhism, Christianity, Islam and Judaism, as well as some less familiar beliefs such as the Bahá'í Faith, and Candomblé. You might stress that this activity will involve the objective comparison of characteristics of these beliefs – the learners should avoid positive or negative evaluations of them.

2   Using the table in Box 13.1a as a basis, brainstorm with the learners a set of key features of those religions with which they are familiar. For example, if the class is familiar with Catholic Christianity, Islam or Judaism, you might check the class's knowledge of the following:

- What is the name of the religion?
- Who are the main figures – the deity, or deities, and prophets?
- Is there a sacred text?
- Is there a special day of worship?
- Where do people worship?
- Can you describe any particular rituals that worshippers perform?
- What are the main religious festivals?
- How is the religious institution organised?

3 Provide copies of the table to learners, and invite them, in groups, to do some research amongst their fellow learners, their e-partners and/or on the Internet into the key features of the religions suggested. (Other religions may be substituted for those suggested in the table.) Ensure that each group of learners selects a different religion to research. A useful website for learners to search for information on is www.simplewikipedia. org

Box 13.1a: Religions: cultural associations

Table: Religious faiths

Key characteristics	Bahá'í Faith	Candomblé	Christianity	Islam	Judaism
Main religious figure(s)					
Some main divisions					
Sacred/key text(s)					
Day of worship					
Place of worship					
Typical rituals					
Symbol					
Main festivals					
Rites of passage					
Institutional structure					

4 In the following lesson, the learners, in their groups, report back to the class on their findings, each group focusing on a particular religious faith. The other learners should then complete the other columns in the table with the information they hear.

Suggested answers for Christianity:
Main religious figure(s): Jesus Christ, the Apostles, the Prophets
Some main divisions: Catholic, Protestant, Orthodox, Quaker, etc.
Sacred/key texts: the Bible (Old and New Testaments)
Day of worship: Sunday
Place of worship: church, cathedral, chapel
Typical rituals: communion (taking of bread and wine), prayer
Symbol: cross
Main festivals: Christmas, Easter, Saints' days
Rites of passage: baptism, confirmation, first communion, first
    confession, marriage, death
Institutional structure: varies – Catholicism has a centralised,
    hierarchical system of Pope, bishops, deacons and priests, while
    Protestantism has a less hierarchical system.

5 When the different groups have completed their presentations, invite them to think about the similarities and differences between the religions they have looked at.

   You may like to highlight to learners that religious beliefs and practices vary widely. Some devout Christians avoid meat on Fridays, but many do not; some Jewish men put on a skull-cap before eating, but many do not. Many Muslim countries discourage polygamy. Generalisations about social groups are therefore very difficult to sustain.

Warning: politics and religion can be sensitive topics for open discussion.

13.2 Being accepted into a religion

Outline	Learners explore the different ways in which members are accepted and welcomed into different religious faiths.
Focus	Describing activities – infant baptism, confirmation, first communion, Bar and Bat Mitzvah, etc.
Level	Upper-intermediate and above
Time	40 minutes in the first lesson and 20 minutes plus in or across follow-up lessons
Preparation	This activity works best when the class includes members of different religious faiths. The activity can be practised in class and then extended to e-partners, if the class is participating in an online intercultural exchange. This activity should be spread over two lessons and includes homework. To give learners practice in asking questions about a religious faith in step 3, be prepared to answer questions about your own or research a religious faith that is different from the dominant one among your learners. Learners will need copies of the reading text in Box 13.2a.

Procedure

1 Explain to the learners that different religions have different ways of accepting and welcoming members. This can happen soon after birth (e.g. some Christians baptise infants) but may have to be confirmed later (e.g. at a confirmation ceremony, or first communion). Some faiths have their ceremonies at a more advanced age, e.g. Bar and Bat Mitzvahs take place in Judaism when the boy or girl is around 13. Islam regards the child as having been born into the faith. Even so, the child's arrival is traditionally celebrated by whispering a testimony of faith into the new-born infant's ear. Later, the family and friends are often invited to a special meal at which lamb is served.

2 Explain that the learners are going to find out about the ceremonies and customs of various religious faiths, by interviewing people who belong to those faiths. They read the text in Box 13.2a and brainstorm the kinds of questions that they would like to ask somebody of a different faith, e.g.

- Does your religion have a special ceremony for new members?
- Who performs the ceremony?
- How old can the new member be?
- Where does the ceremony take place?
- Are any witnesses present?
- What words are said at the ceremony?

- Do people wear special clothes?
- What exactly happens during the ceremony?
- What happens after the ceremony?

Box 13.2a: Being accepted into a religion

Reading text: Hindu welcoming ceremony

Hindus have a 'coming-of-age' ceremony for Hindu boys, between the ages of about 8 and 15. This ceremony is called the Upanayana, or the 'ceremony of the threads'. It is performed by the family priest, usually in the home, where most Hindu ceremonies take place, in the presence of the family. The 'ceremony of the threads' signifies that the Hindu boy is ready to receive religious instruction from a guru. The priest reads from the Vedas, the Hindu sacred texts, and the boy shaves his head and wears three strands of thread, hung from his left shoulder and tied in a knot at his right waist. At the ceremony, the boy promises to obey his guru, and, afterwards, often, he has a ritual bath which signifies a 'second birth'.

© Cambridge University Press 2010   PHOTOCOPIABLE

---

3 If you are willing, and have a religious faith, the class can interview you. Alternatively, you could research a faith and answer questions about it. The class should note down and report back your answers to their questions.
4 If appropriate, the learners, in pairs, find an informant who belongs to a religious faith, preferably one whose customs they are unfamiliar with, and interview them for homework, using the questions they created in step 2. If the class is multicultural, different class members may approach each other, or they may approach e-partners. You could help the learners to contact religious representatives such as ministers, priests or imams in the community. Alternatively, learners can research ceremonies on the Internet.
5 Finally, the learners report back on their findings to the class in a later lesson, or they can write a descriptive account of their discoveries, which they can share with their e-partners.

Warning: politics and religion can be sensitive topics for open discussion.

13.3 Religious services

Outline	Learners explore different religious services. This activity either involves fieldwork or observation of recordings of religious ceremonies.
Focus	Describing activities that take place during a religious service.
Level	Intermediate and above
Time	20–30 minutes in the first lesson and 30 minutes plus in or across follow-up lessons
Preparation	This activity depends on learners being able to find friends who will take them to a religious service in a faith with which they are unfamiliar. If the learners are children, school and parental approval will need to be sought. Alternatively, ceremonies on film and video, for example, as found on www.youtube.com can be sources of information, though media representations should be approached with some caution since they will usually be edited and shortened. Learners will need copies of the observation schedule in Box 13.3a. This activity should be spread over two lessons and involves attending a religious service.

Procedure

1   Tell learners that different religions have different ways of celebrating their faith and that they are going to find out about the ceremonies and customs of a faith with which they are unfamiliar. They will then attend a religious service.

   Warning: learners should be aware that it is not always appropriate in some faiths for outsiders to attend the services and they should check if this is the case. See the Variation for an alternative option.

2   Discuss with the class what aspects of the service they should observe and describe. You can write a list of questions on the board to serve as a draft observation schedule. Questions might include:

   • What is the name of the faith?
   • Where and when did the ceremony take place?
   • How were the participants arranged?
   • What was the sequence of events?

   The learners use the questions on the board to make up their own observation schedule. Or, alternatively, learners can use the model observation schedule in Box 13.3a.

3   In order to attend a religious service, in a faith with which they are unfamiliar, learners will need a contact who is happy to take them. This

may be a friend, classmate, or you might arrange in advance for members of the class to visit a local mosque, temple, church or synagogue. After the ceremony, the learners complete the observation schedule.

4　In a following lesson, the learners then compare notes in groups, and finally they write up an account of their visit. If the class has e-partners, then the accounts can be used as the basis of comparison and discussion online.

Warning: politics and religion can be sensitive topics for open discussion.

Variation
Learners who are unable to visit a religious service might be able to view part of one on television or online, e.g. by visiting www.youtube.com and typing in keywords such as *candomblé, hindu service, mass, mosque, protestant service*, etc.

Box 13.3a: Religious services

Observation schedule: Observing a religious service

Religious faith:
Denomination/branch:
Place of visit:
Date and time of visit:
Brief description of building:
Is audio-visual technology used?
How is the place of worship organised?
- Speaker(s)
- Singer(s)
- Participants: males/females, adults/children?

How does the service proceed?
- Prayers
- Songs
- Dance
- Sermon/lecture
- Community news
- Readings from texts
- Eating/drinking?

Who participates in the events?
- Speaker(s)
- Participants (in full or in part)
- Singer(s)?

© Cambridge University Press 2010　　　　　　　　PHOTOCOPIABLE

Presenting an image

This set of activities turns to the ways that individuals in different cultures present an image of themselves to others. People send messages about themselves through their choice of clothing, scent (whether perfume, after-shave or deodorant) and make-up. The ways that these messages are constructed and understood naturally change from place to place, and from generation to generation. This chapter, then, encourages learners to treat clothing, scent and make-up as forms of communication. *Choosing a wardrobe* (14.1) introduces basic clothing vocabulary, and *A question of style* (14.2) addresses the general issue of 'decoding clothing' with learners exploring what clothes may say about someone, while *Exploring a fashion 'look'* (14.3) encourages learners to explore current fashion trends. The next two activities, *Smelling sweet* (14.4) and *Making up* (14.5), consider the ways scent and make-up, respectively, can be used in different cultures to create an impression. And, finally, *Living dolls* (14.6) takes a more critical look at the issue of body image across cultures, and the imposition of a particular version of 'beauty' on the global population.

14.1 Choosing a wardrobe

Outline	Learners are introduced to some of the basic language of clothes and accessories.
Focus	Language of physical description; clothing and accessories.
Level	Elementary
Time	30 minutes plus
Preparation	Bring to the lesson lots of photographs of different items of clothing and accessories that your learners might like. They could be cut out from magazines, mail-order catalogues, etc. There should be enough for each learner to choose two or three items they like and you can include some more unusual items.

Procedure

1 Tell the class that they are going to choose a wardrobe. On a table in the middle of the classroom, display the photographs of clothing you

collected. The learners gather around the table and ask you the name of any item that they do not already know, e.g.

> *What do you call that/those?*
> *It's a handbag . . . They're trousers . . . etc.*

2   Tell the learners to choose two or three items each that they like, and return to their own seats. You should also choose three items.

3   Show the class the three items you have chosen, using the following formula:

> *I chose . . . , . . . and . . . because . . .*

Your model should include some descriptive language, e.g.

> *I chose the black raincoat, the long, leather boots and the gorgeous handbag because I come from London and it rains a lot there.*

4   Organise the class into groups of three, and the learners practise saying similar things to each other, using their own chosen items of clothing.

5   Bring the class together again. Nominate several learners to talk about someone else in their group, e.g.

> *X chose . . . because . . .*

6   Ask the class to note down three favourite items of clothing or accessories from their wardrobe at home. Again, in groups of three they share their preferences, e.g.

> *My three favourite items of clothing are . . . , . . . and . . . because . . .*

7   If the class is participating in an online intercultural exchange, the learners can begin a discussion with their e-partners. Together, model a discussion opener, such as the following:

> *Hi! I was just wondering what your favourite clothes are? It's very rainy/sunny here, so I like to wear . . . What about you? I look forward to hearing from you!*

or

> *Hi! I'm Linda. I love shopping for clothes. I usually buy clothes from . . . Recently, I bought . . . , . . . and . . . Do you like shopping for clothes? What did you buy, recently? I'd really love to know!*

14.2 A question of style

Outline	Learners look critically at the clothes and accessories people choose to wear, and consider what their meanings might be.
Focus	Language of physical description; clothing and accessories.
Level	Intermediate and above
Time	40 minutes plus
Preparation	Bring photographs of people wearing different types of clothing to class. These can be from advertisements, from a range of magazines for women and men, or from mail-order catalogues. The photographs should include males and females of different ages, backgrounds and cultures. If possible, include ethnic clothing like saris, kilts, turbans, etc. Learners need copies of the questionnaire in Box 14.2a.

Procedure

1 As a warm-up, show the class some of the photographs that you have brought to class, and ask the learners to describe the clothes that the people are wearing.

2 Ask the class what our choice of clothing can tell other people about us. Write a list on the board or project one onscreen, e.g.
   • our gender
   • our age
   • whether we are single or married
   • our nationality
   • our ethnicity
   • our religious beliefs, affiliation or upbringing
   • our occupation
   • our social class, or status
   • our wealth
   • our values or outlook on life
   • our 'tribe', i.e. the group of people we like to belong to.

3 Choose an option from the list below, e.g. 'a male politician or business executive', and with the class describe appropriate clothing, e.g. dark, conservative business suit, white shirt, blue or red tie, dark socks and black, highly polished shoes. Then organise the class into pairs, and ask each pair to describe appropriate clothing for particular people, e.g.
   • a male politician or business executive
   • a female politician or business executive
   • an 18-year-old male going out for the night

- an 18-year-old female going out for the night
- a seven-year-old male or female child

To get the pairs started, you can distribute some more of the photographs that you brought in.

4 Tell the learners that they are going to look in more detail at their own taste in clothes. To do this, the learners are going to interview each other using the questionnaire in Box 14.2a. Distribute a copy of the questionnaire to each learner, and give them time to read it and ask questions about the meaning of anything they do not understand. Then, as a rehearsal, nominate learners to ask you questions from the questionnaire.

Box 14.2a: A question of style

Questionnaire: Buying and describing clothes

How old are you?   10–14   15–19   20–29   30–39   40–49
                   50–59   60+

Gender?   M/F

How often do you shop for clothes:
Once a week?
Once a month?
Two or three times a year?
Less often?

How do you decide which clothes to buy?
I decide myself.
Someone else helps me to decide (explain who).
I am influenced by the media (explain how).

Describe the clothes you typically wear to work or school.

Describe the clothes you would wear for a night out with friends.

Describe your favourite item of clothing.

How important are the following considerations when you buy clothes?
Comfort   (not important) 1   2   3   4   5 (very important)
Modesty   (not important) 1   2   3   4   5 (very important)
Elegance   (not important) 1   2   3   4   5 (very important)

Do you wear branded clothing, e.g. Nike, Prada, etc.? If so, which brands do you like?

Do you wear jewellery? If so, describe the kind of jewellery you wear.

© Cambridge University Press 2010   PHOTOCOPIABLE

---

5   Next, divide the class into small groups, and get the learners to ask each other the questions.

6   When the groups have finished, lead a discussion of the findings, e.g.
   • Do any learners wear clothes that signify membership of a 'tribe', e.g. goths, hippies, business people, religious groups? What kind of clothes indicate tribal membership?
   • Do the learners have a 'public image' (for work or school) and a 'private image' (for home or leisure activities)?
   • Do the learners feel in control of their own image? Or do they feel they have to conform to others' expectations?
   • Do the learners think it is important to be 'fashionable'? Why or why not?

14.3 Exploring a fashion 'look'

Outline	This activity follows *A question of style* (14.2) and involves an exploration in greater depth of contemporary fashions. Learners are invited to reflect upon current trends in fashion and to compare, where possible, fashions across countries.
Focus	The language of physical description, clothing; requesting and giving advice.
Level	Intermediate and above
Time	40 minutes plus
Preparation	Ask learners to bring in their own examples of fashion in glossy magazines (either in English or in another language) or pictures taken from the Internet. You should also bring to class magazine photographs of four or five men and four or five women wearing stylish contemporary fashions and, if you can find them, fashions from the past. Learners will need copies of the questionnaire in Box 14.3a.

Procedure

1   Tell the class that the topic of the lesson is 'fashion'. Ask the learners to discuss the following questions in groups:
   • Do you consider yourself 'fashionable' in your style of clothing?
   • When did you last shop for clothes?
   • Which clothes shops do you consider 'fashionable'?
   • What makes clothing 'fashionable'? (Answers might include the colours, patterns, the cut of the clothes, the textiles used, etc.)
   • What in your wardrobe do you consider 'timeless' and what is 'for now'?

2   Distribute the questionnaire in Box 14.3a. As a rehearsal, ask all the
    learners to look at four or five examples of photographs of women and
    four or five of men that you have brought in to get a general impression
    of what's in fashion. Then go through the questionnaire as a whole with
    the learners, asking them to answer the questions with reference to the
    photographs. Check they understand the vocabulary, e.g. *laces, lapels,
    turtle-neck, flared*.

Box 14.3a: Exploring a fashion 'look'

Questionnaire: Exploring fashion

General questions
What colours are 'in' (i.e. in fashion)?
What colours are 'out' (i.e. out of fashion)?
Are current fashions 'smart', 'casual' or both?
Are there obvious designs, such as stripes or checks?
Are there obvious decorations like buttons, zips, laces, pockets, embroidery?

Upper body
Look at the shirts and blouses. Are the necklines high or low?
Do the models wear ties or scarves? If so, what do they look like?
Are jacket lapels wide or narrow?
Are shoulders padded and wide or narrow and sharp?
Are sweater collars turtle-neck, polo-neck or v-neck?
Are sleeves long, wrist-length or short?

Lower body
Are women's skirts short, mid-length or long?
Are trousers narrow, wide or flared?
Are people wearing shorts? If so, describe them.
What are the shoes, sandals or boots made of? Describe them.

The models
Describe the models' hairstyles.
Is the make-up natural or 'glamorous'? Are the nails manicured?
Are the eyebrows natural or shaped?
Are the models wearing spectacles or sunglasses?
Are the models wearing jewellery? If so, describe the jewellery.
Do any of the models have a tattoo, or another kind of body decoration?

---

3 Next, divide the class into four groups A–D. Each group looks at the pictures/magazines they have brought in and answers the questions in Box 14.3a again.

4 The groups then report back to the class on their discussions of the photographs. Each group should hold up and describe a couple of photographs which for them show what is in fashion. Try to come to a class consensus about what is fashionable. If you have photographs from different periods, e.g. the 1960s, 1970s, 1980s, 1990s, 2000s these can be used too, to give a sense of changes in fashion and how some fashions re-emerge. Learners should then discuss which of the fashions they would/wouldn't wear. If they are in a monocultural class, they should discuss this with their e-partners.

Follow-up

If the class has enjoyed doing an assessment of contemporary fashion invite them to complete a 'Fashion self-assessment', which involves some fieldwork.

1 Explain that the learners are going to do an assessment of their own fashion which will involve them, in groups of four, visiting a fashionable clothes store in their community. They will also compare their own clothes with those that are currently fashionable.

2 Together, discuss possible stores for the learners to visit after class. While the groups are visiting the stores, they should look at the displays in the windows and talk to the assistants, making a note of the styles that are currently fashionable for men or women.

3 Afterwards, learners should look at their own wardrobe and organise it by colour. They should compare their own styles of clothes with the styles that are currently fashionable. Get learners to write a few paragraphs describing the current fashion and their own wardrobe.

4 In a following lesson, the groups present their findings to the class and compare the fashions they found in the shops and their own wardrobes to those they cut out of the magazines. If they are taking part in an online intercultural exchange, they can post their findings to their e-partners.

14.4 Smelling sweet

Outline	Learners focus on the way people might present themselves through the scent or perfumes they choose to wear.
Focus	The language of sensory perception, particularly smell.
Level	Intermediate and above
Time	40 minutes plus
Preparation	You need to bring samples of different fragrances, male, female and unisex, for illustration, and magazines containing fragrance advertisements.

Procedure

1   Ask the class whether they wear perfume or cologne. Find out if the class members can identify names of famous brands and names of perfume or cologne. Alternatively, the learners can be asked to scan some magazines for names of scent for women and cologne for men. The activity should result in a list such as the following:

For women
Coco Chanel: *Chanel Nº 5, Coco*
Dana: *Tabu*
Rochas: *Femme*
Max Factor: *Hypnotique, Primitif*
Worth: *Je reviens*

For men
Azzaro: *Chrome*
Davidoff: *Good Life, Cool Water*
Clinique: *Happy for Men*
Givenchy: *PI*
Hugo Boss: *Hugo*

2   Invite the class to identify patterns arising from the perfumes and colognes they have named, e.g. the names of women's perfumes tend to be alluring (*Tabu, Primitif*), nostalgic (*Je reviens*) or sensual (*Hypnotique*) while male colognes tend to refer to cars (*Chrome*), states of being (*Good Life, Happy for Men*) or exciting occupations (*PI = Private Investigator*). Both reflect the cult of celebrity by naming popular fragrances after the first-name of the founder of the brand (*Coco, Hugo*). There are also some celebrities who lend their full names or nicknames to fragrances, e.g. *JLo Glow* (Jennifer Lopez), *Christina Aguilera Eau de Parfum, Paloma Picasso Eau de Toilette, Britney Spears™ Believe Eau de Parfum,* and so on.

3   Invite the learners to smell the samples of different kinds of fragrance (female, male and unisex) that you brought to the class. The learners sniff the fragrances and answer the following questions:

- Do you like this fragrance?
- Do you think it is for a male, a female or either?
- Which of the following adjectives would you use to describe it?

refined	*feminine*	*exotic*	*attractive*	*light/heavy*
a classic	*pretty*	*soft*	*romantic*	*fresh*
clean	*woody*	*rich*	*lingering*	*crisp*
sharp	*outdoorsy*	*tangy*	*alluring*	*delicious*
subtle	*refreshing*	*warm*	*sensual*	*enticing*

4 Ask the class to reflect on why many perfumes have French names, and
the reasons they gave for evaluating the fragrances as being for males or
females. Possible answers and extra information are below:

While the use of perfumed oils goes as far back as Egyptian
civilisation, modern perfume houses began in France in the 19th
century. Modern fragrances have different strengths, from eau de
cologne (which contains only 4% essential oils) to proper perfume
(22%). The perfume industry today is a global enterprise aimed at
both women and men. Women tend to use stronger and longer lasting
fragrances than men, though there can be variations between cultures.
Many Middle Eastern males, for example, tend to prefer stronger
fragrances than Europeans and Americans.

5 Tell the learners that they are now going to focus on the marketing of
fragrances. In groups, the learners are instructed to look in the magazines
for an advertisement for one particular fragrance and ask the following
questions about it:

- What kind of market is it aimed at? (male/female/unisex, upmarket/
downmarket?)
- What kind of image does the advertiser create for the fragrance?
(clean and fresh, glamorous and exciting or dangerously sensual?)
- How is this image created – visually, through language, or using both?

6 After discussing these questions in their groups, the learners report their
findings to the class.

7 If the learners are participating in an online intercultural exchange, they
can post their findings about perfumes and colognes to their e-partners.
You might note in advance that the same perfumes and colognes are
marketed differently in different countries, e.g. an everyday brand in
Europe might be marketed as a prestige brand in South America, or vice
versa. Learners should be prompted to explore possible differences in
marketing strategy between countries.

Follow-up

Ask the learners in groups to design their own advertisement for a new fragrance – or they can choose to 're-brand' a fragrance of their choice. The learners are instructed to decide on a particular market, and create an appropriate visual identity, name and slogan. Learners should then present their product to the other groups who have to guess what market they are aiming at.

Variation

Learners can examine the names given to other products and explore what the names indicate about the target markets in different countries, their consumers' interests and aspirations, e.g.

- Vehicles: *Buick Regal, Chevrolet Luv, Ford Mustang, Hyundai Sonata, Lamborghini Diablo, Nissan Frontier, Pontiac Parisienne, Reliant Kitten, Renault Clio, Seat Ibiza, Skoda Fabia, VW Rabbit...*
- Mobile phones: *Blast, Curve, Dare, Rugby, Shine, Sidekick, Slash...*

14.5 Making up

Outline	Learners look at the role played in different cultures by body adornment, particularly make-up and features such as tattoos.
Focus	Language of physical description; historical narrative; reading and discussion.
Level	Upper intermediate and above
Time	40 minutes plus in the first lesson and 20 minutes in a following lesson for the follow-up
Preparation	Bring to class magazines featuring advertisements for make-up, and pictures of models (male and female) who have tattoos. Ideally, if you can find photographs of people from different decades and different cultural groups, the discussion will be broader. Learners need copies of the questions in Box 14.5a. Learners will also need one of the 'jigsaw' reading texts each in Boxes 14.5b, 14.5c and 14.5d.

Procedure

1 Begin by asking if the learners can name a famous personality who (a) uses striking make-up, or (b) has a tattoo. If you have magazines that contain pictures of models who have tattoos show them to learners. You can then move the discussion to more general issues such as:

- What kind of make-up do people wear? For example, lipstick, eye-shadow, face powder, foundation cream, henna?
- Do people wear different make-up on different occasions? What do people wear going to work or school? What do they wear when going to a social event? Why should these be different?
- Do both male and female celebrities have tattoos? What kind of design do they favour? What kind of messages? Where is the body tattooed? Is it easy to remove a tattoo?

2 Next, tell the learners that they are going to read different parts of an article about the history and uses of make-up and body ornaments. Different groups are going to read different parts of the article, and then they will share information. When they are finished sharing, they should be able to answer all of the questions in Box 14.5a. Give out the questions in Box 14.5a to all the learners, and check that everyone understands the questions. Then remind the learners that their own part of the article will only answer some of the questions.

Box 14.5a: Making up

Questions: Adorning the body

a) Give four reasons why, historically, people have decorated their body.

b) Which parts of the body does make-up often draw attention to?

c) Explain why some people might suffer pain to decorate their body.

d) Describe the influence of popular culture on make-up between the 1950s and 1980s.

e) Describe how fashions in women's make-up changed from 1950–2000.

f) Describe how fashions in men's make-up changed from 1950–2000.

g) Explain why some people object to the cost of cosmetics.

h) Name two common (but surprising) ingredients of make-up.

i) Explain why the use of make-up might be harmful to the image of women.

© Cambridge University Press 2010   PHOTOCOPIABLE

---

3 Divide the class into three groups, A, B and C. Give Text A in Box 14.5b to learners in Group A, Text B in Box 14.5c to Group B and Text C in Box 14.5d to Group C. The learners read their own part of the text and find answers to as many of the questions as they can.

4   Reorganise the class so that learners from Groups A, B and C come together. Now the learners share their information, so that they can answer all the questions in Box 14.5a.

5   When the learners have finished sharing their information, go through the questions and answers with the whole class. While checking the answers, give the learners the opportunity to voice their own opinions on the topics raised.

Box 14.5b: Making up

Reading text: Text A Adorning the body

People in different cultures have decorated their bodies for thousands of years. Men and women in different communities have scarred or tattooed their skin, pierced their flesh, painted their nails and decorated their faces with a variety of paints, oils, creams and powders. These decorations perform different functions. Often they are to make the wearer seem more attractive, by drawing attention to the eyes and lips. Sometimes the decoration indicates social status, or membership of a group. Sometimes the decoration is purely playful. Sometimes make-up is protective; it shields the skin from the harmful effects of the sun.

Some traditional cultures tend to favour permanent decorations, such as scarring or piercing the flesh. These decorations are for life, and their application often occurs in a ceremony that involves a certain amount of pain. The shared experience of pain bonds the community tightly together, and distances those who have not acquired the decoration.

Facial make-up has ancient roots, in Egyptian cosmetics. Egyptians used make-up to show social status and to combat the signs of ageing. Cleopatra used a face mask of egg white to hide her wrinkles, black pencil to shape her eye-brows, blue and green paint for her upper and lower eyelids, and red powder to colour her lips. Greek men and women both used make-up to indicate that they were members of the court. Using make-up to indicate your status or to draw attention to your most attractive features seems to be a 'natural' human impulse!

Box 14.5c: Making up

Reading text: Text B Adorning the body

In modern times, fashion tends to fit broadly into ten-year cycles and reflects wider social changes. In the 1950s, women's make-up was strongly affected by the arrival of technicolour wide-screen films. Lipstick was bright and glamorous, and 'pancake' skin foundation disguised the smallest blemish so that you, too, could look like a movie star. In the 1960s, women reacted against the 'glamour' look and tended towards softer and more natural pink and peach lipsticks. But people still copied film stars and the eye-liner worn by the actress Elizabeth Taylor in the film *Cleopatra* was worn by famous models such as Twiggy, and then imitated by millions of young women.

The 1970s saw a tendency towards a more natural look amongst many women, while some young men, influenced by 'glam rock' pop stars, such as David Bowie, began to pay more attention to their make-up than their girlfriends did! The 1980s saw women advancing in their careers and adopting 'power make-up' that showed that femininity was not necessarily incompatible with a career. Vivid red lips were back in fashion, but the big decision was 'to tan or not to tan'? People were becoming more conscious of the harmful effect of the sun's ultraviolet rays, and so 'fake tans' grew in popularity. The 1990s continued the trend towards 'healthy make-up' with an emphasis on natural, anti-ageing products and lighter face skin. However, advances in the chemistry of cosmetics meant that young women in the 21st century could take advantage of a wider range of shiny lip glosses, and they and their male partners began to invest their money in tattoos and piercings.

© Cambridge University Press 2010   PHOTOCOPIABLE

Box 14.5d: Making up

Reading text: Text C Adorning the body

While it is true that cosmetics is a multi-million pound, global industry, not everyone agrees that make-up is worth the money that consumers, especially women, spend on it. For religious, ethical or other reasons, various 'anti-cosmetics' groups promote a more natural look, free from lipstick, powders and eye-liner. Real beauty, they argue, is more than skin-deep.

continued

Box 14.5d: (*cont.*)

Some 'anti-cosmetic' groups also argue that the media is responsible for brain-washing women to feel that they must reach an impossible standard of 'doll-like' beauty – a standard that can only be seen in digitally enhanced images of glamorous models in glossy magazines. This brain-washing is supported by the cosmetics industry, which charges ridiculous prices for cheap and simple mixtures of chemicals, dyes and oils. Some people are shocked when they learn that their expensive powders are actually made from ingredients like fish scales and crushed insects!

Other 'anti-cosmetics' groups argue that make-up is one reason why women remain powerless in society. The cosmetics industry encourages men to regard women, and women to regard themselves, as purely decorative. This perception trivialises women, and makes it difficult for them to advance socially and obtain power on an equal basis to men. After all, no-one ever criticises a male businessperson or politician because he has chosen the wrong lipstick!

© Cambridge University Press 2010   PHOTOCOPIABLE

Suggested answers:

From Text A

a) Historically, people have decorated their body to
   • look more attractive
   • show their social status – like Greek members of the court
   • just to be playful
   • to protect their skin, e.g. from sunlight
b) Usually eyes and lips – like Cleopatra
c) People who have shared the pain of body decoration form a close community; people who have not shared this pain are excluded.

From Text B

d) People copied the glamorous make-up of film stars, models and pop stars, e.g. having bright lipstick or eye-liner influenced by Elizabeth Taylor and Twiggy. Men copied singers like David Bowie.
e) Women's make-up was 'glamorous' in the 1950s, more 'natural' in the 1960s and 1970s, indicated 'female power' in the 1980s, turned towards a 'healthy' look in the 1990s, and is making use of new technology in the 2000s.

f) Men didn't pay much attention to make-up till the 1970s, when they were influenced by 'glamorous' rock stars like David Bowie. Men also became more health-conscious in the 1990s, and like their partners adopted piercings and tattoos in the 2000s.

From Text C

g) Some people feel that the cosmetics industry charges too much money for cheap and simple products.
h) Fish scales and crushed insects.
i) The industry encourages women, particularly, to conform to an impossible, doll-like standard of beauty. The focus on surface appearance also makes it difficult for women to obtain power on an equal basis to men.

Follow-up
If the learners find this activity interesting, they can be asked to analyse advertisements for make-up in magazines, or on television. For example:

1   Ask the learners, in small groups, to look in the magazines for an advertisement for one particular type of cosmetic (e.g. lipstick, eye-shadow, or eye-liner).
2   The groups then answer the following questions:
    • What kind of market is the advertisement aimed at? (male/female/ unisex, racial or ethnic group, age group, upmarket/downmarket?)
    • What kind of image does the advertiser create for the product? (glamorous, natural, youthful?)
    • How is this image created – visually, through language, or using both?
3   The learners present their findings in groups in a following lesson, and post their findings to their e-partners. It is worth noting that the same cosmetics are marketed differently in different countries – e.g. an everyday brand in Europe might be marketed as a prestige brand in South America, or vice versa. Learners should be prompted to be aware of differences in marketing strategy between countries.

14.6 Living dolls

Outline	Learners explore the concept of beauty across cultures – how does it vary and how do people attempt to boost their attractiveness?
Focus	Physical description; reading an article on a cross-cultural 'fashion icon'; optional discussion of attitudes to, for example, cosmetic surgery.
Level	Intermediate and above
Time	40 minutes plus
Preparation	If possible, bring a Barbie® doll and a Ken doll, or a photograph of them, to class. Learners need copies of the reading text in Box 14.6a. Learners also need copies of the discussion thread in Box 14.6b for the follow-up activity and the debate conventions in Box 14.6c on the CD-ROM or on p. 196 (Box 10.6b).

Procedure

1 Together, brainstorm the characteristics learners associate with physical beauty for males and females, e.g. hair colour, eyes, body shape, skin tone, etc. Write the physical attributes for males and females on the board or project them onscreen.

2 Ask the class if they have heard of the children's dolls, 'Barbie®' and 'Ken'. How closely do the dolls represent the stereotype of beauty that the class may have described in step 1? If you have a Barbie® doll and a Ken doll, or a picture of them, show the class.

3 Ask if the females in the class would like to look and dress like Barbie®. Tell the class that, some years ago, the makers of Barbie® launched a range of fashion clothing for adults, and that they are going to read an article about this range of clothing. Before distributing the text, ask the following pre-questions:
   * Where do you think the Barbie® fashion range was launched?
   * Where would you expect to find the Barbie® range on sale?
   * Who would you expect to find buying the Barbie® range of clothes?

4 The learners then read the text in Box 14.6a. When they have finished, using the information in the text, check the answers to the questions in step 3 again.

Answers:
   * The Barbie® fashion range was launched in Japan – perhaps surprisingly because it's a typical American doll. The class can discuss

what might make Barbie® attractive to Japanese women.

- In Japan there are special stores for Barbie® clothes; in the USA Barbie® clothes were available in 'respectable' department stores like Nordstrom and Macy's.
- The company clearly hopes that Barbie® clothes will be taken seriously and bought by fashion-conscious adults and young girls.

Box 14.6a: Living dolls

Reading text: Barbie® fashion

In the spring of 2003, Barbie®, the world-famous doll, suddenly came to life. Mattel®, the toy company that produces the doll, chose to launch its line of Barbie® fashion for adult women in Japan, where there were soon over 16 stores devoted solely to selling 'Barbie® couture'. The Barbie® range of clothes was then introduced to Americans at a New York fashion show; and a selection of the Barbie® range of T-shirts, cocktail dresses, coats, handbags and shoes went on sale in US department stores in late 2004.

The move from toy doll to adult fashion posed challenges for Mattel®. The company wanted to present Barbie® to Americans as a 'fashion icon' and not just as a novelty item. For that reason, they selected prestige items from the Barbie® range, like her vintage 1959 T-shirt, and sold it for between $40 and $60 through the 'quality' department store, Nordstrom. However, Macy's in New York also launched a clothing collection for young girls, labelled 'With love, Barbie®'.

The Barbie® fashion range for real, living people is just one example of companies pushing successful global brands in new directions. Other ideas from Mattel® include a perfume and a range of cosmetics – all with Barbie®'s seal of approval.

---

5 Follow up these questions with a few more, e.g.
- What difficulties did Mattel® face when introducing Barbie® fashion to Americans?
- Can you give any other examples of companies or individuals developing a 'global brand' in other directions?

The first follow-up question can lead into a discussion of the difference between a 'fashion icon' and a 'novelty item'. Would consumers purchase Barbie® fashion because they take it seriously, or as a passing joke? The second question can lead to a discussion of other companies or celebrities who have sought to capitalise on a brand name by moving into new markets, e.g. models like Naomi Campbell who 'author' novels; pop and film stars who give their names to fashion, jewellery or cosmetics; chocolate bar manufacturers like Mars® who launch a range of ice creams, etc.

Follow-up 1 for more advanced learners

Learners can be shown the discussion starter in Box 14.6b, adapted from a Taiwanese student's contribution to an online discussion forum, and put forward their opinions about the importance of fashion.

Box 14.6b: Living dolls

Discussion starter: Beauty and fashion

From: Chun-Chen

No doubt, the mass media should take responsibility for women following fashion. But who controls fashion EXACTLY? Is it the designer? Or the model? I don't know. Perhaps there are many people who consider fashion to be trivial. They think women who blindly follow fashion are narrow-minded. What do you think?

© Cambridge University Press 2010   PHOTOCOPIABLE

Follow-up 2 for more advanced learners

One increasingly common type of behaviour in some countries is to use cosmetic surgery to help conform to a conventional standard of 'beauty'. Learners could research the arguments for and against plastic surgery and have a debate. If necessary, go through the conventions of a debate in Box 14.6c on the CD-ROM (or on p. 196 in Box 10.6b) with learners.

Further reading and resources

Some of the following titles are practical introductions to aspects of language and culture, and are intended for those readers who would like to get further ideas for teaching language from an intercultural perspective; others are more academic, and recommended for those readers who are interested in exploring the theoretical foundations upon which the activities in this book are based.

Anderson, W., and Corbett, J. (2009) *Exploring English Online*, London: Palgrave Macmillan.
A textbook for undergraduate university students, introducing the formal study of English through the exploration of freely available, online digital text resources such as the *TIME* Corpus, the British National Corpus and the Scottish Corpus of Texts and Speech. Some of the practical ideas in this textbook inspired activities (5.8), (7.4) and (11.4).

Byram, M. (2008) *From Foreign Language Education to Education for Intercultural Citizenship: Essays and Reflections,* Clevedon: Multilingual Matters.
A typically insightful discussion of current theoretical issues in citizenship and intercultural language education from one of the key theorists in the field. The *journal of intercultural discussions* (1.8) is inspired by the 'Autobiography of Intercultural Encounters' on pages 240–5.

Corbett, J. (2003) *An Intercultural Approach to English Language Teaching,* Clevedon: Multilingual Matters.
A theoretical and practical introduction to intercultural language education. It gives a rationale for much of the present volume.

Council of Europe (2001) *Common European Framework of Reference for Languages: Learning, Teaching, Assessment,* Cambridge: Cambridge University Press.
This exhaustive guide to the aspirations of curriculum and materials designers contains a clear commitment to intercultural language education, and some detailed suggestions on how it should be embedded into European language programmes.

Damen, L. (1987) *Culture Learning: The Fifth Dimension in the Language Classroom*, Reading, Mass: Addison Wesley.
This is another book of theoretical insights and practical examples. It is the particular inspiration for some of the activities involving 'cultural associations' (e.g. 10.2) and 'critical incidents' (e.g. 2.4).

Farrell, T.S.C. (2008) 'Critical incidents in ELT initial teacher training' *ELT Journal* 62/1, 3–10.
This article demonstrates the application of critical incidents to ELT training and provides a useful framework for the activities in chapter 2.

Fox, K. (2004) *Watching the English: The Hidden Rules of English Behaviour*, London: Hodder and Stoughton.
A best-selling work of popular anthropology; this entertaining book covers subjects like mobile phone use, 'petiquette' and dress codes. Contains many good ideas for comparison and discussion.

Fitzgerald, H. (2003) *How Different Are We? Spoken Discourse in Intercultural Communication*, Clevedon: Multilingual Matters.
An accessible, academic study of spoken discourse across cultures; contains practical activities that inspired some of the face-to-face communication activities in Chapter 5, particularly *Gestures* (5.6).

Goldstein, B. (2008) *Working with Images*, Cambridge: Cambridge University Press.
A compendium of ideas for exploiting visual images.

Guerrero, L.K., DeVito, J.A., and Hecht, M.L. (eds.) (1999) *The Nonverbal Communication Reader: Classic and Contemporary Readings,* 2nd edition, Prospect Heights: Waveland.
An anthology of academic studies of non-verbal communication. Useful for the teacher who wishes to know more about research into non-verbal communication.

Hindle, T. (1998) *Negotiating Skills,* London: Dorling Kindersley.
A short, attractively presented guide to practical techniques which can be used in negotiating. Contains a brief but succinct section on body language in meetings and presentations.

Holliday, A., Hyde, M., and Kullman, J. (2004) *Intercultural Communication: An advanced resource book,* London: Routledge.
For teachers looking for a more theoretical approach to intercultural

communication, this resource book provides a framework and readings illuminating the key themes of 'the self', 'otherisation' and 'representation'.

MacClancy, J. (1992) *Consuming Culture: Why We Eat What We Eat and What it Says About Us*, London: Chapmans.
Another popular guide to anthropology, this time focusing on the different kinds of behaviour and value associated with food. Different cultures' attitudes to food is discussed in relation to topics like power, religion, love, health, class, theatre and taboo.

McCormack, C., and Jones, D. (1997) *Building a Web-based Education System*, New York: John Wiley & Sons.
This is a general guide to establishing distance learning programmes via the web, mainly at university level. Comes with an accompanying CD. The advice on 'netiquette' (1.5) is largely based on this resource.

Moran, J. (2007) *Queuing for Beginners: The Story of Daily Life from Breakfast to Bedtime*, London: Profile Books.
Like *Watching the English* and *Consuming Culture* (above), this book takes a popular approach to anthropology. The chapters examine various routines of everyday life in Britain since 1945. Particularly good on the rituals of office behaviour.

Morris, D. (1982) *The Pocket Guide to Manwatching*, London: Triad Panther.
An abridged version of the popular anthropology guide of 1977.

O'Dowd, R. (ed.) (2007) *Online Intercultural Exchange: An Introduction for Foreign Language Teachers*, Clevedon: Multilingual Matters.
A series of case studies, full of theoretical discussion and practical advice.

Roberts, C., Davies, E., and Jupp, T. (1992) *Language and Discrimination: A Study of Communication in Multi-Ethnic Workplaces*, Harlow: Longman.
This is an ethnographic study of the linguistic and cultural challenges faced by employers and employees in multi-ethnic workplaces; it provides insight into the academic study of intercultural communicative competence as well as practical suggestions for devising teaching materials. The 'job interview' activity (2.2) is inspired by a discussion in this book.

Roberts, C., Byram, M., Barro, A., Jordan, S., and Street, B. (2001) *Language Learners as Ethnographers*, Clevedon: Multilingual Matters.
A detailed, theoretical and practical discussion of how to integrate ethnographic techniques into foreign language education at university level.

Scollon, R., and Scollon, S.W. (2001) *Intercultural Communication: A discourse approach,* 2nd edition, Oxford: Blackwell.
For teachers who are interested in the academic study of intercultural communication, this is a useful survey of relevant linguistic theory.

Scott, G.G. (2008) *Disagreements, Disputes and All-Out War: Three simple steps for dealing with any kind of conflict,* New York: Amacom.
A 'self-help' book targeted at business people, this is a useful, practical book that aims to help anyone think objectively about and move to resolve conflicts. Contains exercises.

Spencer-Oatey, H. (2008) *Culturally Speaking: Culture, Communication and Politeness Theory,* 2nd edition, London: Continuum.
A valuable academic study of the way rapport is managed through talk between people of different cultures. The textbook is intended primarily for scholars and university students of applied linguistics. There are examples and exercises.

Tannen, D. (2006) *You're wearing that? Understanding Mothers and Daughters in Conversation,* New York and London: Random House.
Deborah Tannen has produced a series of accessible and popular 'linguistic self-help' guides to illuminate communication between genders and across generations. Others include *You Just Don't Understand: Women and Men in Conversation* (1990) and *Talking from 9 to 5: Women and Men at Work: Language, Sex and Power* (1994).

Trompenaars, F., and Hampden-Turner, C. (1997) *Riding the Waves of Culture: Understanding Cultural Diversity in Business,* London and Boston: Nicholas Brealey Publishing.
Another best-selling, 'self-help' guide to doing business across cultures. Its classification and description of different types of corporate culture may prompt discussion for professional learners.

Wainwright, G.R. (2003) *Teach Yourself: Body Language,* 3rd edition, London: Hodder and Stoughton.
A popular introduction to the meanings of body language, including exercises and experiments. Has a section on 'Body language around the world'.

Websites
Setting up an online intercultural exchange
There are various agencies and institutions that facilitate online exchanges for the learning of language and culture. The following websites give further information:

    http://www.britishcouncil.org/learning-ie-school-partnerships.htm
    http://www.elanguages.org/
    http://www.epals.com
    http://www.tandemcity.com/index.php
    http://www.slf.ruhr-uni-bochum.de/Tandem/tandem/inh01-eng.html

Critical awareness
Some teachers in South America have set up a forum for discussion and exchange of ideas among colleagues and learners – see http://interculturalvoices. wordpress.com

For more advanced teachers and learners who wish to explore the potential of intercultural language learning to foster critical thinking, the Open Spaces for Dialogue and Enquiry website offers a methodological framework and sample activities: http://www.osdemethodology.org.uk/

Searchable language corpora
Digital corpora of texts and speech are becoming freely available in a range of formats. Several of the activities in this book draw on the corpora made available by Mark Davies of Brigham Young University at http://corpora.byu. edu – namely the *TIME* corpus, the British National Corpus and the Corpus of Contemporary American English. Mark Davies' site also has Spanish and Portuguese corpora. The Scottish Corpus of Texts and Speech at http://www. scottishcorpus.ac.uk is another rich source of multimedia documents, including audio-visual conversations with simultaneous transcripts, which can be downloaded free for educational use. Further activities using electronic resources to study language and literature can be found at the WordWebs website: http://www.gla.ac.uk/wordwebs/

Index